FUCK MY LIFE
The Memoir of a Chic Gangster

"When a judge sits in judgment over a fellow man, he should feel as if a sword is pointed at his own heart." ~ Talmud

"If 10 judges are sitting in judgement, a prisoner's collar hangs around all of their necks." ~ Yehoshua Ben Levi

To my beloved children Dylan, Savannah & Dakota, may this book remind you how much being judged is a greater life path than judging. May our story of adversity, survival, love and success inspire others to make it thru the toughest times in their own lives, and help them come out on the other side with humility & gratitude. I cannot protect you from the evil inclination of those who judge you, but our story can certainly help those being judged, turn adversity into success. You three have been my strength, and my reason for living. If I had to do it all again, I would… all I have done I have done out of love for you. I love you to the moon, and the stars in the sky and back. Mom

To my husband, the love of my life Gil. Thank you for loving me for my past before loving me for my present, for giving me a second chance at love, at life and a happy ending. I love you deeply.

To my readers, I have no regrets other than spending many years ashamed of my story. I hope reading this book will help you judge others less, and inspire you to be kind to yourself. Don't lose sight of your dreams, I know it sounds cliché but don't let your past define you, let it fuel you.

To my Savannah, you are the light of my life. You have kept me alive during my darkest times. You have a very special gift, of this I am sure. If it wasn't for your immense courage, deep love, your selfless devotion at the innocent age of 6 and on, as well as your magical 6th sense, I would not be here today to tell my story. Thank you from the bottom of my heart for saving me. I love you, Mom.

DISCLAIMER

I have tried to recreate events, locales and conversations from my memories of them. In order to maintain their anonymity in some instances I have changed the names of individuals and places. I may have changed some identifying characteristics and details such as certain events, legal facts, physical properties, occupations, places of residence and other circumstances.

Chapter 1: J.A.P. Tales

In 1997, I drove a brand spanking new Jeep with a Florida International University vanity license plate. I wore a bikini under my short shorts and tank top, and I drove straight to the beach in between classes during my freshman year at FIU. I was a part-time sales-girl in Bal Harbor Shops, where I never missed an opportunity to tell rich shoppers I was French because it boosted my sales and I worked on commission. I waitressed part-time at the Cheesecake Factory, where my smile and very American hospitality skills got me some really good tips.

I was your typical cliché Miami girl / Jewish American Princess: I never missed a Shabbat dinner at my oldest brother's house in Golden Beach or at my parents' condo in Williams Island. I was 17, and I wanted to grow-up fast, and I did. My dad died unexpectedly and that turned my life upside down. I flew to France to watch him die in the ER and bury him a few days later. His mother arrived at our home there, yelling that my mother and I killed him. I fucking hated that woman; I always have. It always seemed to me she resented God for making my father more successful than her other kids. She despised our lifestyle and pissed on my mother's acts of kindness and generosity towards her and her two unhappily unmarried daughters.

I sat Shiva for one week, wore black, and sat on the floor with my older brothers and sister, thinking to myself: "Oh, my fucking God, I am left to live with this freak show." Luckily, my finals were coming up, and since my parents had already paid both my semesters, my older brother, AKA the new "Godfather", decided I should fly back to Miami to complete my semester.

I flew back to Miami, and never looked back. I would never ever go back to France that was clear in my mind. I arrived at my studio apartment in Aventura to find my then boyfriend waiting for me at my front door. He had flown in from NY so he could be the shoulder I needed to cry on, and I did cry. I cried for my dad, and I cried for myself. I always felt like I was different from my brothers and sister, and that somehow without my father around, they would make my life hell. I was emancipated. My mother, a strong, controlling figure in our household, became weak and submissive, relying on my older brother's guidance and decision-making. She substituted my brother for my father and that was so fucked up. So, three months later, when my Syrian Jew, stockbroker boyfriend from NY proposed, I said YES, feeling a sense of freedom from my overbearing family.

My mother seemed pleased to be getting rid of me. He was Jewish after all, and as long as she could lie to her friends and tell them I married well, it didn't really matter to her if I was happy or not.

I was not happy—I was relieved. I wanted out of my family and out of their constant nagging about the fact that I was born in times when my father was richer and I've been spoiled since the day I was born. It seemed they were on a vendetta to make me pay for never knowing their rougher childhood when my father was a traveling salesman and they were deprived of luxuries I had my whole childhood.

So, the same year my father passed I got married at the Aventura Turnberry Isle Synagogue and Hall. My brother and mother decided to enforce the Jewish mourning guidelines that children and spouses shall not dance, celebrate, nor listen to music for the one-year mourning period. I walked down the aisle to no music, with my oldest brother to my left, wearing his mourning beard (often Jewish men in mourning do not shave), and my mother on my left tearing up all the way to the Chuppah. My older sister didn't show because of family drama from the past year, and we didn't have any music playing at our sit-down dinner. My family couldn't help but whisper some jokes about my in-laws' lack of class and savior-vivre at the buffet. It was a typical Jewish wedding without the celebration. The only thing that was right about that wedding was my Christian Dior Lace wedding gown, custom-made and paid for by my mother. My new husband and I went home to our new apartment that night, and before I could unbutton my Dior, he was already on the bed, opening envelopes and cursing out my "French fucks stingy" family members. He cursed so much that night and was stressed because he borrowed money from his car-dealer grease ball brother Ralph, and he had to return it in the morning. The envelopes wouldn't cover it, and we started our marriage with a debt to fat brother Ralph, and that was bad news. My new husband was not rich, but he was a hustler, who bought his first piece of real estate in Brooklyn at the age of 23. It was a small triangle parcel, you couldn't fit much on it, but he believed in real estate and making it big. He also believed I was a rich girl and I would inherit [LOL]. He waited for that inheritance for quite some years before he realized he bet on the wrong horse. The only thing my mother agreed to help with once I got married were my law studies. She took the Jeep back before the lease expired because she believed a "good Jewish man should buy his wife a car."

Joe and I struggled financially in Miami. He moved there for me because he thought I came from a rich family and they would help us buy a house. [LOL AGAIN]

My older brother and his wife lived a very comfortable life in Aventura, but Joe and I didn't make it. We couldn't live in this rich, fancy community, and we were

5

coming short on rent. My mom helped me pack my boxes and fill-up a U-HAUL Truck that Joe would drive back to Brooklyn. My family didn't hold us back. They helped pack the boxes and waved goodbye without regrets, as an eight-months-pregnant me boarded my flight with a one-way ticket to New York. Well, a one-way ticket to Brooklyn to be exact.

I was accepted to NYU Law School and moved into my father-in-law's basement in Flatbush. I lost my tan, and my short shorts, as my husband fell hard into the Jewish religion. By the time our son was born, Joe was running to the synagogue to pray three times a day. He only wore white and blue, and even said a prayer after taking a dump. He became completely indoctrinated by his religious mentor, and things turned weird as fuck.

Chapter 2: Gimme the Money

I arrived in Brooklyn, eight months pregnant, young and full of hope (well, I thought it was hope-it turned out to be illusion). Our basement apartment had windows high enough to see our neighbors' fat ankles when they walked by our corner. But then, I started my second semester at NYU Law, in the heart of Greenwich Village, and each morning I arrived in Manhattan and took a whiff of NY's energy. I felt like I was in a scene right out of a movie. Often between classes, I wandered around SoHo, had lunch at Da Silvano, glancing at Christy Turlington sitting at the table next to me, thinking she looks exactly the way she did in George Michael's "Freedom" music video.

I took a part-time job at a kinky underground fashion boutique on West Broadway right next door to Cipriani, juggling school and work, commuting to my mediocre life in Brooklyn. Once my son was born, my family came from Miami and France for my son's Brit-Mila at my father-in-law's home in Brooklyn's Jewish neighborhood. Each time these two families mixed, it turned into the most awkward freak show meeting between French wannabe upper-crust-ers and Arab-Israeli aspiring wise-guys. No joke, my father-in-law had a very biblical Jewish first name but insisted on being called TONY (Hello, Scarface much?). Joe and his brothers all had their Israeli birth names changed to Joe, Danny, Bobby and wait for it: one brother took on two new names, Ethan or Sebastian, depending on the situation (Don't ask—I still don't get it). The rabbi snipped my son's penis, and my in-laws devoured my mother's Moroccan meat cigars before the guest arrived, to her dismay. My brothers and my sister posed for pictures with me and smiled graciously, then they all left, and I was left with this life that I perpetually decided made me happy.

The truth was I loved Joe. He was handsome. He had this New York accent and charm to go with it, and big dreams. Until he got close to this homosexual closet case at his synagogue. The guy was the chief-rabbi's unmarried 45-year-old son, and he became Joe's religious guru. He fucked his brain up completely, to the point that the cool long-haired bad boy I married became Mr. Mitzvoth (the religious word for individual acts of human kindness in keeping with the Jewish law). The only problem was there are 613 of these fuckers to comply with and none of them apparently implied supporting and making your wife happy.

As I was living quite the modern life in Manhattan all day, back at home it was the opposite: think religious men sitting at my living room table around amuse-bouches (Kosher, of course), studying Torah and the Parasha of the week, while I stayed confined in another room away from the male scrutiny. I think the first year I may have called my mom three times to ask if I could come home with my baby. She always listened carefully and responded, "With God's Will, everything will be fine. I cannot take care of you and your baby. No Jewish man in his right mind will re-marry you." Each time I called my mom and cried for help, she was only worried about one thing: me asking her for money. I never did. She taught me to be a strong, independent, cash-cow like her. Or, if all else failed, I should look pretty enough to find a rich husband, however bold or fat or old he may be. No fucking way, José!

So, I quit law school, against my counselor's advice. I was the top of class of nearly 300, after all. But, I needed to make money so I started giving piano lessons to the kids in the Syrian community and charged $50 an hour for it. I became as popular as the French (damn, I'm not even that French) piano teacher and even created a teaching method that enabled one to play with two hands in less than two hours. Turns out, I'm pretty good at created teaching methods that can and will get someone to perform something that usually would take years of practice. You'll see all about that later. Joe was still peeved my mother never gave me a dime from my father's inheritance and even more pissed that my family was not helping us buy a house in Brooklyn. I made my position at the Soho shop a full-time gig, until one day the crazy-looking, zebra-stripes wearing, neon red-haired lesbian shop-owner walked into the store and found me too cute and too French to stay hidden underground even though I was her best sales-girl. She took me in as her assistant on her claim-to-fame job as Costume Designer for an up and coming HBO series. I started commuting to the Studios in Queens every day to do everything from walking her dog and getting her coffee to getting assaulted by her then-girlfriend who may have thrown dog poop at me and pulled me by my hair once or twice in a jealous rage. I stayed on the job because she was a fashion genius and picking her brain could get me somewhere in life. I felt it.

I had fashion running through my veins. My parents owned several clothing stores in France and often took me on their buying trips to Paris and Italy. They made it big in fashion. My father went from being a 24/7 small grocery shop owner to making a fortune in the wholesale fashion business. My mother had a knack for fashion, too. Anywhere we went vacationing—the Spanish Costa Brava, St. Barth, or Skiing in St. Moritz—she made friends with strangers eager to dress like her and sold them the clothes off her back. By the time I was 14, she would pack a suitcase full of merchandise that she would wear, keeping the tags on, and sell them to cruise-mates sitting with us at the Captain's table of Costa's most prestigious cruise ship. My mom was so grandiose. She always was dripping in gorgeous jewelry, wearing the latest Loris Azzaro designs mixed with high street items from "Le Sentier", a neighborhood in the 2nd arrondissement of Paris, which has been known historically as the multicultural textile and garment manufacturing district, where my parents bought their merchandise. My mother liked money, power, and intelligence. She still does.

The HBO series was starting to take-off, and neon red-haired boss-lady (I call her Red) was getting tons of press for her fashion genius. The series heroine was becoming a fashion goddess, and I was still a nobody assistant. One day during a production meeting, she says, "We need the 'IT-BAG.' We need the BIRKIN." Of course, she was referring to the HERMES carry-all, rumored to require a two-year waitlist to get your hands on it. At that time, we still sourced clothes and accessories from thrift stores to stay within the show's budget. Fendi was the first important design house to loan us items including the Baguette, but HERMES refused categorically to be associated with a show bearing such a pejorative name. I was there to take notes (hand-written notes) and shut up, but I looked up from my notepad and, in the boldest tone, I said, "I'll get you one."

Red looked at me and said, "From Chinatown?"

Ah! She was underestimating me, but in the most French accent I could mimic (I had a perfect American accent to start with), I said, "Well, I am from France. My mother is currently in Toulouse. She knows the Franchise owner there. She just got her gold Kelly from there." Red looked at me with disdain and said, "Impossible! There is a waiting list longer than the amount of years you were born!"

So, I called my mother and begged her to get me a Royal Blue or Red Birkin 40 cm. She said, "NO way am I buying a Birkin for a teenager!" (I was a few month shy of my 20th birthday). But I never met a no I didn't turn into a yes, so, with some FedEx magic, and a Hermes receipt in hand, I drove to the Silver Cup studios with this $4,000 bag on my lap (yes, that's all it cost back then). I dumped it proudly on Red's desk, who incredulously opened the orange box like it stank of Chinese Noodles from ChiTown. Then, her face lit up, and she promoted me to First Wardrobe Assistant. I took the new job, and the higher pay, with one condition: that I could go back to law school and finish my JDAT.

Fast forward, 18 months later, my second child, Savannah, was born. We moved on up in the real estate game and moved to McDonald Avenue in Brooklyn. You know the aerial Subway train tracks you see in Saturday Night Fever? Well, I lived in a cute little house right under them. The noise of the F train went from keeping me awake at night to putting me to sleep over the years. My husband convinced me this property was real estate gold because it was a commercial property that could be converted into a very profitable commercial building when need be. My little boy spent the next few years of his little life looking out the window at the F train going back and forth from Manhattan Penn Station to the final stop at Brooklyn's Sheepshead Bay. Like the good Syrian Jew that he was, my husband made sure I drove the latest Range Rover, bought at the Mannheim exotic car auction by his car dealer brother, and he occasionally threw a nice fur coat or a diamond my way, so I could shine bright like a good S.Y. wife. S.Y. by the way is the abbreviation the Syrian Jews use for what they consider the elite of their community. They call Ashkenazi Jews the JW (pronounced J-Dubs) and called the off-the-boat Syrian Jews, Chamis. I fought him long and hard to put the kids in private preschool (he didn't want to pay), but ultimately the peer pressure of his rabbi and synagogue buddies got the best of him and we put the kids in Magen David Yeshiva preschool. I was the only platinum blonde, green-eyed, small-nosed woman showing up at carpool. Rumor had it perhaps I was Russian or even worst maybe even a Goya!!! If these pieces of shit low-lives only knew how much more Jewish the blood in my veins was than theirs!

Once, I showed up at Shaare Zion (the Synagogue funded by Edmond Saffra, the tycoon billionaire ironically killed in Monte-Carlo a decade before I moved there), and when I arrived at the door, the Jewish security guard barred me from coming in and asked me if I was lost? He and all of them dark-haired, dark-skinned, dark-eyed, crooked-nosed Syrians were convinced I was a convert.

Luckily for me, the chief-rabbi took a liking to me and checked me out, clearing up the rumors for those who would listen. In those first two years of living in Brooklyn's upscale Syrian community, I came to be liked and accepted, even though they usually disliked Moroccan Jews. But to them I wasn't Moroccan, I was "La créme de la créme" I was Frenchhhhhh! I was stylish. I was a fashion "It-Girl" from Manhattan. Little did they know, this blond fashion girl was fighting the biggest, longest, hardest fight of her life.

Joe was so inconsistent. He could be really generous and loved a Ferrari. Sometimes he would gift me a big cushion cut 9-ct diamond solitaire ring, or a $20K Chinchilla fur coat á la JLO that I didn't ask for, but he could fuss over the price of my haircut... I was never sure whether he had money and pretended to be broke, or if he was really broke and borrowed against lines of credit to get us the finer things he selectively chose to get. I needed to live large. I grew up in wealth and I missed it. I was so driven to make it, and at the same time, I was so not willing to work and give him money so he could sit on his ass and invest it in real estate like he wanted.

Chapter 3: Who's the Retard Now?

My first born, Dylan, is now 20 years old, a second-year law student at the sixth best law school in England. He speaks English and French fluently, and Spanish pretty well, too. You think I'm obnoxiously bragging? You're right... He was born in 1999 and, at the age of 3, was diagnosed with a learning disability on the autism spectrum. All we knew about autism back then was how Dustin Hoffman acted so well as an autistic man in *Rain Man*. You think I'm bragging now? I was 22 when he was diagnosed with a learning disability. We didn't understand it, but we knew it was serious, and I was scared. But part of me didn't believe anything these psychologists were telling me. He didn't look like he had a syndrome of any kind. As a matter of fact, he was perfect physically and so cute. How could it be that this syndrome had no physical aspect at all? Yeah, we were pretty ignorant back then. We associated stuff like this with Down syndrome, but turns out, there is an array of learning disabilities not necessarily visible to the naked eye.

He had autism. He didn't make eye contact with anyone. He fidgeted back and forth inexplicably. He crawled first only using one side of his body, same with going up the stairs. He never alternated to the other side. Worst of all, he didn't speak. But they said autistic children don't show emotions, affection or happiness, but Dylan did. He smiled all day. He got excited when he saw me. He reacted to his environment and he showed so much affection. I refused to take him through the Board of Education's standard evaluations and therapy. They told me if you put him through the system, it will show on his school records till university, and he would never go to Yale or NYU. I didn't wonder if my kid was going to go to law or med school. I just knew he would. My kid was going to do something great with his life, and there is no way we are going to have him labeled with a learning disability on his school records. Who the fuck does that to their child?

So, I decide to cure him privately. All these assholes psych-evaluators looked at me with such pity, thinking this shallow mother doesn't want to accept she doesn't have the perfect child. FUCK THEM! I wish I could find them now and it tell to their faces. The American system is so corrupt when it comes to mental illness and learning disabilities. They want to label everyone with something, then put them on meds to make Pfizer richer. They created a nation of psychotic addicts from young age, diagnosing every child they could with ADD and ADHD. Are they fucking serious? Then they give them those meds that never give these kids a chance to heal. And don't tell me you can't heal those disabilities because my son is proof you can!

I watched CNBC before going to work every morning. I saw this doctor, Dr. CeeCee McCarton. She talked about kids who fidget back and forth, wag their hands uncontrollably, and don't make eye contact. Kids who can't tell the difference between blue and red and won't learn how to speak at the proper age. She was saying how the FDA refuses to approve advanced therapy for those kids and prefer to treat them with drugs. She had opened a clinic in Manhattan to welcome these children, those that didn't fall into any categories of learning disabilities recognized by the National Board of Special Education, and help them find therapies that would help them progress. I realized I had to see her. I had to bring her my son. I found the McCarton center in the phone book and made an appointment. I brought Dylan. We walked into her office, and I told him to sit as she watched, and he awkwardly went and sat on the floor behind us where she had toys. I asked him to come sit next to me, but he didn't look me in the eye and only processed the sitting part, so he sat on the floor behind me. She said kindly it was okay. She spoke a language I'd never heard before and spoke to me about adjustments. She then went to talk to Dylan and, within seconds, said we need a full evaluation. The cost was $4,850 in 2001. Needless to say, I didn't have it and I didn't make it either, but I told her I would find it and scheduled the evaluation. My husband refused categorically to let a quack tell us "what we already knew: he is retarded, but it's okay. I'm retarded too."

I called my big brother in Florida and explained, and he sent me a check. I asked my mother before him, but as always and usual, she said no. "What the hell is a learning disability anyway?" she asked. We got Dylan evaluated. I sat behind one of those aquarium windows that looks like a mirror on the other side and painfully watched his evaluation as he failed every single test the evaluator put him through: building blocks, color coding, climbing monkey. You name it—he failed it. I cried by myself in my aquarium as I watched my perfect little boy, challenged and unable to perform the natural skills of life. I wiped my tears when I met him on the other side of the door, and he told me he had fun. HE HAD FUN? Fuck!!!

After the evaluation, we came back for the report, Dr. McCarton told me my son was not Rain Man, but his distant cousin. He is on the spectrum, she said. He has some of the symptoms but not all, and he can function much better than Rain Man. But if we didn't catch it at 3 1/2 years old (that's the earliest), he would end up in assisted living as an adult. She scanned my eyes, looking for open-mindedness, and she found it. She then said, there is a program that is not FDA approved. It involved a different therapy protocol than mainstream psychology. It's called Fast-Forward for reading and processing information, but it's still in the trial process, and it's a customized therapy. It is not reimbursed by insurance and cannot be done on school premises, because the government won't have it, but she believed it could help Dylan develop normal skills, by teaching him everything again, like re-entering the information into a computer. In other words, he would learn every social, mental, physical skills through learning induction, skills that usually come to us naturally as children. She said we are re-programming him to think like the rest of us, but we will keep his special abilities if we can.

Yep, by the time he was six, Dylan was a genius. Like Rain Man, he could memorize the phone book, a license plate during a hit and run, the number of each and every player on the Yankees. The protocol was costly and would run about $1,500 a week, and I could do payment installments. So, I agreed. I gave 10 checks (I had no money in the bank), and we started the therapy: educational, physical, occupational, and other kinds of cognitive therapy. I taught piano every night after kids came out of school till 10pm. I worked during the day on the HBO series set, and I sold all my expensive jeans on eBay.

From the age of three to the age of eleven, Dylan's disability was tough. He looked so normal to the rest of the world. When you spent fifteen minutes with him and started to realize something was off, you just thought he was awkward.

His brain didn't function like ours. It worked at superior speed, bypassing every aspect of social skills and normalcy. At first, therapy was excruciating. It was hard to watch and hard to put him through. I took night classes for a semester at Brooklyn College, studying special education to help me better cope with Dylan and speak a language that would help him progress. His progress reports were shit till he was six. I told him, "Dylan, look at that red truck!"

I waited a few seconds and then asked, "Dylan, what color is the truck?" He'd answer, "BLUUUUUE."

I tried over and over again till tears would come gushing out of my eyes. I fought the private Jewish school system that was trying to send him to schools for mentally retarded children because he didn't fall into any mainstream categories. I fought it and fought the system in court, arguing that putting him in a school for mentally retarded children would cause regression in his progress, since he was on the spectrum of a syndrome that had nothing to do with retardation. A Jewish social worker helped me argue my case, and the Jewish school he was attending agreed to launch a program for kids like Dylan, with "mild to medium learning disabilities."

They said if I could get seven kids for his grade the program would exist, and Dylan could be in it. So, I started to advocate, and speak to mothers, bringing awareness to these moms who thought their kids had ADHD, ADD and dyslexia, convincing them there is a better place for their children to possibly matriculate into regular programs someday. The First Grade Academy (that's what they called the program) launched in September, thanks to Dylan's condition.

Today, many of these children he went to school with, from first grade to fourth grade, have been "mainstreamed" into regular classes and programs. Dylan was mainstreamed in the fifth grade and started following the regular curriculum with normal children.

When I decided to move to Monaco, Dylan was 12. His doctors told me he will never be able to learn French ever. BULLSHIT. He read and spoke Hebrew perfectly, but still doctors said the delays, caused by his learning disability although they were now corrected, would not allow him to learn French well enough to go to school and graduate in a foreign country and school system.

Today, Dylan speaks French fluently. He took the equivalent of SATs one year after arriving in Monaco and passed with a B. He then took the French portion of the Baccalaureate and again passed with a B. He is a valedictorian, straight-A student in the French school system today. All that without ever taking any prescription drugs. Do you still think I'm obnoxiously bragging now? Well, you bet I am! But I don't think it's obnoxious. I think it's our reward, for this long journey we took to get here.

Do you wonder at all how I paid for this trial therapy? (Remember I gave 10 checks to start with?). Oh, I paid alright. This is where my story really begins.

I worked union on that HBO series. I gave piano lessons evenings and weekends, and once I sold all my designer jeans on eBay. I realized my eBay sales generated more revenue than my other two jobs combined. So, I went to Daffy's (if you are from NYC you remember their ad campaign "the Bargain for Millionaires") and to Century 21 outlets all over the city and Brooklyn, and bought all the Juicy Couture tracksuits, True Religion, Seven, and Rock & Republic jeans I could get my hands on, and I opened an eBay store. My margin was 40%, and I started to make a killing. My sales skyrocketed to $5000 -$8000 per month. I quit giving piano lessons, and every night I would spend hours replying to buyers and watching bids go up on eBay. I packed and shipped out of my kitchen and spent my days on my AOL dial-up connection, listing and monitoring bids and sales on eBay.

Chapter 4: Where the Fuck is Virginia, Anyway?

I no longer had any issue paying for therapy. I employed two nannies and housekeepers and had both my kids in one of Brooklyn's best Jewish school. I also started doing wholesale sales. I made deals with local retailers like Clothes Horse in Brooklyn to sell me their premium jeans and Juicy Couture at a small discount, and I still made 40%, selling abroad to Europeans coveting the latest crystal-embossed Seven For All Mankind jeans. I made so much money that I was considering leaving my union job at HBO. But I stayed because I wanted a career in the fashion industry, and I hated sales.

Ultimately, I quit eBay and selling jeans, and I made it big in the fashion industry. Bill Cunningham snapped my street looks. WWD wrote articles about me. Anna Wintour kind of remembered my name. We left Brooklyn and moved to a neighborhood called NEPONSIT, on the nicest beach block in Belle Harbor, NY. If you don't know, that's the fancy part of Rockaway. We bought our dream house. Everyone talked about that house, that's how big and imposing it was. By then, my third child, Dakota, was six-months old, and I got to spend more time with her than I did with her brother and sister. My career was thriving. I was my own boss. I dressed movie stars, styled Vogue editorials, and did my share of freelance styling jobs on Hollywood motion pictures. I took summers off and spent them on our beach with the kids.

It was 2006, and I hadn't sold a pair of jeans on eBay for the past four years. One September morning, I dropped my 2 big ones to school and was home in my kitchen with my baby girl, in my dream house. I wasn't set to pop up at the office in Soho till later that afternoon. My doorbell rang, and my life—our lives—changed forever. I swung open the door and saw six armed men, with bullet proof vests, in FBI marked windbreakers and caps. Six cars surrounded the house, and I found out later, six other guys were covering all of the house's exits.

"We are the FBI," one told me. He identified me by full name, including my middle and maiden names.

Immediately, I thought it was something Joe did. "Yeah, I don't know what my husband did, but he isn't here."

The lead agent, Greg Shitzman, quickly corrected me. "We aren't here for your husband, ma'am. We're here for you. Ma'am?"

Where the fuck was this asshole from? Who the fuck says, "ma'am" in New York? Well, Greg Shitzman did because he came from the Virginia FBI Field Office. Wait, what? Virginia? Where the fuck is Virginia? And why was this asshole crossing state lines to come for me? Did I commit a fashion crime? Did I wear the wrong Louboutin's? No joke, I had no idea. He says ever so kindly, "Can we come in? We will explain everything."

I am a law school graduate, and I watch enough TV to know to ask for a warrant. They have one; they have a search warrant. Twelve suits come into the house and start something between a rampage and a witch hunt. They take my Dell computer; they take my cellphone while I'm holding my baby; and they go into my closet—my shoe and clothes closet. They try to take my jeans, my very own jeans. I stop them and tell them that doesn't match the "merchandise" description in their warrant, so they put my stuff back. They're looking for new designer jeans I once sold and Juicy Couture tracksuits circa 2001. They find nothing because I haven't sold online for the past four years. Shitzman starts reading an indictment (apparently, I was indicted by a grand jury in the state of Virginia). He reads names of "victims" I've never heard before, who say they were defrauded online. The charges: Non-delivery of goods, wire fraud, and bank fraud. I don't ask for a lawyer because I'm innocent (I am also so fucking stupid because I also went to law school and I know better than that). Some of the statements were true. I recognized some transactions, but the facts around them were fabricated. I felt like I was in the twilight zone.

My baby starts crying while the suits are rummaging through my house and find nothing. Shitzman says I should talk or I will have to "go downtown" with his NY field office colleague. I then say, "Okay, I'll come with my lawyer." The New York agent was not happy being there, as he left he said they are just here as jurisdiction protocol, but if it was a New York case, they wouldn't even have agreed to execute such a ridiculous search warrant. Shitzman and his cheap suit left rudely. The NY agent left apologizing. I just thought, it's the "good cop, bad cop" act. I read my indictment a hundred times over. I sat there in disbelief... Seven counts of fraud... bank fraud, wire fraud, non-delivery of goods, impersonation (whattttt?) - total amount $27,000... witness A.F... 82 victims, many of which are in Germany... WHATTTTT??? I knew just the lawyer to call in NY. I knew the whole scene: the best lawyer if you carried a weapon, the best lawyer if you got a DUI, the best lawyer if you are P. Diddy and you got yourself in major shit at a club and your girlfriend, Jennifer Lopez, got arrested. How did I know? I interned in the best law firm right out of law school.

So, I go to Brafman and Associates, and I'm sitting in the client's chair. I am told I don't get to be represented by Brafman because he is the big Kahuna of state crimes. I get to be represented by Marc, as in Marc D'Angelo. He has won some of the most complex federal cases in America. As a former supervisor at a United States Attorney's Office and former Manhattan Assistant District Attorney, he fucking wrote the RICO ACT. He served as lead trial counsel on complex and serious criminal cases, investigations and financial regulatory matters in U.S. District Courts throughout the United States, in state courts in New York and New Jersey, and in other countries. He has represented nationals of other countries charged with spying against the United States and with violating Iranian sanctions. Generally, he handles high-stakes criminal cases involving securities, mail, wire, insurance and bankruptcy fraud, money laundering, construction and labor union matters, foreign corrupt practices act violations, racketeering and enterprise corruption, international arms dealing, anti-trust, bribery, kickbacks and criminal tax investigations, specializing in sensitive and high profile matters, including United States Congressional investigations. Do you know why I copied and pasted his bio on here? No, this isn't a plug for Marc, he lost my case... It is to point out how fucking unreal and ridiculous my situation was. I sold jeans. I fucking sold denim and Juicy Couture on fucking eBay!

So, here I am with my indictment on the table, watching Marc go through it, and say, "Hmmm. Seven counts. This is bullshit. This can't go to trial. But then again, the new guidelines, in the district of Virginia, can have you behind bars for a maximum of 4 years. But I've never seen it happen. I would think you would end up on home confinement for 6 months. Oh, and you would lose your license."

At that point, that was the worst news ever. Home confinement and losing my license? I was ashamed, a little scared, and I didn't want to lose my bar license, even though I didn't even practice law. Never in a million years did I think at that moment that I would end up in jail. The game at that point was to wait and see if we could squash the indictment and if we could fight the venue. I mean, why Virginia? I had never even been there. Why Virginia? I'll tell you why... because there was no precedent on internet fraud and the Commonwealth State of Virginia was all into having this precedent and having it fast.

Napster's prosecution was paving the way for new precedent on "internet crimes" and was being prosecuted in Virginia the year before in 2000. Virginia was on a mission, to grab all the internet crimes it could, and make it a case for the books. After all, in all federal cases tried in Virginia, 99% of them ended in the guilty verdict. Not guilty verdicts are as rare as fucking unicorns in Virginia's federal courts. Do you think my lawyer told me that? Nope, he didn't. I take a second mortgage on my dream house and give all the money to my very expensive lawyer. All 150K just for pre-trial. I hoped the case was to be dismissed, as he said, on the basis that it's fucking ridiculous. We fly to VA, to go to the first of many court hearings, and the Virginia probation department that interviewed me on the phone submits its pre-trial report, failing to mention I am an upstanding citizen, a respected member of my community, a member of my kids' school PTA, and a leading member of my local Autism Speaks organization. It also fails to report accurately on my son's current health and the fact that he has a serious learning disability that occupies hours of my day in taking him to therapy and caring for his special needs. Instead, it notes that I am not just an American citizen, but rather importantly a French national, who has already received the outspoken support of the French government and drew the interest of the French Diplomatic Attaché in Washington. The report notes that the ambassador of France has shown much interest in these legal proceedings, and that made me extremely predisposed to be at "FLIGHT RISK."

I am panicked, but I look over at Marc. I mean he is like the John Wayne of the courtroom. He fucking defended spies and shit… and he looks serene. He argues against me being a flight risk, and he tells me when the judge asks you how you plead to say "not guilty." Wait a minute Marc, I have to plead not guilty? Like what the fuck is this? Ally McBeal goes to VA? It was more like Paris Hilton screaming, "I'm a celebrity get me out of here." Except it was me saying, "I'm a mom who sold jeans out of her kitchen and takes her son to therapy every day after 3pm, get me the fuck outta here."

"Not guilty," I squeak instead. The judge says I have a right to a speedy trial, so my trial starts in two weeks. Of course, Marc pointed out that the alleged crime goes back a few years, that we didn't even get discovery from the prosecution, that there are 82 transactions to look over so he asks for the trial to be a few months later. Granted. I am released on my own recognizance, until the trial. Wait, the judge did say the word "released"? Like was I under arrest before that? Is that why there was a marshal behind me holding handcuffs while the judge was deliberating on my bail? HOLY FUCKING FUCK!!!! I flip out, I cry, I literally shit myself in my expensive Wolford black synergy stockings.

"Okay," Marc says as we leave the courtroom, "we need to go to pre-trial and you have to give them your passports."

"The American government cannot have my French passport, fucking fuck them," I say.

"Yes, they can and you're going to give it to them or they will arrest you and you will stay in jail till your trial date which was just pushed off 3 months," he says.

So, I hand over my passport, and I cry when the prosecutor, that big fat greasy scummy asshole, smiles as he takes my French one. We fly home. Now what? Marc says now you continue living your life, and we meet weekly to prepare for trial. And that's what we do. He convinces me I won't go to jail. He convinces me the jury will see right through this insanity. He convinces me the judge is obligated by the guidelines to take into consideration that my child has very serious special needs and this should come into play if I was to get sentenced. It was excruciating. The discovery was years old. Some of it didn't come from my computer and I knew it. Some originals had been tampered with, some numbers had been changed. Some so-called victims, "customers who bought jeans", from my business partner and I couldn't be found by our investigator. A lot of things smelled bad. But instead of scaring me, it reassured me. I believed in the land of the free, where the truth always wins. Bahahahaha. Okay, Laura Ingalls... I mean Ingrid. We were prepared. I had the BEST of the BEST federal defense attorneys in the country. My case was ridiculous; I sold jeans! I may have to pay a fine for bad accounting, but no-one goes to jail for years for selling $28,000-worth of jeans on the internet.

Jury selection was like in the movies. You assess who is most likely to be favorable to you. Whoever will have an open heart for a mom who struggles with a child who has a severe learning disability? A mom, who works two jobs, and was a good citizen until now. BULL-FUCKING-SHIT! In Virginia, the juries are mainly composed of government employees: policemen, mailmen, mail room employee at the FBI in Langley, social security office employees. You name the agency, you bet your ass one of the jurors at least worked for one. The only guy who didn't was a Pakistani taxi driver, but he told us he came to VA originally because he aspired to be a CIA employee. FUCK MY FUCKING LIFE.

The trial lasted two days. Marc and I often thought we had mini victories, where little glimpses of truth would come out. The feds deemed it a scheme to defraud, even though 80% of our customers got their orders (this was ironically mentioned by my defense team many times). And the 20% of customers who were unhappy could rarely be found. My defense team hired a forensic investigator and could not find the supposed purchasers from Germany or Sweden who were "defrauded." This is what you call being railroaded by the federal justice system.

The prosecution's main witness (my ex-business partner) felt bad lying and sending me to jail at the last minute. She went back on her testimony. I don't know what they had promised her, but she looked scared. She was from Virginia, and during the investigation, she had been visited by the FBI and prosecutor a few times. Marc and I also came to see her to get documents from her because she ran most of our operation, and when we left her house in VA during the time of pre-trial, we thought she was just scared but wouldn't lie.

She cried on the stand and refused to say whatever the prosecutor promised her to say. So, the judged asked her if I intimidated her. She said no. She said she felt sad because she knew I didn't do anything, and she knew she shouldn't say what the prosecutor and her agreed she would say. They read her her rights and started waving the perjury card in the air. The judge told her she has to go back in the chambers and talk to an attorney before she perjures herself and ends up in jail like I will. She left and came back...and delivered the testimony the prosecutor wanted in a frail and sobbing voice, looking at me with very sorry eyes. They flew a German lady from Germany, who had supposedly bought a pair of Rock & Republic Crystal Jeans from me, and never received them. I didn't know the lady. I didn't remember her transaction. I'm not even sure she was really one of my alleged victims. They convinced the jury this specific transaction was fraudulent because I didn't accept credit cards and asked to be paid by bank wire. Except I'm not the one who took payments, my partner was. My job was to source the jeans I found in discount stores like Century 21 and Daffy's in NYC and to ship them to the customers. Each piece of evidence has been twisted and turned to look a certain way... BAD.

The prosecution found a loophole to prevent us from showing that all my revenue went to paying for Dylan's very expensive therapies. Instead, they found a receipt for a Chanel Bag I bought on eBay for a client and showed pictures to the jury, saying I used the money to buy Chanel, a bag that cost more than 6 months of salary for many of the government employed jurors. I felt the contempt. I felt the judgement in their eyes. I felt their jealousy and even hatred. I decided I'd testify against my lawyer's advice... but I wanted to speak the truth. I wanted to show I was human and not vile. First, my attorney put me on the stand, and that went well. The questions were tough, but a lot of it was about how desperate and distracted Dylan's condition made me. The prosecutor didn't care about Dylan. He said, if every mother with a handicapped child was to steal, what would this world be? Was I above other mothers? What made me so special that my kid had to get private self-paid therapy?

"Oh, I see," he said. "You are from NY. You are rich and famous." And then, the biggest shocker, he asked why I didn't pick up the phone on Saturdays when customers called.

"I am Jewish orthodox. We cannot pick up the phone on Saturdays, it's Shabbat," I said.

He smiled an evil smile and said, "AH! You are Jewish? You are above everyone else, and religion came first."

I was silenced. I couldn't believe the enormity of the fucking anti-Semitism of the statement. My lawyer said, "Objection, your honor. This is unacceptable."

"Sustained," the judge replied. "The jury will ignore the prosecution's inflammatory statement."

But the jury didn't ignore it. Virginia is very anti-Semitic. After September 11th, many in states like VA blamed the Jews for the terrorist outburst in America. I had just been railroaded by a political landmine. We took a break... and I went to the bathroom with my mom. I was in one of the stalls, and I heard two jurors, females speaking.

"She doesn't feel remorse," one said.

"She is so entitled," the other said. "Did you see her expensive haircut? She doesn't deserve any pity, whether she meant to do it or not, she needs to pay."

I fucking peed in my underwear. I remember I didn't have time to take off my stocking and panties. I peed myself. My mom came out, but she didn't understand because her English isn't good. I started to cry as I washed my stockings and dried them under the hand drier. I told her, "Maman, they are sending me to prison." Reality didn't hit her. It didn't hit Joe. I don't even think it hit my big shot lawyer, for he had seen such bigger crimes gone unpunished, thanks to his skills. Deep down, I knew I was going to jail. Court was adjourned.

Closing statements the next day were reassuring. The prosecutor, in his cheap suit, with his big fat belly, made small talk with the judge (is that even legal?) about their golf tournament at some fundraiser for fucking President Bush, as we waited for the jury to come out. Isn't the judge usually supposed to arrive after the jury? WTF is going onnnnnnn!?

Then, Marc addressed the jury.

"My grandparents always bickered," Marc said. "She told him to put the toilet seat down, he told her he forgot. She replied he shouldn't forget and it would burst into a big fight."

Marc, where are you going with this?

"So my grandfather would always shout as he slammed the door, 'Nancy, why do you always make a federal case out of everything?' and this is exactly what the prosecution is doing here. They are making a federal case out of a case that belongs in small claims court. And the prosecution is about to affect some very important little lives, especially Dylan's in doing so."

That was fucking good! I felt golden!!! Marc had the last word, and he made Mr. Fucking Grease ball look so petty and fucking crazy. WE WON. We went back to our hotel across the Justice Department Building and waited for deliberations. I ate olives and bread and had a glass of wine... Marc's phone rang after two hours. The jury has a verdict. He panicked. "What do you mean?" he asked his interlocutor. "The bailiff gave them 16 boxes of discovery to look over, so how can they have a verdict in two hours?"

He doesn't look me in the eye, but I know it's not good. I decide that my best bet is to be found guilty on one count out of seven and it wouldn't be so bad. We return to the courtroom. I stand up to hear the verdict. The room is spinning around me. I feel lightheaded, and my heart is pounding so hard I can hear it loud in my ears. The U.S. Marshal stands behind me and holds my arm, with one hand on the handcuffs attached to his belt. I move my elbow to release my arm from his grip, but Marc tells me to leave it.

"On the first count of wire fraud, how do you find the defendant?" the judge asks.

The foreman, a CIA analyst, reads his little paper. "We find the defendant guilty, your honor."

"On the second count of wire fraud, how do you find the defendant?"

Again, the foreman reads his little paper. "We find the defendant guilty, your honor."

"On the third count of mail fraud, how do you find the defendant?"

"We find the defendant guilty, your honor."

At this point, the voices sounded so far away, I wasn't really listening anymore. I was trying desperately not to faint. Was I going to go to jail right now? Was the marshal behind me going to slap those handcuffs on his belt on me? I was going to hyperventilate. "We find the defendant guilty... fifth... guilty...guilty...guilty."

"Marc, can we appeal?" I asked him in a furious whisper. "Marc, appeal now. Marc, tell the judge we are appealing."

20

He ignored me. "Your honor, my client needs to be with her children till the sentencing hearing. She needs to prepare her child for her potential absence your honor, please show the children some grace and let my client out on bail until sentencing."

The U.S. Marshal gets ready to hand-cuff me, but the judge waves him away and says, "Defendant has respected the terms of her pre-trial release. She will be under the supervision of pre-trial services until the sentencing hearing, and she will be expected to report to her pre-trial officer in NY until sentencing."

I turn around and I see my mother, who understood I had been found guilty. She smiles and whispers, "It's going to be okay." Joe looked terrified and angry.

We fly back to NY. Sentencing is in three months. Life is sucked out of me. I hug my children tight. Dakota is not even a year old. I take her to bed with me and sleep with her. I smell her. I cry in her hair. I'm scared I won't watch her walk for the first time. I'm scared I won't hear her first words. I'm scared I won't see her grow. I'm just plain scared.

That fear still lives in me. Even though I'm done now, I've been scared of being separated from my children every day for the past 12 years. That fear is still living in every particle of my body today, even though they are 2 adults and a teenager.

But, back then, I hadn't even been separated yet. I flew to Washington DC every week, to interview appeal lawyers. The meetings are scary. They say VA doesn't fuck around, and I'm definitely going to jail. They say the sentencing guidelines work against me. Sentencing guidelines are mandatory minimums that federal judges must follow.

They say the federal prosecutors are making an example out of my case. It's a NY case, but it's federal because I had an AOL email address. The alleged crime was committed crossing state lines, via the internet. I have fallen into the very opaque cracks of the system. We hire Nathan Levine, the fucking HOLY GRAIL of Supreme Court and appellate court litigators. He says I have a strong appeal. We have to wait for sentencing, before filing the appeal. We get the motion to appeal ready to file the day of sentencing.

I'm scared, but I hold on to hope. I believe the lawyers. Joe takes a third mortgage on the house and a line of credit with his bank to pay my lawyers. At that point, I tell my mom I'm going to jail. Can she help pay for lawyers? She says no. God is great and will help me. I'm not surprised she didn't help. She never felt like I needed help. She always thought I'm like a cat, that I always land on my feet. And even though she taught me to study and work hard, she also believed that when you have nice tits and ass you should be able to find a guy rich enough to pay for you.

She always despised that I didn't use my looks to get ahead. She didn't say it like that but she often noticed, how "uglier women we knew, got bigger rings on their fingers, and unlimited funds AMEX cards." Joe was my one and only support system. He knew I was innocent. He knew I worked hard for our son, and he knew I was a good mom. He was determined to keep me out of jail. I think he was also terrified to have motherless kids. He lost his mom to cancer, and it left him very opinionated about the mother-child bond. His dad beat up his mother her whole life, so much so that when she died of bone cancer, her kids were relieved. I believe Joe wasn't a good dad because he felt dads are disposable, like his own freak of a father (I fucking hated that man for mind-fucking my husband so much, he didn't have one paternal fiber in him).

*

So for three months, I hugged my kids a little tighter. I prepared them for the unthinkable. Except Dakota. She was just a baby, still drinking from the bottle. She was my baby. I still hoped and prayed. Joe went into psycho fucking religious mode. He started bringing these weird rabbis around my house that would do these fucking strange rituals. They gave me some strange parchment papers with Hebrew Scriptures on them, and he was to sleep with them under his pillow, but he had to remove them if we were to have intercourse. He made me throw out all the tomato sauce I had in the house that wasn't marked Kosher. He claimed one rabbi told him I was going to prison because I kept non-kosher food in the house.

Fuck, even my Tide laundry detergent had to be kosher parve. One rabbi told him I needed to sit and admit to any lie I may have told since I was bat mitzvah-ed at the age of 12. I was like, "Okay, fuckers— newsflash, I didn't have a bat mitzvah." I could puke just thinking about the level of indoctrination he underwent. In the meantime, my older brother went the political route. He reached out to Washington's Jewish Coalitions and lobbyists. They got to Senator Schumer and Hilary Clinton and the French government. Diplomacy worked for and against me here. The French government was up in arms. My case was transmitted to the Quai D'Orsay, where my case was tried by French judges, who determined the charges against me were not crimes in France. The French embassy in Washington DC petitioned on behalf of President Sarkozy, requesting my immediate release and exoneration, on the basis that often the US requests that Americans found guilty of crimes be released to US custody for trial and due process. But something was up, this case, my case seemed to be something else—something political. Nothing and no-one seemed to be able to help. Letters of good moral character by Dylan's doctors, school deans, rabbis, employers, affluent political figures (close to my family), nothing worked. Someone in Virginia wanted me in jail and wanted my case to become textbook precedent.

Chapter 5: Orange is the New Black

My sentencing day came, and I was sentenced to four years in FEDERAL MEDIUM-HIGH security prison: Danbury Federal Correctional Institution. Why MEDIUM-HIGH and not Martha Stewart's camp cupcake across the street? Because the French got involved, and that made me a flight risk. Like the fucking French government was going to send BLACK OPS to break me out of prison. What the actual fuck? Why such vigor in incarcerating me for a white-collar crime under $30,000?

I was to turn myself in on October 27th, ten days after my birthday. So, I had the summer to care for my kids. That meant three months of freedom. How is it humanely possible to live knowing you are going to turn yourself in on a given day to be incarcerated for four years? I would not see Dakota take her first steps or say her first words. I wouldn't even see her go to preschool. I would be out in time for Dylan's bar mitzvah, but I may come home to a child that regressed. That's what his doctors predicted. They said my absence will cause regression. Regression in autism spectrum disorders is well documented; the attribution of regression to environmental stress factors may result in a delay in diagnosis. The apparent onset of regressive autism is surprising and distressing, especially to parents. Dylan regressed so much when I went away that I suspected severe hearing loss because it seemed he didn't hear what I said when I spoke to him. They said his mental development was at risk, and they were afraid he would go from being on the spectrum to being severely autistic.

In the three months leading to the beginning of my sentence and the day I had to turn myself in, I lived with hope. Lots of hope... that's probably what held me back from fleeing the country and becoming a fugitive.

I fantasized about running to Mexico with the kids, getting new identities and raising them as little Mexicanos. Their dark-complexions and hair definitely would make it easily believable that I was a GRINGA who had kids with a Mexican man. The scenario played well in my head, but, man, living on the run was scary. It also meant

23

that growing up my kids would always have to look over their shoulders and fear passport control. I worked so hard to give them a good life... growing up with a fugitive as mother was probably not the way to raise successful adults.

The French President was involved, and through his diplomatic liaisons, he asked for my release on French diplomatic immunity grounds. When that was refused, the French ambassador offered to open his doors and house me and the kids under diplomatic immunity, until my appeal would go through. They also offered to fly me to France, where there is no extradition treaty with the US, and where I would be safe from extradition and further prosecution. It was all so tempting because I didn't want to be separated from my babies. I didn't care about going to jail. I didn't care about not living life as I knew it. I didn't care about my freedoms being taken away and being incarcerated with scary people. All I cared about was being separated from my babies. I lived for every morning, waking up to kiss them, smell them, and care for them. My life, regardless of my successful and glamorous career in fashion, only revolved around them. I had been a mom since I was 21. All I knew how to be was a mom. I lived and breathed motherhood.

I played the scenario in my head: I fly to DC and find diplomatic shelter at the French Embassy. I get escorted in a diplomatic vehicle to the airport, where their jet would be awaiting... I imagine the private jet to look like US Air Force One, because why not? I mean it's a scenario in my head, so I can imagine whatever the fuck I want anyway.

The night before I was to turn myself in, we had been with my lawyers on the phone countless times, and they attempted to file a motion to keep me out of jail while awaiting my appeal. It was denied. Any attempt at staying out failed, and I realized going to jail was inevitable. It was a Sunday night, and I started hyperventilating. We put the kids to bed, and Joe took me to a doctor, some fucking weird doctor's office in Borough Park. Some Rabbi's friend of some Rabbi said I can go there, and if my vitals aren't good, and he would write to the Bureau of Prisons and request we push of the date of my surrender.

The doctor was Russian, an Orthodox Jew, and shady as fuck. He called the Bureau of Prisons at midnight, asked for an urgent contact email, and got the email ready. We get on the phone with my attorney, Nat Lewin, and his daughter and co-counsel Aliza. They both advised against this move. I heard the words resonate in my head, "Fugitive...warrant out of your arrest... obstruction to justice... lengthening your sentence... incarcerate you far from home."

Joe and I went home with our tails between our legs. I went home, kissed my kids, and cried all night. I woke up from my sleepless night and got the kids ready for school. It was picture day for Savannah. The kids went to Magen David Yeshiva in Brooklyn, the prestigious Jewish school of choice for the rich Syrian Jewish community. I curled her hair. I put in beautiful satin bows. I helped her put her ivory stockings on and her Lili Gaufrette ensemble, an ivory silk shirt with pretty ruffles and a peplum skirt to match. We bought her outfit at Lester's, the week before in preparation for picture day. As I do her hair, I tell her I may have to go for a few days... and Dad is staying with Berta (her beloved Mexican nanny). I told her she has to be brave and take care of her older brother for me because he is not strong like her and he is special. I tell her to give Dakota lots of kisses, especially when she gives her baba (her bottle of milk) before bed. I tell her I'll be back soon, and I prepared a Post-It with Dad's number, Jimmy's, and Bobby's (Joe's brothers who were so much part of the kids' lives) and Berta's. She asks if she can call my number. She knows it by heart; she sings it to me. I've had this number since NYC Phone Company VoiceStream existed, then I migrated it to T-Mobile, then to Verizon, and people still call us wanting to buy this number from us, because that's how cool that number was in NYC. I tell Savannah not to call me because I'll be busy but that I'll try to call her.

Dakota woke up, and I can still remember her delicious smell of baby eau de toilette Mustela. I breathed her soft baby hair as I grabbed her from her crib and hugged her. I made her baba, took her blankie, and went to help Dylan get dressed. I warn him less than I did Savannah about my absence. He can't handle it... He probably can't understand it, either. A lot of what I tell Dylan at that point goes in one ear and out the other. He is better than last year but still has a severe auditory processing disorder. Instead, I hug him. I tell him I love him so much.

He starts talking about his baseball cards.

He is OCD, too. Having obsessive compulsive disorder is typical to children on the spectrum of autism. He obsesses over baseball cards, and that's all he will care to talk about, even if it's off subject. He will say the same thing repeatedly. He is upset the last pack had two of the same Derek Jeter Cards, but he still didn't get an Alex Rodriguez card, and he needs it.

I tell him I'll buy him all the baseball cards in the world next time we go out together. I also tell him he looks so handsome for picture day today, but he won't be deterred.

"I need a new pack of cards," he said, not letting the discussion of baseball cards go. "When will we go get it? I have two Derek Jeter's Number 2. Did you know he is number 2, but I don't have Alex Rodriguez. I need it? When will we get it?"

"I don't know when I'll get it, Dylan," I said. "Mommy has to be away today. Maybe Dad can get it."

He doesn't realize I tell him I won't be here. "Then, you tell Dad he has to pick me up because when he finishes work the store is closed and I need it today."

"Okay, Dylan, I will tell him."

I drive them to school in my Range Rover. Shit, I look like such a suburban housewife. I don't ever drop them off at carpool. I park on the street behind the school, and I hold their hands tight as we walk the rest of the way to school. I hand Savannah the Post-It with the phone numbers, and I tell her, "Anything you need, you call Dad first okay? If he doesn't pick-up, call Uncle Bobby (He is a sergeant in the NYPD at the precinct next to the school). Don't call me, okay?"'

I fix the ribbons and bows in her hair. I adjust her curls and I start crying as I hug her so tight she can't breathe. She is so small, so tiny. She is six years old. She hugs me and taps me on the back.

"It's okay, Mommy," she tells me. "You will be back soon, and we can go to Dunkin Donuts to have munchkins after school."

At that time I worked part-time, I had come to a point in my career where I opened my freelance fashion consulting company in NY, and I could be working for Vogue or on the set of an HBO series for three weeks, and then I could have two weeks off. So often after school, we would go to Dunkin Donuts for Le Goûter (French snack time). I'd have coffee with my best friends Julie and Valerie while the kids ran around the donut shop eating munchkins.

I grabbed Savannah's hand and put Dylan's hand in hers.

"Take care of him for me," I told her. "And if anyone bothers him, you kick their ass okay? Just like mommy does. And also wait for him after class, so if Dad is not on time to pick you up, Dylan isn't on the street alone, okay, baby?"

She nodded her head and hugged me tight. It was insane to ask my six-year-old to take care of her eight-year-old brother. I don't think she knew she would not see me again for a while. I don't think she knew she wouldn't have me home for a long, long time. Savannah is wise beyond her years. Often, I looked into her eyes and wondered if she wasn't the reincarnation of my grandmother, Zohra. She has her smile, her wit, and her dutiful sense of overprotectiveness. Now, when we speak about October 27th, Savannah who is now an adult says, "It was picture day. You gave me a yellow Post-It with Joe's number on it. You never came home. We didn't speak to you for days, and when we did, a weird recording came on right before we were connected."

The fucking recording...the recording that told my kids exactly where I was, when I was trying not to tell them. "This is a call from an inmate at a Federal Correctional Facility..." FUCK MY FUCKING LIFE and fuck my kids' life while you are at it, too.

I went home, held Dakota in my arms, as I sat in my den, getting my long blonde locks chopped by my hairstylist Tony. I told her I'm surrendering to prison today, and I'm scared of looking too feminine and attractive. I'm scared of getting gang-banged by serious offenders. I was going to medium-high security prison, for selling fucking True Religion Jeans and Juicy Couture Tracksuits on eBay. She shook her head...in disbelief. These are New Yorkers for you. They don't judge you for this kind of SNAFU shit. They actually support you and tell you about their uncle who is incarcerated at the moment for turning back the miles on a few car's odometers.

Back at home, I look at myself in the mirror. My platinum blond hair is chopped. I took off my diamond eternity wedding band, and my 9-carat, cushion diamond engagement ring. I took off my diamond Rolex, my push present from Joe, for Savannah's birth. I put on black leggings, and a tee shirt, some flats, and hugged Dakota one last time as I handed her to Berta before slipping into the passenger seat next to Joe. Before leaving I briefed Berta, in Spanish... I speak her Spanish fluently. She is Mexican, and the kids speak Spanish too. I tell her she is not to leave while I'm away. I know she dislikes Joe and the idea of being alone with him and the kids. He is tough, not pleasant, and doesn't smile much. He isn't warm. I promise her that for each month she stays I will pay her 1000 dollars extra when I get back. I don't tell her they put me away for four years. I believe I will win my appeal. I believe I will be out in a few days. Do I really believe it, though? I'm numb. I don't know. My heart hurts.

I look over at Joe and I have mixed feelings about him, too. What the fuck is his deal? He is supportive in hard situations but such an asshole in pleasant times. He doesn't say I love you unless you say it first. He gets pissed off about crumbs on the floor (fuck, he is so OCD about that, I threw a CRUMB FEST party when he went to Israel to bury his rabbi, and I invited all my friends, to eat all over the house and make crumbs). Joe is an enigma... I met him when I was 17 and he was 26. I was in law school already (I skipped a few grades when I was younger, and two years of college by getting the equivalent Baccalaureate in France that same year).

My roommate Nurit and I went to South Beach with some friends. We went clubbing. I had a fake ID, but I also was Roger's little sister... My big brother was notorious in South Beach, doors open the second I said I was his little sister. We went to this nightclub called the Living Room on Collins Avenue. I didn't drink but Nurit, who is older than me, did. She went on to wander around the club while I stood in the crowd... This older guy comes up to me and speaks to me in English with a horrible French accent, "Hay hough aaaacheeee youuu? I'm Patrickkkkk." He looks Jewish and very French. He's not particularly good looking, not dressed well, but he acted as though his name should get me to get on my skinny little knees and suck his dick right then in there. Well, I was a virgin, and I was not sucking any dick and certainly not an ugly French guy's dick. Turns out he was a huge celebrity singer in France: Patrick Bruel. I kind of knew who he was, but I didn't recognize him. I wasn't living in France, and he was plain ugly, and that accent? Wtf! He shouldn't be allowed to speak English with that accent. He went back to his hot Eurasian piece of ass, and I impatiently waited for Nurit to want to go home. At 4 am, she finally pops back up, her beautiful cheeks flushed, and her eyes sparkling like she just scored. She drives a Volkswagen Golf, the latest model. She is cool as fuck, and she is my bestie. I admire her so much. She is part German, part Israeli, and a few years older than me. I feel so innocent and a prude compared to her. She is so gorgeous. She has higher cheekbones than I do and looks like Romy Schneider in Sissi Young Empress. She is as voluptuous as I am skin and bones and boobs. Nurit is always on a quest to lose weight. Under our beds are all the ABS-Crunching devices she bought on late night infomercial shopping sprees. I think she is motherfucking fabulous. We're driving home from south beach to Aventura, and she makes a U-turn, and says, "I am hungry. Let's go for a sandwich." Me, in prude mode: "It's 4 am. Let's go home. Who the fuck has a sandwich at 4 am?"

Nurit and her friends do. They drank. I didn't. She speaks of this fabulous French little kiosk in South Beach called, "La Sandwicherie." We pull up Miami Vice style, in our brand spanking new Volkswagen (same car she lent me to take my driving test), and as we get out of the car, I hear a loud Hebrew conversation between two guys.

"Ma pitommmmm..." I look at Nurit, like I just threw up in my mouth. Israeli men aren't my cup of tea. They are loud. They are promiscuous. They are pushy and hairy. She smiles and turns into a vixen. We sit at the counter. She orders a huge baguette sandwich with the other two girls, and I order a Perrier. Why do I mention the Perrier? Ah … Perrier changed my life. I feel someone standing by my side, with a glass of Perrier in his hands. He looks like Andy Garcia but better looking, a little bit of Al Pacino in Scarface. He has John Travolta's hair in Saturday Night Fever (if you are a millennial, just use Google). He is smooth. A smooth operator… NY accent and all.

"Hello, beauties. Oh, you are drinking Perrier. You must be French?"

WTF! Nurit and I spoke English to each other and sometimes German (she helped me practice my German, and I think the last time I spoke German was with her). I was rude. I was a rude-ass bitch. I looked at him, dashing, handsome, and then I had a flashback to 15 mins before, like wait a minute… isn't that the guy who was saying "Maaaaa pitommmm" (what the heck?) to his friend. How is this guy so well-spoken in English, with his sleek hair and NY accent, and he sounded Israeli two minutes ago?

I look over at Nurit. She is eating her sandwich and pauses. Her eyes are glistening with excitement. Mr. Al Pacino Junior's charm isn't wasted on her.

"This guy is so sleek, with the French comment and all, but he is Israeli as fuck," I whisper to her.

P.S.: half of my family is Israeli, so no need to send the Mossad after my ass when you read this. It's just that in Miami they are as obnoxious as Adam Sandler's character in the ZOHAN.

Joe laughs and doesn't lose his cool. He tells us he is a stockbroker on Wall Street, and he is from Brooklyn. Nurit starts blabbering, she is a fashion designer. She tells him she is European. She says a few words in Hebrew. I just roll my eyes and sip on my Perrier. I think I even started chewing on the lemon slice. I glance over at his friend. Now that guy is really Israeli, and he has bushy eyebrows. I hope Nurit is not planning a double date because I ain't going with Mr. Bushy over there.

Joe smoothly, moves his attention on to me. "And you? What do you do?"

I flip my hair. I smirk and knowing he won't find me as sexy or old enough to be taken to bed like Nurit was. I say, "I'm 17 1/2 (you didn't forget the half when you were underage) and I go to law school. Oh, and I work in a boutique called Bisou Bisou. I'm an assistant manager there, in Bal Harbor Mall. And what the fuck is a stockbroker anyway?"

His eyes lit up. He flashed the biggest smile. "Ooooh la la, a lawyer, so young and pretty, and are you Jewish too?"

Fucking stupid questions, deserve stupid answers.

"No, I'm Krishna. Of course, I'm Jewish. Didn't I understand your whole Hebrew loud rant with your boyfriend before?"

Joe was whipped. "Oooh, feisty, relax, that is not my boyfriend, that's my cousin Joey! First of all, and second of all, why are you so rude?" Ba-ha-ha-ha-ha, Joe and Joey, Laurel and Hardy same fucking shit. Nurit, is impatient. She wants the attention. And she deserved it. She was the right age. She was pretty, single and ready to mingle. So, Joe proceeds with such a Swiss solution. He proposes we give him our numbers, and he calls us to take the two of us to dinner before he heads back to NYC in a few days. We say okay. Weirdly enough, I meant it. I wanted to see him again. I was intrigued.

Nurit slips him her "fashion designer" business card, and I pull my usual stunt. I give him a fax number. I absolutely loved doing that, the thought of the guy calling and getting the fucking annoying ringing fax tone in his hear. It would wipe out the stupid "I just scored" smile off of his face. Let Nurit be the "easy-one."

He somehow finds my move too easy, so he goes, "Is this really your number?"

He got me. "No, it's a fax number."

"Is it your fax number at least?"

"No, not even."

"Why won't you give me your number? Your friend did."

"I don't give my number to strangers. I don't take lollipops from strangers, either. I'm underage."

"C'monnnnnnn." There goes the Brooklynite in all of his splendor. I had heard that accent on West Side Story. I had never met a guy from Brooklyn before. I didn't even know where Brooklyn was, except I'd seen it in the movies. Turns out, I had met someone very similar to the wolf of Wall Street.

The next day, I woke up thinking about him, thinking about Nurit on the way home, with all the car windows down, and her hair in the air á la Farrah Fawcett, still buzzed and saying, "Omgggg. He is soooo cute."

"I still think he is Israeli," I said. "I don't buy his American accent."

She was right, though. He was cute. He was 26 years old, handsome, from NY, and when he paid for my fake French sparkling water, her coke and her sandwich, he took out a wad of cash. I liked that. He was an adult.

I went to class in the morning and went to work that afternoon, at Bisou Bisou. It was an upcoming fashion brand at the time, in the very ritzy Bar Harbor mall. I was behind the counter and the phone rang. "Bisou Bisou, Bonjour, Ingrid speaking how can I help you?"

"Ya bonjour whatever," Nurit said. "The guy from last night called. He invited me to dinner, and he said you are welcome to tag along."

Okay, so Nurit got a date with Al Pacino Junior, and I'm welcome to tag along as a third wheel?

"Yeah, no thanks, Nurit. I'm not going to tag along. He can go fuck himself. Are you sure that's what he said? Did he ask for my number?"

"Yes, he said you can come if you want because he promised to take us both out, and no he didn't ask for your number. Did you want to give it to him?"

"Yes... well, no, I don't know, Nurit. Just go enjoy the date. You were more excited about him than I was, anyway." I went on with my life, kind of pissed. And then I forgot about him. I figured Nurit, who is sexually active already, would please him so much he would never look back. She was very sensual, and she was liberated. I knew men desired her and I was sure he would love her ways.

At that time, my parents had moved back to Miami from France and asked I leave the apartment I shared with Nurit to live with them in Williams Island, a luxurious and upscale gated community. So, when Nurit went out with Joe, I wasn't sitting on our couch waiting for her to tell me all about her date. I actually didn't call her the next day. I didn't want to seem like I cared.

The phone rang at my parents' house. My mom said it was for me, someone American.

"Hello?"

"Hi, Ingrid? It's Joe. Remember me? Nurit gave me your number."

"Yeah, I remember. She gave you my number? Why? Didn't you guys go on a date?"

"Yup, she said you didn't want to come. She said you were offended."

"I wasn't offended. I was told I was welcome to tag along on your date."

"Wait, what? No, I called her to invite you both to dinner in Coconut Grove and asked if she will call you or I should. She proposed to call you and arrange to drive you to me."

I understood Nurit wanted a chance at a date alone with the guy, and she took her best shot. She wasn't wrong. I acted so casual and uninterested. Why should I fuck up her chances of getting with him?

"So you went on a date with Nurit, and now you are calling me? Why? Didn't you like her?"

"Well, to tell you the truth, I like you more. You are more my type. I really want to take you out."

I'm fucking 17 years old and the Wolf of Wall Street wants to take me out. My heart is pounding, and I'm about to turn into a really bad friend.

"Okay, but before I say yes, where did you leave it with Nurit?"

"She kissed me, but I didn't kiss her back. I told her I had to go. So, then she understood and proposed to give me your number."

FUCK, FUCK, FUCK, FUCK, FUCK... a really bad friend. "Okay. Where are you taking me?"

"I'll take you to dinner. Wear a nice dress."

"Don't tell me what to wear! Besides, I'm French. I always wear a nice dress." We agree to go out the next night. I called Nurit, and she explained her ego took a hit. She didn't want him to just settle for her because he didn't get to meet me, so she gave him my number so he can make a decision. I told her that I'd go out with him on a date. She said to go and have a good time, but I think she was pissed. I also think part of her thought I was too young, not yet sexual, and too uninteresting for him to choose me. Part of her thought he would call her back after he had a boring night with me.

That afternoon before our date, my dad and brother got into an argument, and my dad had chest pain. When I came home from school, my mom said my dad had been in the ER, and he is resting in the bedroom, but she had a scare. I felt uneasy going out

30

on the date... I confided in my mom. I told her I met a handsome, Jewish young man from NY, and we were supposed to go on a date tonight before he flew back to NY the next day. She said call him and propose lunch the next day. I called him and told him my dad just had a mini heart attack. He thought I was standing him up with the lamest craziest excuse.

"It's okay if you don't want to see me but don't lie about your father," he said.

Then, I proposed the lunch, but I could tell he was a temperamental guy. He said he will think about it and call me back. He called back a few hours later and said he was okay for lunch, but I better not stand him up. I had the motherfucking upper hand. He thought I was going to stand him up. The next day came, and I went to pick him up in my brand spanking new Jeep, FIU vanity plate in the back and the Williams Island resident plate in the front (I'm not showing off there is a reason I'm telling you this), in Hollywood (not California, but Ft Lauderdale), at his cousin Joey's house.

I pulled up in the typical all-American driveway, nothing like Aventura, or Golden Beach where I lived, nothing impressive. I felt right then and there, we aren't from the same world. He came out, and, man, people look so different in the daytime. He was still handsome, but not shiny and bright like that night. He was different. It was early for lunch, so he said let's go to the mall. "I need to buy sneakers," he said.

I thought to myself: is that what older guys do? They take you to the mall, maybe to buy you something? I felt awkward. I drove back to Aventura because fucking Hollywood felt weird as fuck. It was not the same neighborhood as mine. Everything still looked like the 1980 there. We went to Aventura Mall. We went to Foot Locker, and he really tried sneakers on. He didn't find anything. I told him I want to go to Wet Seal. It was like H&M at the time, and we walked through. I found a top or two and went to the register. He asked me if I wanted him to pay, but I said no. He stayed back and let me pay. BIG FUCKING MISTAKE. I've made this mistake with every man in my life ever since. But more about this later.

He asked where we should go for lunch. I took him to Lehman's Plaza, Prezzo's Italian restaurant. It was the cool spot in town. My friends and I always went there for lunch and dinner. It was the place to be and be seen, casual but very en vogue. I ordered the Cobb salad and fries. He hesitated so much over the menu and literally looked like he couldn't eat anything. He ordered some fish filet. The food came. I started to eat. He watched me eat and didn't touch his food. At first, I didn't notice. We had easy conversation, although he did ask a lot of questions about my family and my parents' financials. He seemed to care a lot about money. Half-way through my salad, I find out he eats strictly kosher and some places he doesn't trust enough to even just eat the fish. I felt awkward eating alone. I felt awkward answering his questions about my parents' money, or how expensive it was to rent in Williams Island.

I took him back to his cousin's ugly house, on time to get his luggage and fly back to NY. He kissed me and said he would call me.

And he did. He called me that night from his landline on my parents' landline. We didn't have cellphones yet. We spoke hours on the phone. He was pretty straight forward. He started to fly back to Miami weekly to see me. It was a courtship, a real one. He was my first... He bought me red roses (I now hate red roses); he took me out to dinner every weekend, and I taught myself how to cook for Shabbat dinner, for him on Friday nights. He met my parents. He came to my father's 56th birthday. My dad just stared at him, but my mom was all smiles. My parents moved back to France for a short time, and I got my own apartment in Williams Island. I lived alone. I was emancipated.

One day, I was called back to France. My dad had a heart attack, and it wasn't good. I went to Toulouse the next day, after a long flight. Went to see my dad on his hospital bed, attached to tubes and wires. It wasn't good. He was unconscious. I had not seen him since the Jewish holidays a few months before, but I spoke to him daily. My parents were moving back to Miami a few days before his heart attack. We slept on chairs in the waiting room, and one by one, we would go into his room. I did, all by myself. I touched his hand. I cried and begged him to wake up. I was his baby, his favorite. He bought me everything and anything I wanted. When I was 16 and got my license, he bought me a brand-new Jeep, with the big red bow, and asked our building's valet to pull up in front of the entrance. He handed me my keys, and I took him for a drive. He bought me my first Dior bag when I was 18. He got me my favorite and expensive Free-Lance boots every fall. He still scratched my back even though he thought I was too old for this. He still hugged me and told me he loved me. I learned to play the piano just for him. He would sit by my side, smoking his cigar, while I played Beethoven and Chopin for him. He bought me Elton John's Yamaha Piano at auction when I was 10. He called me Tiger or Tiggy in French.

I reminded him of all this, as I held his hand and cried warm tears on his soft cheeks. I laid in bed next to him, waiting for a nurse or my mom to come yell at me any minute. No one came. He started to move his legs uncontrollably, but he was still unconscious. I was scared. I wiped my tears and called for the nurse. By the time she came, the machine showed his heartbeat had become a straight line. Everyone came into the room, my mom, my brother, asking me what happened. I kept saying, "I didn't do anything. I was just talking to him, but he didn't hear me."

Till today, I hope it's not the memories I told him about, or my cries that killed him. Till today, I am scared I did something when I laid next to him, but I swear, I didn't touch anything except his hand and his face. I also touched his hair. He had the thickest, most beautiful dark hair. I have his hair texture. I have his cheeks, you motherfuckers!!! Those cheeks you all like to scream plastic surgery about, they're my dad's cheeks!

I loved him, so much. He and I had a special bond. He knew a lot of my secrets and I knew many of his. He died. My youth died with him, and my life collapsed. I felt like Cinderella must have felt when she was left to live with her stepmother and stepsisters. Except, that was my real mom and siblings. Only once he died, it didn't feel like it.

We sat Shiva for seven days. According to the Jewish religion, the deceased wife, children and siblings must wear black, rip their shirt, not shower, and must all sleep and eat in the deceased's house on the floor. That's what we did. My grandmother arrived from Israel, his mom, on time for the funeral. She was a piece of shit, and I never liked her. I had one good grandma (Zohra) and one bad one (Dina) I fucking hated her and her name. That's my middle name. I hated her for reasons my siblings don't even know. My dad and I spent a lot of time together when he got sick. He once told me that when he was small, during the war, he was the middle child of six. She would always choose to send him out in the dangerous streets to get milk for the family, leaving him at the risk of being shot or blown up by a bomb. He told me he felt like the black sheep. I believed him. My dad was self-made, born to low-income parents. His dad was a butcher and his mom a stay-at-home wife. He went to work at the age of 13 when his dad became a paraplegic. He left school, worked, and brought the money home to feed his older brother and younger siblings, as well as his parents. In the Jewish religion, such sacrifice comes with reward. The Torah says that God takes a liking to those that suffer a great deal, and so he did. My dad worked hard, and he also was an autodidact. He read books. He watched the history channel and the geography channel. He did all he could to appear smart and cultivated. He landed a job at LOREAL in Morocco and climbed the corporate ladder to become their chief of import/export and a renowned customs general. He moved to France, leaving my mom and older sister in Casablanca, where he opened a sort of 7-11, open 24-hours a day. He slept during his downtime and worked hard enough to buy a small apartment in the southwest of France in Toulouse and bring them both his mom and sister to France. He married well. My mom was the daughter of a wealthy man, but my dad refused his help. He made it on his own. By the time I was born, he was 40 years old. He owned several clothing stores and lots of real estate, and he had built his dream home. So when he passed, his evil mother came, and regardless of the fact that he kissed her ass during his whole life, bought her anything she ever requested without a mere please or thank you, she came into my parents' home to spit the last of her venom and said to me and my mom that we killed him. I was so young; I fainted. When I got back up, I went to see her and I said to her, "Cursed is the woman who lives long enough to bury her child. May you live the longest most painful life and die a long painful death."

I never saw her again. My siblings loved her. They still went to see her, and they still gave her money. I found out recently that my mom did too for a while...which is so fucked up considering how much this woman hated my mom. I still can't believe I was named after this fucking bitch. You are probably wondering how I can write all this, what will my family think?

Well, my family knows. I always spoke my mind, and I always acted accordingly. I never saw my grandmother again, nor any of her daughters that I thought did us wrong.

Shit, I get carried away...So, anyway, my dad died. I sat Shiva for seven days, then I flew back to Miami for my finals. When I landed in Miami, my brother's friend and business partner picked me up. I got the sense that he was also hitting on me but couldn't be sure. Men are weird when you're vulnerable. I went to bed and cried myself to sleep. My bell rang, which was so weird because in Williams Island there are three security gates that call you to let visitors in. But no-one called. It was Joe. He took the first flight out of NY to be with me. He held me all night while I cried, and the next day and the next day.

He went back to NY and came back the following weekend. He gave me a cell phone, my first one ever. It was a Motorola and state of the art. He got one too, so we can be in touch all the time. When I went to look for the plug in his suitcase, I found what looked like a ring box. Omg. Omg. Omg, he got me a ring. I didn't open it. He was visiting family in Ft Lauderdale. He called me on my new cell.

"So how do ya like your new phone?" he asked me.

"It's fantastic! I'm so excited to have one," I said.

"Okay, I have something else for you. Go in my bag and look for a small box."

I act like I have no idea. "Okay, omg. What's this?"

"Well, what do you think? What do you say?"

He rings the bell. He is at the door. I answer the door while I'm still on the phone with him, and he asks me what I think. So, I say, "YES, but really? ... YES."

He puts the ring on my finger. He didn't go on one knee, but it was good enough. He took me to dinner in South Beach and said he needed to talk to my older brother and ask for my hand. That was backwards, Joe, but don't worry, I didn't think my family was going to give two fucks. My brother, Gilbert, did give a fuck, though. He took on the role of the patriarch—The Godfather as I called him. He wasn't particularly nice to me. He thought my skirts were too short. He never complimented me on my academic achievements. He barely smiled at me. I think he thought I was a nuisance. He liked and still likes my older sister, Corine. She is two years older than him. They are respectively 17 and 15 years older than me. I was too young. I wasn't part of the plan in their sibling bond. Corine always lived in France. She never followed my parents to the US, so while I got to grow up with her part of my life, there is a huge part where I didn't get to see her much. She is the one I'm closest to, though, and for good reason. She has been there for me through thick and thin. I sometimes felt like she was my mother.

Back to how Gilbert gave a fuck about me getting married to Joe. Gilbert clocked him right away. He found him money hungry, and thought he lacked good manners. He was not for me. But, Gilbert, if you are reading this, it's not like you made me feel so welcome, either. I truly felt like I needed to get out of your hair (when you still had some). So Gilbert sends me to Brooklyn, to get a sense of who my in-laws were, and where Joe is from.

Before Joe proposed, I went to NY, with my expensive Free-Lance Boots, my Chanel bag, and my skinny jeans. Joe came to pick me up in a nice car. He said it was his brother's Ralph's and not to think it was his because he has no money. Joe liked to remind me he had no money. We arrived in his father's driveway, and some weird woman, who I now know was Lourdes, jumped Joe. She was manic! She screamed and yelled and broke his finger, till Joe's dad came out and got her off him. He invited us in before we made our way to Joe's basement apartment. My ex-father-in-law's house was tacky. The couches were brand new but covered in protective plastic, so were the dining room chairs. He had a brand-new kitchen, a fancy one too, but he didn't use it. He used the sticky old one in his basement.

We had dinner. He cooked, and served us some Middle Eastern specialties like goulash, and another one with okra (all Syrian cuisine recipes from his deceased wife). Only one problem, I didn't have a knife. They only ate with old stainless-steel forks, no knives. I had not learned how to eat and cut my meat with just my fork. I was so out of my comfort zone. I watched all of them eat and tried to copy them and my meat flew across the table and fell in the beetroot salad bowl. Joe understood and got up and gave me a butter knife. Geez, thanks!

I could see what Gilbert wanted me to see: we didn't come from the same world. We didn't have the same upbringing. We didn't necessarily like the same things. Joe argued on the porch with his dad. He thought I didn't understand Hebrew, but I did. I have a thing for languages, and while I speak a few, I understand many. Hebrew is one of them.

His dad was already putting pressure on him to marry me. I'm from a good family. They have money, he says. Joe argues that he is not ready, and I'm not really his type. He is not ready to give up his shenanigans with women, and he liked what he called "white-trash." I definitely was white, but I was not trash. My teeth were straight and white. I brushed my hair, and I didn't snort cocaine, nor did I drink Johnny Walker black like he did.

We go back to Joe's small basement apartment, and I tell him what I heard. He says he is confused, and his dad is pressuring him. I ask about Lourdes. She is Puerto Rican, and he had an on and off thing with her, but he left her because she is not Jewish.

I was so young. My dad had just died, and I didn't feel I belonged with my family. They were burdened by me. My dad and mom had me when they were older. I only knew them in wealth. My brothers and sister didn't. Sometimes, I felt they resented me for being the golden child. Joe may have jumped the gun with the ring. He didn't necessarily love me. He hit the jackpot was more like it: a Jewish American Princess, with a French background and a wealthy family, living the American dream in one of Miami's nicest gated neighborhoods. I was eventually going to be a lawyer racking up the big bucks.

I went back to Miami and lied to my brother. I told him I was marrying into a wealthy and distinguished family. But, things weren't a fairy tale. Joe told me often he didn't like my appearance. Specifically, he didn't like my cheeks, and if you think I have prominent cheekbones now, you should have seen me before I turned 20. I had the cheekbones and the baby fat on top the cheekbones. I was all fucking cheeks. Joe said I looked like a fridge once. I stopped talking to him for a few days. He flew in to see me. I still wore my 3-carat engagement ring. He often spoke about money (obsessively) and told me the ring cost him 10k, and he was still paying for it, but he couldn't get me something smaller or my brother would not agree to let us get married.

Each time Gilbert saw Joe, he noticed how much Joe was infatuated with money, and the price of things we had and what we paid. In the meantime, I was still going to law school and working 2 jobs. I worked at Bisou Bisou, and I worked at the Cheesecake Factory as a waitress. Why, you ask? My parents were loaded, so why didn't I inherit?

That's a fucking loaded question, but long story short, when my dad passed there was a new sheriff in town. My mom, who was the most powerful woman I knew, became a vulnerable blob and started leaning on The Godfather for all major decisions. It was almost disgusting and incestuous how she looked at my brother like he was her new husband. And in the course of the following months after my dad's sudden death, Gilbert started to set new rules. They would stop paying my rent, car lease, and insurance the way my dad had. I had to pull my own weight. So, I tried. But even with the two jobs, it wasn't easy. And sometimes I would overdraft, so when the money in the account was there to pay the car lease, the check would bounce and Gilbert would call me and summon me to his office and terrify me.

He did this while his new wife enjoyed a lavish life and was not expected to work a day in her life. Not that I'm comparing, but you could say Gilbert was teaching me how to be a strong woman. No! His wife was pampered by both Gilbert and my mother, and for some odd reason, I was cut out. My dad didn't do things right. He didn't amend his will to include his children, but considering my mom worked her whole life to contribute to his fortune, it only made sense that she inherits all the money, and she did... He wrote a letter, though, and he asked that my mom to please give me our home in Toulouse.

 He felt there was enough other assets to compensate my siblings, but this home I had a special attachment to, and he knew I wouldn't sell it. He thought I should inherit it because he built it for my birth and I loved that home. Gilbert and her laughed off the letter found in his journal, and even though it was dated and could have been challenged legally as an amendment to his will, they said he was pre-surgery and losing his mind when he wrote it. I didn't argue; I didn't care about money. Hell, I didn't even care about them.

They sold the house, and when I didn't sign for the sale, they "worked something out" with one of my old French IDs. It was okay, though. It was my mom's house, and she worked her whole life alongside my dad. He often said she "made him." I was not mad.

Gilbert cared so much about Joe not getting his hands on our money, that I never ended up getting anyways, that he tried to give Joe a check to disappear. I think Gilbert did care about me and thought I deserved better. Joe came back to my place after meeting him and said, "Let's take the twenty grand, act like we are separated, and elope."

But I'm rebellious, not fucking stupid. Like I said, I didn't care about money. I still don't. My dad had plenty and he couldn't stop his heart disease from killing him. Money sucks, and people suck when it comes to money. Joe refused the payout, and we organized the wedding. You know how my wedding went—it was as bad as my marriage. My family and Joe's family were worlds apart.

Joe and I were worlds apart, too. Did he love me? Yes, he ended up loving me. Did he love me from the start? I don't think so. I truly believe he thought he scored: Jewish, good family, good genetics, and most importantly, a good bank account. Bahahahaha ... I had nada, zero, and I was getting nothing. As a matter of fact, the day I got married, my mom stopped paying anything for me. Joe and I struggled financially a great deal. I was going to law school, and we made ends meet with my two part-time jobs and his small income from some real estate deals.

Turns out, he was not exactly a stockbroker. He was just studying to get the license to be a day trader and interned at a firm on Wall Street where everyone ended up getting arrested. Shortly after he gave up on that dream. Note to fucking-idiot-self: never marry a man who thinks your face looks like a fridge and who asks daily how much money your family is worth.

Fast forward ten years, and he is driving me to prison. I look at his profile from the corner of my eye and seek reassurance. He is silent. He says he will pray and call the lawyers, too. He will go see some holy rabbis for their blessings.

Source: BOP

We arrive at FCI Danbury in Connecticut. I tell him to make a U-turn. I tell him my brother Roger can get me out of the country through upstate New York and the Canada border... He would have, if I was serious, but I wasn't. I thought of the kids, what their life would be if we became fugitives. I would fuck up three lives forever for selling fucking Swarovski Crystal-embossed Seven Jeans on eBay. FUCK MY LIFE, and fuck my kids' lives, too.

The prison is a big barb-wired property, lots of green and also lots of concrete. It could almost pass for an army base. There are cameras everywhere, and I see a metal door that says R&D... that is the door you dream of, once you are inside.

We go to the front desk first on the other side, and we are greeted by a CO. She was no fucking Daisy. She was mean, and I felt tears coming. She says to sit in the waiting room and someone from R&D will come get me. We should start saying our goodbyes. We sit, and I feel I could pee myself. He holds my hand tight and says nothing

Seven or eight years later, Sheryl, one of my old cellmates sent me a message on FB and said to turn HBO on and watch Orange is the New Black. As I watched, I felt complete déjà vu.

It was exactly the same thing. It's like Piper and I had the same exact nightmare one night and she just sold it to HBO. Even the waiting room was accurate. Turns out, the girl who wrote the book the show is based on went to FCI Danbury, but she went to the camp. We, on the other side, called it "Camp Cupcake" or "club fed" because it was for sissies. They had more freedom and were treated much better than us medium-high security serious offenders. In Camp Cupcake across the street, you didn't have lockdowns, and you didn't have "controlled movements." Those bitches were in Club Med compared to us. What's controlled movements? Movement through the facility units and corridors are done only during a specific ten-minute interval. You are only allowed to move to recreation and other places within this time period. You must stay at your location until the next controlled movement before you can return to your unit. These movements will be announced over the P.A. system. "Ten minutes move, 10 minutes move..." At that point, you have to get out of your unit (or cell) and move to the next building. Once the move is over, don't be caught outside or you'll get a strike and possibly be sent to the SHU, solitary confinement. So fucking exciting right? WAIT, you haven't heard anything yet. I'm not even inside.

The R & D (Receive & Discharge) C.O comes and calls my name. He is Caucasian but wears a beard trimmed like observant Muslims and he wears a religious beanie. He has compassion in his eyes. He looks at me. I see shock in his eyes, too. He looks at Joe, and says, "Say your goodbyes. I'll give you a few minutes...give him anything you don't want to let us take from you. Any jewelry—anything. All you can keep is a simple gold wedding band."

I give Joe my pocketbook. I look at my old yellow gold wedding ring he gave me under the chuppah. I dug for in in the safe when I took off my diamond eternity band that morning. We hug, kiss, and Joe says, "I'll see you tomorrow."

The C.O apologetically interrupts, "You probably won't see her tomorrow or the next day. Once inside, she has to submit a list of pre-approved visitors, and only once the warden approves it can you come visit. Visiting days are only four days a week.

She will call you and let you know when."

I do the math quickly in my head and it sounds like I won't see Joe or the kids for 4-5 days, but who cares? My lawyer said I'm going to get out. He is filing another motion for release while awaiting appeal. I beg Joe to call my lawyer and pressure him to file the appeal. The motion is pages and pages long. We need to hire an investigator to challenge all the discovery presented by the prosecution at trial. My appeal is not really going to be submitted and won in the next five days, but I hope it will. Somehow, in this crazy situation, my sense of reality is at its lowest. Reality doesn't hit you at all. Actually, everyone in there is completely delusional, some to the point of being mental cases.

The kind CO (probably the kindest during my whole incarceration, and he probably saved my life, too. You'll understand why soon), walked me to the R&D metal door. I felt like I was going into Area 51. He buzzes us in. I didn't look back at Joe till the first door started to close. I looked back at the cars driving away, and Joe walking back to my Range Rover. Little did I know, I wouldn't see this sight for a fucking long-ass time? I was waiting for the CO to handcuff me, he didn't. We stood in between the first metal door and the second.   He waved at the camera and said: "INMATE SURRENDER."

We were buzzed in, and he walked me into a weird, very dark space. There were some cages to the right with metal toilets and weird metal hooks and chains on the floor. I could tell those were to attach handcuffs and to the left a sort of room with ugly linens, blankets, and orange uniforms. He is reassuring. He says reassuring things, but I can't remember what. I want to cry. He says he has to put me through the system, and then my counselor will come to go over my report. I had no idea what that meant. It was all so scary. He said I have to change into an orange set, even the underwear had to be federal property underwear, and I had to wear the navy-blue espadrilles. He mentions I will be called the next day to get my real uniform and steel toes. I don't know what steel toes are. I'm scared.

I change, and he gives me privacy. He puts my clothes in a bag and says it will be shipped to the address on my probation report.

"Wait, but what if I'm released tomorrow? I have an appeal."

He is sympathetic again, and says, "When you win your appeal, your family brings you clothes or ship it here, and we give it to you when we release you. You see this is where you come in, and this where you get out from."

I will actually never ever get out a free woman from this R&D, but I dream of this for months and months to come, as I watch women being released, finding out the day before their sister sent a package with some sleek tracksuit and good lingerie. I fantasize about that for months to come.

The CO asks me my religion for the report.

"Jewish," I say.

"What languages do you speak?"

"English, French, Spanish, German, Italian, and Arabic, and a few others but not well enough to mention."

His eyes light up. "You speak Arabic? How come?"

"My family is from North Africa, and I took classic Arabic in school." I pause, and ask him, "Do you speak Arabic?"

He tells me he is American but converted to Islam, and only knows the prayers but doesn't understand any of it. He says I'm lucky. His demeanor changed towards me, and he becomes firmer and preps me for the jungle, like he just became some kind of honorary protector of our brotherhood. I'm thinking to myself, "Didn't he get the Jewish part?"

He took my mug shot and said from now one you don't really have a name; you have a federal ID number. It will be on a red ID card. "Learn the number by heart," he told me. Up until five years ago, I still remembered that number by heart. It's so quiet in R&D. I don't feel at risk. I'm just in some weird Twilight Zone. "You speak Russian?"

No, motherfucker. I speak six languages and Russian ain't one of them. I shake my head. "Are you Russian?"

What is he a fucking retard of some sort? My report says explicitly I'm part French! I shake my head again. He gives me a piercing look, and says, "From now on, you are Russian, you hear me? You are Jewish and you are Russian."

Okay, is this guy fucking nuts? Is he an inmate escaped from the mental ward? Or is he mind-fucking me already? Like it's part of this conspiracy or what.

He stays firm. "Listen, in there are 2,489 female inmates. It's a jungle out there. Ninety-nine percent of them committed the crimes they are here for, and most of them are dangerous. You do not talk about your case to anyone. You do not trust anyone. You do not say where you lived until now. You do not show fear. You do not look down. You look women in the eyes."

I start to weep, and he says I need to cry one last time and be done. He is going to call someone who will help me adjust. "I don't need anyone to help adjust. I'm coming out soon."

He gets on the P.A. system "BINDELAD... to R & D, BINDELAD report to R & D immediately." I couldn't make out the name he called. It sounded like a German or a Jewish name, or both. I didn't know if it was an officer or an inmate.

He gives me a pillow, a blanket, two sheets, two towels in a pillowcase and says, "Wait here, and don't forget what I told you. Chances are you will never see me again till the day you leave this place. Be strong, may Allah be with you."

He buzzes her in, a tall woman with a gorgeous long silky TV commercial mane of the most beautiful hue of red I've ever seen. She has huge tits, long legs, milky porcelain skin, and piercing cold blue eyes. Her voluptuous lips looked like meaty berries, and they do not smile. She has a very superior way about her, so she just tips her chin to the C.O as if to say, "What's this about?"

"She is one of yours," the CO says. "She needs help. Take her to Unit 5. Help her the best you can." She gives me a stare down, sizes me up, and with a very heavy Russian accent, moves those sensual naturally bitten-colored lips and says, "Come with me." We are buzzed out into a completely empty, humongous courtyard. There is no-one, it looks to me like a deserted concentration camp, like the one I visited in Auschwitz on a class trip when we were studying Anne Frank in French literature. I'm having a hard time juggling the pillow, sheets, and towels, so she grabs the pillow from me. "ты русский?" [ty russkiy] ... "No, I am not Russian, but I'm from Brooklyn, so I understand some."

Didn't the C.O just tell me to lie and say I'm Russian? Well, fuck him, this woman is terrifying. I'm not going to lie to her. She looks at me with interest "Funny, I thought you Russian, CO say to me you Russian... You Jewish?"

"Yes, I am."

"Ah, okay, that's why he call me. I'm Jewish, too, but some people here are fake Jewish. Don't trust everyone who say they Jewish."

I look at the floor as we walk slowly along the units. Tears start coming up. I can't control them. The scary yet gorgeous blue eyes strike me with a terrifying look, and with the most Russian accent I've ever heard she says, "You NOT CRY. You stop this shit now, you hear me? You cannot cry here. You put head up and look everyone in the eye. I don't help you if you cry."

I want to cry even more. What time is it now? Are the kids coming out of school? Did Savannah listen to me and avoid calling my phone? It probably went to voicemail, and it never goes to voicemail for the kids. I forgot to tell Joe to take Dylan to buy baseball cards, and I promised.

"Can I call my family?"

"No, not yet. You need the special number first, and you need to put money in account or you can't call. You only will have 300 minutes per month." I suck in math, but I quickly calculate that's 10 minutes per day for 30 days, and that's horrible. Tears are burning my eyes again.

Russia, we call her Red-Russia... (Yup, just like the character in Orange is the New Black). She starts explaining that she is not in my unit and that she will have ten minutes to take me to my unit and quarters, and then she will have to leave me there and will see me at chow time. Chow time? Like Mr. Chow, the restaurant I love in NYC? Or like Jimmy Choo? ... What's chow time?

In prison if you are notorious or cool enough, you get a nickname. Red-Russia said I have to make my bed, get my uniforms in order, make sure my family sends me commissary money. My head was spinning. We got to a metal door. For all I knew, there was a gas chamber inside. I swear, the inside of this prison looks like a concentration camp. A CO comes to meet us at the door. She shows him a slip she got from my Muslim good Samaritan, and he opens the heavy door with one of those huge key rings you've seen in the movies. We go up a flight of stairs and into a corridor, where it looks like a hospital. There are inmates in khaki uniforms going about their business.

No-one looks at me just yet, even though I'm the only one wearing orange. Red walks me to a sort of dormitory/room with bunk beds. It's so small, and there are six bunks and metal lockers. Four inmates are in that room. One of them is an old black lady, sitting hunchbacked on her bed; one is sitting on a top bunk with her towel over her head, looking like she is praying. Wait, is she a woman? She looks like a boy...it can't be a boy, though. This is a female facility. The black lady has a hoarse voice. She sounds like she is from New Orleans. "Well, Russia, who do we have here?"

Russia gives her a stare down and says, "Which bed is hers?"

Some other name points to the bottom bed, under praying boy, but another inmate jumps in front of me, grabs my sheets and says, "No, you can't take a bottom bunk when you are new. They will bother you, if you do, and we won't hear the end of it. Take the top one on top of Ms. Walker. She is old and quiet; she won't bother you except she snores. Let me make your bed for you, that way we pass inspection."

Russia looks at me and says she will see me later as my "bunkies" will help me adjust. I wanted to hug the cold bitch, and cry in her arms. I wanted to beg her not to leave me here.

I was on the defensive. I had been warned not to trust anyone, that it was every man for himself, and that anyone's kindness would mean a favor is owed. I remember feeling scared of accepting help.

"Do you have slippers? You need sleepers. In the shower slippers are a must, or you will catch a disease."

A crackhead voice in the background startles me. "That's right, blondie. We don't want them germs of yours in our showers." I turn around to find the crackhead voice and find a small he-she character sitting on a bed, staring at me. She was so dark, with short dreadlocks. All I could see was the threatening white of her eyes scrutinizing me. Was he-she looking at my ass? Chills run down my back. I need to puke. But they rush me, something about an inspection. If we don't pass it, Precious will be upset. We are going to be last for chow, and Precious doesn't like to be last for chow.

WHO THE FUCK IS PRECIOUS??? What the fuck is Chow? Is Mr. Chow here? I'm so confused and I'm so scared. The closest I've ever been to sleeping on bunk beds with strangers was when I went to summer camp. This was not summer fucking camp. The other girl, who grabbed my covers, starts making my bed. I argue that I can do it. I know it's not a five-star hotel, but she still says I'm going to fuck it up and we will fail inspection. So, I watch and learn instead. I know how to make fucking beds, though, I'm not that prissy. Another nosy girl comes in. I realize I'm the minority in prison. There are so many African Americans, so many Hispanics, and less Caucasians. White privilege is so evident here. It's the first of many injustices I start sensing.

I look over my head, over my bunk bed, and the young man who I assume has a vagina because, fuck, it's a fucking female facility after all, is still holding a prayer book, swinging back and forth with a towel on his/her head. He looks like a Jewish man with a talit on. It looks like the way Jewish men sway back and forth to pray. Ms.

Wilson, the old black lady sitting on her bed, has a scraping, deep voice. She sounds like Tina Turner. She sees me interrogating that praying situation.

"That is Gabriel," she says. "She is Jewish. She spends her time praying. Do you know about Jews?"

I reply in a low voice, "Yes, I'm Jewish." Gabriel's head emerged suddenly from under the towel. He looked at me with big eyes, and in a Spanish accent he says, "You are a real Jewish person?"

I nod. Gabriel comes off the top bunk as fast as possible. Literally jumps off the ladder and appears in front of me. He has kind eyes, and he looks like a young man. He looks like he is 20 something years old. He has facial hair, a small mustache, bot a beard, but facial hair like a premature teenage boy mustache. He has the corpulence of a man, and I cannot really make out whether there are breasts or not. He has a manly-ish young voice.

Miss Walker said, "Be careful. Gabriel has crushes on young little things like you."

Gabriel was my bunkie. After my bed is made, I'm told it's my turn to wash the floor by the others. Gabriel shakes his head. "They are assholes," he whispers. So I decide it's time for my coming out: "No necesitas hablar en ingles conmigo, entiendo Español perfettamente." His eyes light up...He starts speaking Spanish with a Mexican accent. It's my Spanish, too. I speak the Mexican dialect fluently. And then just then, I hear a hint of felinity in his voice, like something warm and homey. Gabriel starts sweeping the floor and doesn't let me do it. "Todas estate mariconas te van a acabar en tu primer dia si las dejamos." (All these lesbians are going to eat you up alive on your first day if we let them."

By the time the cell is clean, my bed is made, and my almost-no-belongings are in my small metal locker, it's inspection time. We are told to stand by our beds, as intimidating Cos, a man and a woman, search our belongings, under our mattresses, and check on the hygiene of the whole unit. You are supposed to be quiet and speak only if spoken to. The female CO is an asshole. She starts with me from day one. She is African American, and her huge ass is sausaged in her polyester inform pants. She has long acrylic nails with silver and gold designs and a weave á la James Brown's. "You new? Or you just got out of the SHU?"

"I'm new. I don't know what the SHU is."

"How did you end up in general population without going to the SHU first? You sufmin special we should know about? You come from the camp?"

I try my best southern accent. "No, ma'am. I self-surrendered."

Laughter erupted. "Ms. Walker here, she is doing life in prison. No-one surrenders to medium security. I'll have to check your probation report out and figure out your deal."

I don't feel like crying now. I'm angry. "With all due respect, ma'am, I don't think you need to figure out anything out. I surrendered in compliance with the judge's order. I can have my attorney talk to you."

Ms. Walker chuckles and gets all ironic on the overzealous CO. "Uh-oh Ms. Perkins, it looks like someone here knows her rights."

Our cell passes inspection, but we hear chatter in the rest of the unit. The bathrooms were filthy. There was a sanitary pad full of blood sticking on one of the stalls. Well, that may have been a rumor because whatever you hear in prison is often a hoax. Inspection ends, and the stress is palpable. It's been weeks since Unit #5 has been first for chow.

I meanwhile figure out chow is like "chow down" and it means eating. It comes from chew. Excuse me, I think I left some brain cells at R&D.

I am just obsessed with one thought: making phone calls. I inquire with Gabriel. He takes the only paper I got with me and shows me a code. He says with this code and my Fed ID#, if I have money in my account, I can call home, but the number has to be on a pre-approved list of numbers.

"At the next move, you need to go to unit #4 to see Mrs. Wilson," he says. She's my counselor (as shown on the paper).

"Wait, isn't Ms. Wilson the lady sitting on the lower bunk there doing life in prison?" (Poor lady).

"No, your counselor is white. She is okay, and if she likes you, she will be good to you."

A voice on the loudspeaker booms, "Ten min move, ten min move."

We stand by the unit door and expect it to be unlocked any second. We have 10 minutes to move to the next unit. Gabriel takes me, and we walk fast next door. Gabriel is not allowed to stay. Mrs. Wilson isn't his counselor, so he can't be in that other unit.

It's strange. There is an office with her name on the door, in the middle of a huge dorm with bunks lined up. I knock on the door, and my bladder is about to explode. I needed to pee before, but I was scared to ask. I was scared to go. I know newbies get sexually assaulted. Yes, women assault other women sexually. It's reality. There are also many lesbian couples and loads of drama... There is tons of sexual activity.

Mrs. Wilson waves me in. There is a small window on her door so you can look inside to see if she is there.

Source: BOP.

"Hello, I'm Mrs. Wilson. I am your counselor?" She seems kind of nice. She is dressed like a police officer with a rank, but I wouldn't know which one. I don't really know what a counselor is. I should have read a guide to federal incarceration before coming here, but I didn't think I was staying. I didn't think I was coming till the day before. I give her the paper. She scrutinizes me.

"Oh, yeah, you are the one with the law degree. I know your story, wire fraud, non-delivery of goods, and you are an immigrant."

What?

"No, I'm not am immigrant. I'm from the United States, but I also have a French passport."

"Same thing. You are in medium security because you are either a serious or repeat offender or you are deportable."

Whitty? Is she nuts? How can the US deport their citizens? I wonder if she is one of those people not to be trusted like inmates. Should I let her talk? Or correct her? She seems to come to her senses without my help.

"Well, now I see, you have dual citizenship. You can't be deported, but you are a flight risk. However, it says here you come from middle-upper class background, with a degree, which puts you at the lower-risk point here inside."

Does that mean I'll have more freedoms? Not at all. So what does it mean? It means Mrs. Wilson looked over my probation report, and she knows how much I make. She knows I have a very expensive beach front home in Neponsit, NY and she knows, compared to her, I have had a dream life till now. Strangely, she is not making me pay for it at all. Throughout my incarceration, this woman was kind to me. She treated me as an equal. She recognized my level of education. She gave me good advice and often even awarded me more privileges than other inmates.

I started to cry when she softened-up and spoke about reading about my children in my report. "I have children, too," she said. "I know this is hard. A lot of women here cry for their children. Try to be strong for them. I will allow you one phone call for five minutes home now, until we get your account activated to start making calls." She hands me the phone and says it will be recorded like all inmate phone calls are. She steps out, and for a second, being in that woman's office holding the phone, I feel back in the shelter of civilization.

Joe picks up the call. "Hi, I spoke to your lawyer. Have the counselor set up a call with him tomorrow. It's a privileged call, so it can't be recorded. The kids are alright; they are asking for you. I told them you are at work."

I stay strong. I speak to Savannah and Dylan. Dakota is too small, so they put me on speaker, and I say, "Koko, Mommy loves you." I hear her little squeaks and happy laughs. Then, I cry, and tears keep coming and rolling down my cheeks. They taste salty. I hang up. Mrs. Wilson comes back in and says, if I need to cry, I can come see her, but it's better if I don't cry in general population.

General population, what a weird concept.

She also tells me that I can apply to be a piano teacher or work at the law library. You have to have a job and it is determined on your level of education and professional skill set.

I'd much rather be a piano teacher. I'm told only long-timers can take piano lessons. Which is scary because someone doing hard time or life is not necessarily the type of person I want to spend time with. I apply for both jobs.

"You speak several languages," she says. "Not one inmate here speaks this many, but many are aliens (as in illegal aliens) and don't speak English. I may call on you to help translate some of the handbook. We are currently changing some of the regulations."

"Sure," I say.

I'm thinking to myself I won't be here long enough, so no need to get all chummy with me and think I'll be here to do translations.

I have to wait by the unit's door for the next move. "Ten min move, ten min move."

It's my first time walking the yard by myself in general population. I'm scared, as they are all wearing beige-khaki uniforms, and I'm wearing orange. I try not to look down like I've been instructed, but it's hard. Some of these faces are scary, and most of these women committed crimes I only heard about on TV. I make it to my unit. It's next door, 30 steps... Now, the stairs, and I hope I remember where to go. But it's a huge cell, with hospital-like corridors, and that one room with the six bunks. Apparently, this is the room where newbies go, and then, eventually, you are moved to a cube with slightly more privacy in the general room. One hundred and ten beds, 110 inmates per unit. I go to my bed and I sit.

"How old are you?" asks Mrs. Wilson.

"I'm 29." All five sets of eyes turn to me. The skinny girl, Karla, is pretty, but she has ugly teeth. She starts speaking to me in Spanish, since she heard I can speak Spanish. She says I look 20. I know I did, with my short blonde hair, no make-up, no indication of having any fashion sense. We all chat, and it's not so bad. I look at the time, and I know exactly what I would be doing and what the kids are doing at home. I want to be home.

I finally work up the nerve to go to the bathroom. I get into the stall, but there is no lock. I go in the next, and there's no lock. In the next? No lock. You aren't allowed privacy not even to take a shit. So, I crouch down to pee, but I don't sit on the toilet seat, and I hold the door at the same time. I mastered wiping and pulling my pants up with one hand after a while.

What time is it? There is a clock on the wall, and it reads 6:20 pm. Gabriel takes my hand and pulls me, hurries me, to get on the queue by the unit door. We have to be first to get out for chow. And there are plenty of inmates already with their nose on the door, waiting to be let out, like hungry dogs.

"Chow Time, Chow Time, Unit #6." Those motherfuckers passed inspection again. Some big person, and I say "person" because I don't know if it's a male or female, pushes everyone to be let through to the front door. It's Precious. "She don't queue." She has a metal front tooth; it's not a grill, but almost.

The door opens, and again I'm hurried into the chow hall, where there is a line of inmates. You have to get scanned, so you don't come to eat twice. I follow the lead, grab a tray, and grab the bread. They are serving nasty mystery puddles made of what looks like dog shit. Gabriel says, "Don't worry, we get the kosher tray." We go to a special spot and line up, with the Muslims, and we ask for our special kosher trays. They are carefully wrapped in cellophane, with bread and other plastic containers, containing what looked like less elaborate but hygienic food: a piece of cold-cut, bread, beans, an apple. We sit, and I'm numb.

"You need to know the water plant here is maintained by inmates who do life in prison. The rumor is that a few of them have AIDS, and often cut themselves to let their blood infect the water we drink from the sink. You need to buy drinks from the commissary instead." I look at my glass of water. I'm thirsty, but I don't drink. I eat a piece of bread. Some inmates start eyeing my tray. Gabriel notices and says that whenever you have "special trays", you make special friends, and you don't want

47

those friends.

WTF? There is less food than the regular inmate meals. Why is that?

Gabriel tells me it's not potentially infected with illness. Rumor has it, inmates in the kitchen stick all kind of horrible stuff in the food they prepare, from spit, to feces, to pubic hair to Ajax powder. FUCK MY LIFE!

Chapter 6: You Can't Sit with Us

Russia (Red) found me in Chow Hall. When she walks by, inmates have a way of clearing the passage for her. She is like an amazon moving through the wild. Her eyes are a cold blue, her lips scrumptious and plump. She goes to get her special tray and sits across from me and Gabriel. She ignores Gabriel and asks how it went in my unit. She barks instructions at me. I have shit to do: get uniforms, get commissary, and get an email address... What? Hmm, no, Russia, no email for me. I'm not allowed to have one.

Long story short, they know I'm too good with computers. I can hack. I know my way around the web, so they made sure to restrict my access to email. I would have my 300 phone minutes per month.

Russia glances around the mess hall. "You see that blonde tall lady who looks like you? That's Vika. She won't like you because she is a piano teacher here and now you want her job. She says she is Jewish. I don't believe her. But we used to know each other in Brooklyn."

Russia's English is very broken, so I make her repeat important information to make sure I didn't miss anything. Russia only hangs out with Eastern Europeans, Ruta and Tati—they are younger. Like me, they are somewhat under her wing. I'm instructed to stay away from the other Russians. This woman from Belarus in particular. I forget her name, but she manages to still run scams in prison.

Russia glances at me. "Why you no eat your bread and your apple?"

"I'm not hungry."

Her ice blue eyes scold me. "Stop acting like baby," she barks. "You have to eat. If you get sick, you don't get visit from the kids. EAT NOW."

I start chewing, but I want to barf.

*

My first night in prison was terrible. I can still feel a burning sensation in my heart. I cry silently for hours, afraid of being heard. I hear the unit door opening a couple times, as well as the sound of keys and the heavy steps of the guards. I remember the light of the lamp in my eyes, the stress of that guard, nearing the bed. The breathing of strangers around me continues nonstop. Ms. Walker snores.

I want morning to come so my lawyer can get me out of here. I don't even know if it's morning yet, as there are no windows in this room. Time doesn't pass. I will soon find out that time simply doesn't pass behind bars. If you are a jailbird, time stops. Most of the female inmates in Danbury medium security prison learn to leave their lives behind. They create a new life in prison and never think about "outside." Some of them even create "new families." Some of them have a "Jail mommy" or a "Jail daughter" or a "Jail son... Yeah! Some of these ladies are legally entitled to continue their hormone treatment when they started transitioning to becoming a male. Many of them have nicknames: Red Russia or Red, Karla was Flaca, Gabriel was Gordo (fat guy), some other girl was Sassy, another was Dirty.

I had two names, one bestowed on me by the Latina community, which I got to belong to (I'll explain how later). They called me Flaquita (Very skinny girl), and the other name given to me by the African American community, at least the ones I was tight with, "Blondie." It came a time when I heard "Flaquita" or "Blondie" called out across the yard and would turn and answer to like it was my actual name.

The first few days, I was living on standby, waiting for that call announcing I'm being released. I walked the yard, sobbing under my breath, probably making ugly faces, attempting to hide the fact that I was a sissy. I was not terribly scared most of the time. I was desperate. I missed my kids, terribly, excruciatingly. I didn't know how to live or to be without them.

I heard my name and unit number called on the loudspeaker. I was told to report to visiting. What? But Joe can't visit today. Gabriel rushes to me and explains I need my uniform. I need to put my steel toe shoes on, and I need to report to that building over there next to the warden's office. I report, and I'm let into a back room. I'm told I need to get naked, and I'm patted down by the female guard. Then she says take off your panties, squat and cough. What??????? WTF is squat and cough?

At first, I don't feel embarrassment. I feel sheer panic. I heard things about female prisons, about inmates and guards. I look around, wondering if there was a broom stick she might stick up my ass and rape me. I legitimately thought so. No one gives you a fucking handbook before you go to jail, and there is no fucking orientation explaining procedure. She is a fucking cunt, too. It's CO Perkins (Keesha Perkins). Right before she asked to see my asshole, she commented on my nails.

I hadn't had time to get my acrylic short square nails removed, so I was wearing a chic and fancy French manicure. She asked where I got it done. Fuck you, you cunt. I get it done in a place you will never even go! I tell her to go to 10 Perfect Nails in Brooklyn and ask for Vanessa. Vanessa probably wasn't the girl's real name. She was Chinese, and like every girl in that salon, she changed her name, like strippers do: Vanessa, Amy, Sally, Dolly...

I squat and cough while the cunt examines my asshole. I can tell she takes pleasure in it. Not sexual pleasure, mind you. She just enjoyed my embarrassment. Like all of the prison staff, she read my probation report and knows I come from a rich neighborhood. She enjoyed the power trip. Many COs did.

A huge metal door separates us from a visiting room. I can see it's empty from the little window. I'm scared. Why am I being brought to visiting on a no-visiting day?

This woman waiting for me is dressed conservatively. She's very tall and thin and is standing there in a separate room. She has a briefcase. I come in, and she introduces herself. She is here on behalf of the French ambassador to check on me. I'm dumbfounded. The French government is concerned she tells me. My incarceration is the subject of discord between the US and France. The French government will use all of its diplomatic privileges to make my incarceration easier and to plant as many diplomatic obstacles up the American government's ass to motivate my early release. I spend time with the French consulate lady. Over time, she will visit me 3-4 times a week, on non-visiting days to allow me to spend some time "away from general population." She says we can chat, or I can bring a book and just relax in her diplomatic presence. The room we are in is privileged, which means no recording devices are supposed to be planted to listen to conversations.

I pass messages to Joe through her to my attorneys, and we discuss my next legal steps. She eventually becomes a friend. She tells me about her kids. We speak French, and we have a lot in common. She is genuinely compassionate and outraged that I'm behind bars. She asks me questions about the inside. The inside is a parallel world. I tell her about lesbian couples, women who are actually men. I don't name names. There is a code about that, I honor it.

The first visiting day comes five days after I went in, but it seems like one month passed. The notion of time is like Groundhog Day in there. I try to look decent to see my babies. I'm stressed. I hear that if it gets foggy, visiting is cancelled. If there's bad weather outside, visiting is cancelled. If someone picks a fight with me, visiting is cancelled. I walk a straight line because I fear the cancellation of visiting hours, and I will live with that fear for the length of my incarceration.

On that first visiting day, five days after I went in, I walk into visiting after squatting and coughing out of my asshole, and here they are: Dylan, Savannah, and Joe with my baby Dakota in his arms. She is one year old and still in diapers. I start crying at the sight of them. The kids are dressed so strangely. I can see Savannah put her outfit together by herself, and she mixed colors pretty badly. Joe has a five-day-old beard and looks exhausted, like he hasn't slept.

"Mommy, Mommy! What happened to your hair? Why is it so short?" Savannah is the one most shocked by my appearance. I lost weight immediately. I look thin and frail and she comments on my smell. She thinks I smell weird. I remember that smell. It was a weird smell like the uniforms were washed with plastic or rubber.

I am allowed to hug the kids and hold them, but I am only allowed to kiss Joe once when he arrives and when he leaves, and we cannot touch nor hold hands, and that's okay because he is not that affectionate to start with. But he warns me; he is afraid they would stop the visit. I'm telling you we lived in fear of visiting being cancelled. It terrorized me more than rape. I hold on to Dakota the tightest. She smells like my home…I inhale her as much as I can. She needs a diaper change, so I ask for the bathroom. The guard, a male, one of the rare kind ones, looks at me with compassion.

"You aren't allowed to take her," he informs me. "Joe has to change the diaper."

But Joe doesn't know how—or at least can't do it as well as I can. I want to change my baby. I start sobbing uncontrollably. Joe takes Dakota and Savannah and goes to the changing room. Savannah helped him change the diaper. She is six years old, but she is literally a little homemaker. They come back. Dakota reaches for me and cries till I cradle her, and she falls asleep. Dylan wants to discuss what's for dinner. Joe will make spaghetti and meatballs, and Dylan is pleased. He does not ask why I'm here. He asks when I'm coming home but dismisses my answer. He jerks his body back and forth. I touch him gently like I used to when he would do this, but it doesn't stop the jerking.

I start crying again. It's only been five days and he is regressing. I feel sheer panic, and I start crying and crying. Savannah is desperate to see me smile, and she holds my face in her tiny little hands.

"Mama, you are strong," she says. "You have to be here. It's okay. I'm going to come back tomorrow, Mama."

I stop crying. I should be a better mom. I should stop selfishly panicking my kids with tears. Joe gets impatient with me, and he tells me to stop crying and pray. "Say tehelim," he begins.

"Fuck you, Joe, and fuck your fucking religion and your voodoo rabbis. Fuck you, Joe."

We argue, and then he apologizes. It's 2:45pm, the clock on the wall says. The other CO, that bald asshole Mr. Hitler (He legit had Hitler's mustache, though his real name was Mr. Hayden) announces, "Ten minutes."

Visiting Day is ending. My heartbeat accelerates, my legs go numb, and my hands get sweaty. Dakota is still asleep on my chest. I squeeze her so hard. I feel like my heart is about to be ripped out of my chest. I try to wake her, but Joe says she hasn't slept this deeply since I left the house. Fucking kill me now. I wanted to die. The guard comes to the few visitors and says he is going to start the lineup. We have to say goodbye. Dylan gives me a tight hug. He communicates emotions at that point, and says, "I love you, Mommy. Please, come home. This place gives me a stomachache. I need to go poop."

Dylan's digestive system is fucked up. Being on the spectrum starts in the gut. He is intolerant to cheese; he often needs to go to the bathroom for number two; and usually his stress level dictates his bowel movements. Savannah, my angel, with her beautiful long brown hair and those big exotic brown eyes, looks up at me like I'm her hero and hugs me tight.

"Mommy, you are going to come home. I won't go to Dunkin' Donuts without you, I promise. And we will go do your nails because I've never seen you with your nails looking so bad. I love you, Mommy."

"I love you, too, baby, and don't forget babies, Mommy loves you all the way to the moon and Hashem in the sky, around all the planets and back."

Hashem is god in Hebrew. They say it at the same time as me.

"Like Buzz Lightyear, Mommy?" Dylan asks.

"Yes, baby, like Buzz Lightyear."

"Will you buy me a Buzz Lightyear?"

"Yes, baby, I will." The hardest moment in my life comes next, one I don't wish on any mother living on this earth. My baby Dakota, I wake her gently, and I smell her again. My tears are dripping on her chubby cheeks... her baby fist is gripped to my ugly prison uniform's shirt, and I try to open her first to release the fabric and hand her to Joe, but she resists and grabs my shirt with all her might, and starts screaming,

"Noooo, nooo! Mama, Mama! Nooooo!" she cries hysterically.

I am going to faint. My heart feels like it is being ripped out of my chest by a strong, evil bare hand. Joe grabs her abruptly, and I want to kill him.

"Be fucking gentle, no? She is a fucking baby."

"You cunt, you want your visiting rights to be revoked?" Joe snaps.

He apologizes again. Joe is verbally abusive, and he can't help it. His father is a fucking monster, if you ask me. It's sheer luck his boys didn't become serial killers. Joe's father was a wife beater, and a violent one at that, with the venom of evil instead of a tongue.

I go back inside, but not before I'm stripped naked, and have to squat and cough again. They check my tongue and throat, too. I don't give a fuck. I'm too ripped to shreds to care. When you get out of visiting, it's not movement time, so the yard is empty. I walk back to my unit, crying, and by day five, I've cried so much I noticed I lost almost all of my lashes. Like I fucking care. I am let into my unit, and Karla and Gabriel run to me.

"How are the kids? Como te fue con tus bebes?" I cry, and cry and cry. I skip dinner. Nothing anyone can say or do matters. I don't shower. I don't change. I cry. The skin around my eyes is red. I get a rash from crying so much. Somehow, no one notices. I cry, but I hide it well. When they ask about the rash (all these fucking parasites in there are scared of bacteria and contagion—how fucking ironic!), I tell them I have allergies to the detergent.

The Dominican ladies find out I am a lawyer and I speak Spanish. "Flaquita, me ayudaras con mi appelacion?" They want me to help with their appeals. I say yes. I spend my days when I'm not crying in the law library typing habeas corpus motions for the Boriqua and Dominicanas doing hard time for drug crimes, many of them on conspiracy charges. I know it probably won't go anywhere. The law isn't on their side, and the system even less so, but I file them anyway. In there, they live for the new laws being passed. There is one they are all waiting for that could release them immediately. I give them hope.

One of them reads tarot, and she reads my cards. "Jajaja mujer tu no the quedas aqui, hay un hombre poderoso que te va a sacar pronto," she says. Holy shit, there is a powerful man who's gonna take you out of here. You aren't going to be here long. I press her.

"Pero cuando???" WHEN?

The cards aren't certain.

*

Russia comes to my unit. She is not allowed to, but she is here and plants her tall body in front of me, and her huge tits in my face.

"You eat today? You look too skinny and sick! You wanna be sick for your kids' visit?"

I shake my head. She pays people who work in the kitchen to steal fruit. She brings me an apple and an orange and stands there to watch me eat. I want to puke, but this bitch scares the fuck out of me, so I eat both. She smiles. HOLY FUCK, this mega bitch smiles. Fuck—

if me eating a fucking orange makes her smile, I'll eat one every day. Russia is the only person who ever gave me something like food, or make-up or tea, and never ever asked to be paid for it.

My next visit, Karla (Flaca) comes to me.

"You know you need to wear make-up for your babies," she says. "They need to see how bonita their mama is, so they don't worry." She tells me her story. She has two daughters. She passed the border illegally twice and got caught. On the third strike, she got four years in prison. But the kids and dad live in the US, and she needed to be with them. She can't get a green card because she has a record. So, Karla says she is in jail for being an illegal alien and repeat offender for coming into the US illegally.

I believe her but I don't at the same time. I sense there are drugs involved, but she does look more like an innocent mule than a drug dealer. She shows me her kids and husband. Unlike her, they all look so American. She says her oldest has cancer—leukemia—and her name is Vanessa. My heart dropped. She cannot visit at the moment because she is undergoing chemo. But they will bring her the following week on a non-visiting day. She is attached to tubes and a mask when she visits. I'm devastated for her. I hold her hand, and for a second, I thank the God I lost faith in when I walked into jail for keeping my kids healthy.

I let Karla do my make-up. Yes, inmates can wear make-up. They sell some Revlon expired shit in commissary. I go to visiting, and right away Savannah's face lights up.

"Mom! You are okay. You are wearing make-up." Visiting is harder each time. It is always the same song and dance. I press Joe for news from my lawyers. Sometimes, he is full of hope. Sometimes, he makes it sound like they threw away the key and I'll be here for four years. Then he tells me, "If you didn't use non-kosher tomato sauce, and if you went to the Mikvah like you were supposed to, this wouldn't have happened."

YOU DUMB FUCK, you are telling me I'm in prison because of fucking Hunts tomato sauce and missing going to a purifying Jewish bath of rainwater after my period? YOU DUMB FUCKING FUCK!!!! I remember thinking *what is going to happen to me if my life depends on Jewish fucking cult shit*? He is totally delusional.

On a visiting day, Savannah told me there was a weird gathering with black-hat rabbis in my house, and they were doing weird stuff around the dining room table, using some of our pictures in our picture frames. I was scared. Each time Joe came to see me, he would speak of a mystical Rabbi Weinberg he met, and when he goes to see him, he comes out knowing I will come out. I literally imagined he had been recruited in a sect like the Manson Family.

Inside, I dodge bullets and bitches who want to fight. Others want to fuck, and some start conspiracy theories.

"Blondie, why you getting visits on non-visiting days? Are you an undercover cop?"

"Yeah, Mandy, I'm an undercover cop, you dipshit." I acted all tough, but the truth is I was scared. Sure, when I was feeling attacked, I acted tough. But all I had to do was think of a fucking mop and what another inmate could do to me with it. Around here, mop handles were weapons. They weren't just used to clean toilet floors.

Speaking of toilets, Blondie had to be on bathroom duty like everyone else. The day I found out it was my turn, I chewed my acrylic nails and ripped them off. I fucking gagged my way through every stall. Imagine shit on the floor, shit on the walls, period blood splattered all over. We used hygienic pads to wash the floor and that was epic. You know what else is epic? Taking a shower with a bunch of HE-SHE lesbians, who were horny as fuck. It took me months to not be scared of being gang-banged in the shower. I showered with my underwear on. Nothing ever happened to me in the shower, but I dodged a few bullets.

When I couldn't protect myself, Russia handled it for me. She scared those mother-fucking ghetto bitches, and when she didn't scare them, her bunkie, a big black woman, scared them till they shit their pants.

Gabriel was a nut job, everyone said it, but I found him kind. I believed his story about being in love with the wrong girl, who was herself under a pimp who got them both in trouble with drugs. Gabriel said he was driving the car when they caught him, and he never saw her again. He said he was raising her kids with her, so he didn't mind she never contacted him or tried to help him out of jail. Gabriel prayed every day.

I asked if he was bar mitzvah. He said no. He became a boy later, and when he sees his parents, he wears a skirt. His real name is Sylvia. I only find out he is Sylvia when they call his name at mail call.

I'm shocked. I storm out of the unit. Gabriel runs after me and begs me to let him explain. He never made the transition. He is all woman, except the voice, and the facial hair. He only started meds before he got in, but they weren't legal meds, so the Department of Prisons won't allow him to continue the treatment. Gabriel talks crazy tales, but in prison it's the Twilight Zone, so you believe it.

Karla often tells me, "No hablas con el, es un loco," don't talk to him he is a nutjob. In fact, everyone dodges Gabriel because they think he is weird. I belong to a few posies. The Latina Mamas, the ones who got in trouble helping out the father of their kids, The Latina Gang ladies, who are doing hard time and will probably go right back to their gang activities if they ever get out, and the Russians. I have a few African American buddies. Sheryl is one of them. I'm still friends with her today.

A few months down the line, Gabriel makes his move on me. I since have uncovered his many lies and also discovered he was in the psych unit before they moved him to five. His brother came to visit him and spoke to Joe on the way out, and it wasn't good news. The brother said his sister is delusional. Sylvia is nuts. I walked away from Gabriel, and he fell into a deep depression. But like Russia said, it was better this way. Some people were speculating I was Gabriel's new wifey.

Chapter 7: 300 Fucking Minutes

Every month, your phone minutes are renewed. The first week in, I wasted my minutes. I mean 300 minutes is nothing, if you think about it. Ten minutes a day wasn't enough to hear from my three babies, to hear about their day, to try and get some reassurance from someone, anyone: Joe, my brother, my cousin who is a celeb psychic. I was desperate for anything they could tell me to assure me I was about to be released.

On Day 12, I had twelve minutes left. Twelve fucking minutes. I don't like to count, but I could count that was literally one min per day for the next twelve days, or I would spend twelve days without speaking to the kids. So, we decided I won't call them on days they visit me. But I wasn't disciplined. I had horrible urges and needs to hear them, to wait by the phone booth for my turn, for a moment of privacy in that booth, to hear those sweet voices, and listen to the sound of home.

I asked anyone and everyone with a little bit of seniority there if there was any way to gain extra minutes.

"This ain't *Jeopardy*, Blondie. You don't win extra minutes here," said Ms. Wilson. She said she wishes she could give me her 194,294,051 unused minutes because she sure as hell never called anyone. Didn't she have family, I wondered?

Someone in the law library pulled a newspaper clipping out of a book sitting in the back shelves. Mrs. Wilson was notorious. She killed not one but two husbands in cold blood. It is clear no one from her family wants to talk to her, so she had minutes (more like years) worth of phone calls to spare.

I lived in constant stress and sorrow. Nothing during the day brings relief, except perhaps the visits, but then again the visits were a source of stress too, I was scared something would happen, like fog, or an issue when the family goes through security and the visit would be cancelled. Then, stress because the clock was ticking too fast during my kids' visits. I couldn't enjoy it or feel an ounce of happiness. The second I saw them, I hugged them and smelled them, and I started to feel the pain in my gut and in my heart, that strong pain of separation looming over our heads.

Inside, so much stressed me. Some of the inmates are terrifying at first. Then, comes a point you actually wish you could die, so you are less scared for your life. Going to the bathroom stressed me. Showering was excruciating. I had so many unknown fears, apprehensions, and uncomfortable situations. I was in a place where many inmates were here for life; they had nothing to lose, except perhaps some privileges, but that was not enough to stop some in their hostility.

I walk around the yard with Russia, and she speed walks. She is your modern-day Jane Fonda. Somehow, she makes her uniform look sexy. I often wondered if she had a gifted inmate take it in for her to make it look more couture. Turns out, she did, and proposed I do the same. It could make my butt look perkier and my boobs more prominent. Um, no thanks! Why the fuck would I want that?

A) I'm not staying here long enough to care what I actually look like and B) I don't need to get gang-banged by a bunch of HE-SHEs.

At night I fight the urge to pee. I hold it for hours and sometimes the whole night. At this point I was moved to the general dormitory, and my bunkie is a 500 lbs monster of a woman. Word is she killed a few people. Each time she moves, the whole bed moves, so much so I almost flew off my top bunk. I get down that ladder, and she grabs my ankle. She calls me a tight piece of ass and asks if I want to take a nap with her. I'm light and quick on my feet, so I jump off, throwing a kick her way, and free myself of her grip.

I go to the bathroom, and I hear some heavy breathing and grinding. 2 girls are fucking in the bathroom stall. I make a U-turn. I'm too scared they'd grab me and force me to participate. I'm told some girls become lesbians because they are scared for their lives and do it in exchange for protection. See, some inmates are what you call separates, which meant they are serving time for the same crime. They are witnesses in each other's trials, and often that's a problem. While the Bureau of Prisons usually makes sure separates aren't incarcerated at the same FCI, sometimes it happens, and it ain't pretty.

I often tell Russia I'm scared. She says she has to teach me self-defense and how to keep weapons. I don't want a piece of plastic or glass sharpened into a knife. I can't afford to end up in the SHU and miss my visits; I'd die. No worries, she said. What she means is another kind of weapon. We have these huge locks for our lockers. She tells me to put it in a sock and swing it in your assailant's face. Great! Fuck my life!

Day 15: I'm suicidal and I inquire on contraband meds. Maybe an overdose is the answer. I'm friendly with this girl, Briana. She is a violinist but is here because she is a terrorist. I met her in visiting. Her sweet little girl, Kallyope, visits often. When we leave visiting, we both cry, and our eyes meet. I finally find someone who understands my pain. We bond over the pain of motherhood behind bars. She too was found guilty many years after the crime, and she, too, was taken away from a tiny little baby.

She was already in for two years, and her daughter lived in California or Seattle—I can't remember. Briana said I can't try suicide. If I do, they will transfer me to a mental correctional facility out of state, probably in North Carolina, and visits are suspended for those on suicide watch.

Still, I once went to the bathroom and put a plastic bag over my head. It was a Jewish holiday, and since Joe was so religious, he didn't drive on those days. This holiday had five days of driving restrictions (you can't touch electricity, you can't drive, you can't work, and you can't speak on the phone during those Jewish high holidays). It had been five days without seeing or hearing from my kids.

I knew all Jewish families got together for holiday lunches and dinners, and my family did too. Desperation would take over on those long days. I felt less like me and more like the other inmates. This was my life, and I may never come out. I was hearing stories about girls coming in for a two-year sentence but still doing time because of trouble on the inside twelve years later. Anything that can go wrong behind bars will go wrong. Innocent, doesn't mean shit there... You are at the same risk of having charges filed against you whether you stole a few thousands or whether you cut your baby up and microwaved it. Gruesome, I know! I only mention it because that monster was in Danbury with me.

Did you ever hear of this woman who cut her baby up, cooked him, and served him to her husband for dinner? I was incarcerated with her. Only I sold True Religion jeans to get there and she killed her baby. This to me was terrifying, not so much the fact that she cut that baby up and cooked him, but the fact that you can be put in the same category as those people. The reason why I'm having this talk with you, my dear reader, is to express why, as a mother, you can come to a point of wanting to die, suicide the only relief you can think of.

I attempted suicide a few times for twelve nanoseconds, only to let my maternal instincts and common sense take over. I didn't want to miss my visits because I was on suicide watch.

*

Day 16: "You do not have any credit left. Please, hang up and try again."

I hang up frantically, and then entered my code again like a mad woman. The same automated message comes over the phone. "You do not have any credit left, please hang up and try again."

No, no, no, no, no, no, no, no! My heart started pounding so hard I could hear it in my ears. "Yo, Blondie, are you making that phone call? I gotta call my man. Get the fuck out if you ain't gonna start talking in that phone."

I come out. "Fuck you, Precious! Fuck you!"

She grabs me by my hair. "No one talks to Precious that way." I elbow her in her fat midsection.

"No one this ugly should call her fucking self Precious, but, hey, it still happened! Don't fuck with me, dumb bitch! I can't talk to my kids, so I might as well kill someone."

I guess I was hoping she would kill me and put me out of my misery. Instead, she was amused...and she never fucked with me again.

"Ohhhh, Blondie is mad; she finished her minutes like a rookie."

You are probably smiling about this anecdote, but you won't smile long. I got desperate. The Jewish holiday was ending after five long days without contact, and I had no phone minutes left to hear my babies. I went to find Gabriel.

"Gabriel, me tienes que ayudar, necessito mandar un mensaje a mi familia ahora!" *Gabriel, you have to help me, I need to send a message to my family NOW.* Gabriel was in love with me and I knew it. I knew he/she would do anything for me. She had been incarcerated for three years so she knew the rules. She warned me if she called another inmate's family member she would get her phone privileges suspended. I begged. I cried. I told him I wanted to die. My heart was in burning pain. It truly was.

I now realize I was being selfish and reckless towards Gabriel and really risked sending her to the SHU. She agreed to the alternative of calling her brother and giving her brother Joe's number to tell him I'm okay and ask him if he is coming to visit tomorrow. Joe was coming to visit, and I should have just been okay knowing that, but no, my urges to get confirmations of things were compulsive. I needed to hear it. I needed confirmation. It was a form of getting a weird instant relief, at any cost, even at the cost of getting Gabriel and myself into trouble.

Gabriel called her brother and did as we planned, and then she called him back and he confirmed that he spoke to their "amigo" and he is going to visit. They spoke in codes because the phone conversations are monitored, and if it was understood I got someone to call my family to pass on a message, I would get a strike. A strike is an infraction ticket that can get certain prison privileges suspended, or get you sent to the SHU, or even could extend your prison sentence.

The next day, we heard Gabriel's name called on the loudspeaker.

"Inmate Sandoval report to the captain's office immediately." It was Captain Sanchez. I recognized her voice. She was terrifying. Gabriel left, in silence, looking at me like, I told you so.

I think I shat myself. I remember having to wash my ugly prison underwear that day. Gabriel may not come back, she may be sent to the SHU, and it would be all my fault.

She comes back after an hour, and says kindly, "I told you we would get caught; they catch everything." She had gotten her phone privileges suspended for three months and a strike. Thank God, she wasn't sent to the SHU.

I pressed her to tell me what she said, and she claimed they knew she was calling for me, but she didn't confirm and denied the whole thing. One hour later, I was called to the Captain's office. I tried to deny it. After all, Gabriel didn't call Joe. She called her brother. I got my phone privileges suspended for three months and a strike.

But the captain said she knew I got visits all the time and could suspend them but won't this time. Weirdly, I was relieved about that and didn't feel the sense of devastation about my phone privileges until the following days.

My incarceration went from bad to worse. The phone privileges suspension is lot more emotionally charged than you may think. Something happens and you start feeling like people in your life, those that are part of you, are becoming a mirage, a far-away memory and this life inside becomes your only reality. You start forgetting what normal people look like or what walking on the street is like. Prison life is like living in a parallel world, where the other world really does not know you exist.

My desperation is obvious on my face, and I develop a rash under my eyes, from rubbing the tears off with a scrappy piece of tissue, day in and day out. I cry in silence, under my rough sheets every night.

By then, I was not a rookie anymore. They moved me into the general unit with 80 others. It's a huge cell, with bunk beds, separated into cubicles... called cubes. You have no privacy, but you are sharing that cube with a cube mate you didn't pick (it is not summer camp). My bunkie is a serial killer. I don't know how many she killed. She is doing hard time—probably had a 40-year sentence—but that is not something you ask, and even if you do, everyone lies, so you probably won't know the truth anyway. Each time she turned in her sleep, the bed moved.

I'm sleeping on top and I feel like a leaf, look like one too. There are very few mirrors in prison, and the ones that are there are made out of plastic to avoid inmates breaking them and using them as sharp weapons. I can see myself, a distorted image of me in one of them. I'm wasting away. I'm becoming thinner and thinner... In the shower, I feel my vertebra poking out. I'm literally skin and bones, and my hair is falling out a little, too. I stop having my period for months.

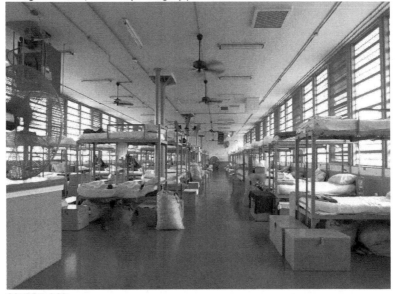

SOURCE: BOP

My cube was maybe on the sixth row here. This is an older picture, but it hadn't change much by the time I was there, except the bunks were separated by ugly peachy colored Formica walls into cubicles. Not the "We-Work" feel, either.

*

Russia puts me in a corner like she is going to crush me with her huge chest and pulls out two oranges and one apple from her pocket and stuffs them under my shirt.

Her accent is getting rougher around the edges, and she is speaking less and less English.

"EAT NOW," she tells me. "I got this stolen from kitchen for you. You eat it or I hurt you." She also tells me to sleep with that lock she mentioned I can put in my sock. She tells me to just take a swing at whoever decides to come fuck with me. I may have used it once, when an inmate tried to sexually assault me, thinking I was fast asleep.

The truth is I never really slept. I didn't sleep for a year. I slept for minutes and kept an eye open. I heard every sound. I heard every count time. I heard bitches fucking. I heard someone sobbing. I heard guards walking by with their huge key holders clinking.

Russia saved my life. She gave me the tools to survive. She helped me eat, helped me learn to fight, helped me to hide my emotions, and taught me how to suck up to the right people. She was a gangster and so badass.

Throughout my whole incarceration, I know she cared about me but not in a cutesy kind of way, more in a burdened, dutiful way. It's as if some sort of unspoken pact put her in charge of me the day she was called to fetch me from R & D, and now she had some sort of duty to keep me alive. She never showed weakness, except when she would be in visit with Andrew, her gorgeous brown-haired, blue-eyed boy, and she would wave at me when I was visiting with my kids. I always tried not to pry, but once she walked over to the food machine in visit with Andrew and introduced us. She said my kids are beautiful, and she understands now why I cry so much.

It's 2:55 pm. Hayden, the Nazi correctional officer, starts telling the visitors it's time to go. It is always the same song and dance. Dakota's little baby fists tighten around my ugly smelly uniform and she starts crying. Dylan can't wait to leave. Savannah's strong little expression hardens, and tears start rolling down her cheeks. She reassures me as she reassures herself. "It's okay, Mommy. We will be back soon," she says.

I hold my tears until I go line up by the doorway back to hell and turn my back to the visitors lining up to leave, returning to the free world. It's only then I burst into tears. Russia is strong, but I can see her icy blue eyes turning wet and red too. She was hurting for Andrew and I think a little bit for me, too.

"Come on," she says. "We will go and make some chai and play cards, yes?"

I nod my head. She teaches me a Russian card game she plays with Ruta all the time.

*

Connecticut is so cold. Its knife-sharp cold, a cold I feel in my bones, on my face, and in my soul. I dread an element I never thought of before: I am scared of the fog. Fog is what can ruin my life behind bars. It causes general lockdowns, and if it is thick enough, we will be locked in our units the whole day, only let out for chow. Rumor has it, inmates have escaped on bad fog days, but I wasn't terrified of being locked down all day with a bunch a cabin-fevered psychopaths. No, that didn't scare me. What scared me most was the cancelled visits.

Your family could drive to FCI DANBURY (a three-hour drive for my family) just to be turned away due to foggy conditions, and that was the worst thing that could happen to me. I cannot explain it. When you are on the outside, a cancelled visit with your kids sounds bad, but not deadly right? Well, on the inside, it felt like death.

I felt like they may never come back if visiting got cancelled. I felt like I couldn't go on breathing if visiting was cancelled for the day. And if it was a Friday, that meant I may not see them till Sunday, and if it got foggy again Sunday, it meant I wouldn't see them till perhaps the following Friday or Sunday, if they had school. I lived through a chain of anxieties that would build up into trauma. The trauma would devolve into depression and that would then lead me to suicidal thoughts.

Every day that passed, I would lose hope...

Chapter 8: I Love You All the Way to the Moon and the Stars and to the Hashem

Months pass and my phone privileges are still suspended. It isn't called a privilege for nothing. You do not understand how phoning home makes you feel a little less like E.T when you are incarcerated. I have so much on my mind.

I feel like my special boy is slipping right through my hands. He hardly shows up anymore, and he has chronic stomach pains. We think it's the thought of coming to see me that causes the pain. His OCD is really bad, and he over washes his hands. He goes to the bathroom incessantly, even though he doesn't need to, and he is consumed with his bowels. He asks to leave class almost every hour to go. I wrote the kids letters every day. I became artistic and drew cards. I used commissary goodies or even paid some inmates for contraband art supplies like crayons, paint, paper, and glitter.

I wrote them lies. "Mommy will be home soon!" These lies, I believed. I would cut out anything I could find from old magazines. I'd promise them I'd buy them this or that we'd go on vacation. I found a cool blackberry phone. I cut it out, and in my letters, I would promise Dylan to get it for him the week I would come home. I would find Bahamas Atlantis Hotel ads with pictures of giant slides in the vivid blue lagoon pools, and I would these cut out and promise Savannah we would go on that trip for her upcoming birthday.

I made sure they got letters from me every day that the postal service would deliver it.

June 2nd, 2009 (40 days to your BIRTH DAY)
❤ My angel ❤
My princess, my love, my precio[us]
jewel, my goddess, my baby gi[rl]
Sooman ❤

I miss you so so so much ❤ I think
about you all day long, I dream
about you every night ❤ I just
can't wait to be with you, to
squeeze you hard, to smell you[r]
hair, to nibble your arms, to biss
your face, to bite your pretty nose,
to hose you nibble my back while
we lay in bed ❤ I miss all that so
much ❤ And we're going to do it
all again soon ❤

Love you so much, everyday that
goes by, I love you more & more ❤
[we] will be together again soon ❤
[...] soon ❤ You will see much [...]
[...] will never be alone ever ❤ [...]
[...] going to go to Ahh [...]
[...] & France [...]
[...] you, [...] ❤ ❤ [...]

I would always end these letters with, "Mommy is coming home very soon, I promise. I think and dream of you every night. You are the love of my life. I will hug you so tight when I come home, and I will never go away every again. I love you from here all the way to the moon and the stars that twinkle in the sky and to Hashem."

I still reference the Hebrew God, even though I was angry at Him. How could I believe in a god that separated three small innocent children from their mom? A mom that moved mountains for them, a mom that one of them needed desperately to function pseudo-normally in a world that already categorized him as abnormal. What monster is that god?

Yet, I wavered in my crisis of faith. I went from days of praying, reading the psalms of David Tehelim, and hoping that I too would be set free, like King David was when he recited those psalms... and then the next day I would believe there is no god.

All the inmates read *The Secret*. What a fucking crack of shit book that was. How do you fucking manifest anything behind bars and expect it to happen? A sentence is a sentence, no fucking manifesting or Tony Robbins bullshit was gonna open those motherfucking doors. I was angry ...

I saw a lot of shit inside, and dementia was a big one. There was a unit (Unit 3), which was literally called the mental unit. All those inmates on anti-depressants or with serious mental illness were in there. Then, there were the crackheads that just arrived and going through the detox phase without any assistance or meds. All the ticks and symptoms were recognizable. A mouth twitch I then learnt is common to crack addicts in withdrawal.

I met this beautiful young woman. She really looked like a girl, with long legs. She was a bit too skinny, but she had gorgeous blue eyes and stunning hair. Her name was Jessica. The minute I started being seen with her, all the gossipers came to me to say she is nuts. So, yeah, she was in Unit #3, but she was well-spoken (maybe too well-spoken). She was kind and seemed so educated. It was actually nice to be with her even though she was seven years younger than me.

I didn't trust easily. When Joe came to visit, I asked him to Google Jessica and find out what she had done. When asked, she just said some boss didn't pay her her due and she threatened him. Joe delivered and brought me the story.

"Twenty-three-year-old high school dropout Jessica was sentenced to 21 months in federal prison this week after pleading guilty to extorting $125,000 from a married business executive she met online and threatened to expose as an adulterer."

The business exec in question was the then CEO of Pepsi. I was relieved! So that idiot fucked her and then probably dumped her, and so she got mad. So what? At least, she didn't cut up her child in pieces and microwave him for dinner like that other psycho we were incarcerated with.

I never told Jessica I knew what she had done. She had a cute (very young looking) smitten boyfriend who came to visit her as much as Joe and the kids visited me, and she seemed to get a lot of money for commissary. She was generous with her food, and she was so fucking human.

When I told her I'm dying inside that I couldn't call my children because my phone privileges were taken away, she commissioned Jude to meet up with Joe in the parking lot after a visiting day and exchange numbers so he could code-speak to him and pass messages or just give me news.

She was smart and conniving, in a way that whoever was supervising the phone calls never put two and two together. She became a real friend, a lifeline. She was so young, but something told me she had a rough past. And she'd grown up and matured really fast. She would come out of the psych ward unit, and it was like an angel appeared in front of me, with her pretty hair, her freshness, her beautiful face and allure.

She wasn't fazed by prison at all. She had a short sentence, and she made the best of it, or maybe it is whatever pills she was on. Some people said she was bipolar, but frankly to me she was the most normal person in there. She would rush to me and say, "Jude spoke to Joe. Everything is okay. Your lawyer is going to call you, and Dylan's evaluation went well."

"But how the fuck did you get all this out of Jude without mentioning our names, Jess?"

"We speak in coded language. Jude knows I don't need to speak to my lawyer since I didn't appeal. I plead guilty, so he knows I'm talking about yours, and we called Dylan 'the boy.'"

Smart cookies those two, and they had so much humanity. Strangely, she never asked for anything in return. I kept waiting for her to ask but she never did. Not even when I went home. I figured she would find me and ask me for something for all she had done. She never did, although today we are friends on Facebook and Instagram. We watch each other's lives and applaud each other on making it through. We didn't get in touch until I moved to Monaco because the federal laws prohibit convicted felons from associating with one another for the time of their probation, and I think she had a few years left after I left Danbury.

But once I arrived in Monaco, she said she would visit. I remember seeing a pic of her all gorgeous, posing with a fluorescent Yellow Birkin on place du Casino in Monaco the year before I moved there. She said she was a sommelier when I met her. I don't know if it is true, but she sure knew a lot about wines, and she did own a vineyard or wine business with this guy, Cal, who visited her often and kept her informed on the business and also sent her money on commissary. I was kind of captivated by her story, although I knew she didn't tell me everything. She had a pure heart towards me and for that I am forever thankful to her. She did alleviate a lot of my anxiety and pain.

I'm smirking as I'm writing this because I never thought of Googling Jessica (Jess, if you are reading this, I am so sorry I Googled you, it took me 11 years to do so myself) since, and just now when I did, I just find out she could have avoided jail. The newspaper wrote: "Jessica was arrested last year and pleaded guilty to extortion. She was released on bond, but a judge issued a warrant for her arrest after she hit a woman in the head with a glass in a bar in Seneca Falls. Police arrested her after she gave them a phony name and Social Security number. She also cut off the electronic monitor attached to her ankle, according to court records. Under the terms of her pretrial release, she was allowed to leave her home only for school, work, or court-ordered mental health treatment. The nasty CEO has since left Pepsi Bottling."

Ah, now I understand why she was in Unit #3. I never wanted to Google her before. I didn't want to judge her. I still don't judge her, other than positively for the way she acted with me. Maybe she made amends while in prison, or maybe she did want to punish the Pepsi CEO for being a disgusting cheat (as she claimed in emails to him). I don't know and I don't care. She didn't really deserve to be in medium-high security federal prison because some CEO couldn't keep his dick in his pants and she tried to make a buck for sleeping with his nasty ass. Isn't that what sugar babies do?

Isn't that what most young women marrying old rich men do? If I have learned anything from all this, it is that I will never judge anyone until I walked in their shoes, or unless they committed murder, molested a child, or anything else of gruesome nature...

But, fuck, was she a badass. She beat up a woman in a bar? She cut off her electronic bracelet? Fuck, when I wore my electronic bracelet, I was scared of breathing on it and get a probation violation.

I also am not going to judge her for sleeping with a married man because I did too.

Now as you are reading this, I need to remind you I am not looking for sympathy. I am not justifying my wrong-doings, but I am also not looking for absolution from my readers or anyone for that matter, except maybe for Joe (but he already forgave me, and said he now understands why it happened).

The spring before my incarceration (six months before), Joe and I bought our dream home in Neponsit's Far Rockaway, NY. We moved into the mansion-like home after years of living in Brooklyn's Jewish neighborhood in Flatbush. Years of struggles, hard work, and raising three small children right under the F train Railroad. Yes, under it—not over it.

This is where I raised my three kids. There was a cute little house on this horrible commercial street in place of this building. I got this picture from Google Maps.

Our house was right on this road, with the F train line passing over our heads all day and all night. Eventually, you get used to the vibrations and noise of the trains.

So now, let's get past the sob story. I still drove a Range Rover living on that street. I had beautiful jewelry and furs Joe showered on me with (even though he could be such a stingy asshole with other basic needs of life), and I drove into Manhattan every day to my office on West Broadway, thriving in the world of fashion.

See? This little house under the railroad was a commercial property. Joe bought it was an investment, living in it was a temporary thing that would eventually make us rich and have us move to a very upscale beachfront mini-mansion someday. When you are from Brooklyn, you know you gotta eat shit to leave the shit hole someday. I mean, 50 Cent did it, right?

So, we moved on up to Neponsit, 145th street, prime residential location of the wealthy New Yorkers in the know. The owners of Jordache Jeans lived right down my block and held fancy fundraisers for Senator Charles Schumer that would block my driveway at times.

Remember this small detail for later, as it will make a lot of sense (No, I did not have an affair with Senator Schumer, not even close).

Joe was at the peak of religiousness. He had fallen deep into what I like to call ignorant-orthodoxy (I made up the word— it goes for orthodox and toxicity), and it stands for those that never learned anything about the Jewish religion but keep on adding stringent rules of practice without even knowing why. In Hebrew, they call them "Baal Teshuva." The term baal teshuva is from the Talmud, literally meaning "master of repentance." In my language, it means master of idiocracy and lack of tolerance, which itself goes against every fundamental of the Jewish religion.

I should know; my grandfather Joseph was a Talmud scholar. His passion and knowledge for the Jewish religion made him so wise and a well of tolerance. He particularly insisted we don't practice rules we don't understand and truly, convincingly believe in. He taught me the religion I loved, respected, and believed in. When I was young, he read me the Torah, as I would sit on the floor. By his chair, he was a mystical, spiritually powerful man, with his feet so grounded in reality. I'm not at all into spiritual quack shit. I'm more of a Cartesian. I don't believe unless I see. However, today I believe I used to sit on the floor so much in a quest for stability. I used to sit at my grandfather's feet because our feet are our rooted in survival, security, and stability. When you don't have that foundation, you feel ungrounded and lost.

The foot is an important energy center that supports you in standing and living your truth. Still today, when I micro-blog or create a post sharing my truth, I will sit at the foot of my bed on the floor while finding my inspiration and publishing my post. I stand and live my truth.

Sheesh, I get sidetracked … probably because it is time I open up about my affair, and it is not my proudest moment, but here it goes…

So, Joe and I finally moved into our dream house, our mini-mansion in Far Rockaway, NY, and we have to introduce ourselves to our neighborhood. Like good Jews, we select the synagogue that fits our traditions and rites best. We put our best outfits on. I curl Savannah's hair and put pretty bows on. I dress her and Dakota in exquisite European designer dresses with chic ruffles, not the tacky kind. I dress Dylan in Ralph Lauren pants, a dress shirt, and Todd's moccasins, and I dress to impress, modest-chic, not orthodox-like but still respecting the basic rules of Jewish modesty: my skirt to my knees and sleeves a bit over my elbow, insanely high-heeled Louboutins, and my very long platinum blonde hair styled by one of Manhattan's star hairstylists.

I tried to downplay my sexiness as much as I could. Joe wore his usual perfect Italian cut custom suit and crisp shirt, looking dashing. I remember us, walking in like the perfect family where a small congregation of people just stood there, first sizing us up and then putting their best foot forward to welcome us. I already knew some gossip about some of them because Joe's brother, Bobby, who was a sergeant in the NYPD, had a friend, a fellow officer who's very wealthy uncle and cousins lived there and belonged to that community. They were often mentioned at my table when Bobby and the cousin would come over to dinner.

Somehow in Brooklyn, if you are rich people gossip a lot about you, and you are a point of reference. This guy always referred to his rich uncle in Far Rockaway as a point of reference that he thought made him relevant, like his mother's brother's son's wealth was supposed to impress us. It didn't.

Joe is holding my hand. We look happy (but the truth is we aren't, well, maybe he was, but I wasn't), and he points to a tall, handsome guy and says, "That's the cousin. Handsome huh?"

I wasn't the kind of wife that looked at other guys, I really wasn't … but he was definitely built. I could see that, and much taller than Joe, and definitely handsome, but I don't remember being smitten or anything. I remember thinking, *he doesn't look Jewish, kind of like me.*

It's true in this community we belonged to in Brooklyn and Belle Harbor, every single Jew was Sephardic (The Sephardim are from Spain, Portugal, North Africa and the Middle East). The term "Sephardi" comes from the Hebrew word for Spain. Alternatively, the term "Ashkenazi" comes from the Hebrew word for Germany. Most American Jews today are Ashkenazim, descended from those who arrived from Europe in the mid-1800s and early 1900s.

I looked more Ashkenazi or non-Jewish and so did the rich cousin. Like me, he was light-eyed, light-haired with a small nose. His wife came to greet us, after giving me the head-to-toe scan, with the biggest, fakest, prettiest Stepford-wife smile she could fake. She knew exactly who we were. I am assuming someone from Brooklyn had briefed her. She was pretty, tall, dressed expensive but tacky. She fancied Diane von Fürsternberg signature wrap print dresses to my horror. I couldn't stand those dresses, so already I wasn't inclined to like her. But she was pretty, I'll give her that... prudish, though. She most resembled the character of Charlotte in *Sex and the City*. She urged her husband to rush over and give us a proper greeting. She introduced us, and Joe, of course, mentions we are tight with his cousin (personally, I couldn't stand that idiot meat head cousin but whatever).

He was polite, maybe a little shy, and starts chatting with us. He introduces us to his cute kids. We find out he is 27, just a few years younger than me. Our kids start playing together even though they aren't exactly the same ages. He didn't look at me any different than most men when I went to the synagogue. I was used to the stares. I handled them. After all, what did I expect? I was platinum blonde, with voluptuous lips, big breasts, and long legs, and no matter how modest I tried to dress, I still wanted to be stylish and sexy, and I failed at camouflaging that savage side of me. So, did he look at me a certain way? Yes, I think so, but I was used to it. Most men in a religious setting do, and I became oblivious to it. I mean I had a handsome husband. If good-looking men could make me happy, I had that at home, thanks very much. The problem was good-looking men didn't do shit for me because Joe was as bad a husband as he was handsome.

*

Over the next couple of months after our move, I became friendly with his mother, Jaffa. She lived on my street. She was sassy, cool, and was wonderful with my kids. She told them to call her Safta (Grandma in Hebrew). I saw her after work. I'd go over her house for coffee, and she would come over to mine. Sometimes she'd come for the Mexican girls' night that I threw once a week for a few of my girlfriends. I served frozen margaritas, tortillas, and salsa, and we would sit in my backyard laughing over light girl talk till the wee hours. I got so close to Jaffa. She was kind to me. She was a little bit like a surrogate mom and also a best friend. In parallel, I got friendly with her son...Gil (the rich cousin). We had a lot in common. He took amazing care of his kids. I admired that and loved that about him while I was always alone with mine when I wasn't working. We would often bump into each other at the beach (on my block). My house was on the beach block that everyone wanted to come to because it was the nicest... I bumped into him and his kids at the Aviator, the neighborhood's sports center where Dylan took up ice hockey and kickboxing and Savannah tried ice skating and gymnastics. We obviously and very organically and innocently friended each other on Facebook and often would message each other about the kid's schedules at Aviator or taking them to the beach. It stayed a really nice friendship for a long time. We got personal. He told me how he felt trapped in

73

his marriage and felt he was forced into it by familial pressure. I told him how unhappy I was with Joe, who had not a paternal bone in his body, and was mentally abusive.

His stories made me hate his wife, and I think mine made him hate Joe. He described her as a tyrant, and sometimes I wondered if she was capable of hitting him. Why did he stay? He loved his kids, and he knew she would do everything to take them away, and also he said that she didn't sign a prenup. She fought him tooth and nail to not sign it. He was concerned, since everything he owned really was his father's and getting selfishly divorced from the dragon lady meant giving her his father's money.

Meanwhile, he was an amazing friend. He boosted my confidence, where Joe would tear it down. He played ball with Dylan while Joe refused to do anything with him. He admired my career in fashion while Joe called it outrageous, stupid, and unhealthy because of all the gays I worked with, and all the boozed up parties on rooftops I was invited to (and often didn't end up going to because I knew he would accuse me of being a whore for going).

Gil looked at me with kind eyes; he was sweet and gentle, and he was almost my age. I related to him—our parents' backgrounds were very similar. Both our fathers were Moroccan Jews. The food we grew up on and the education we received were very similar. I had always been faithful to Joe, and it never crossed my mind not to be, except when he would refuse to take the kids and I on vacation, so I would book us on exotic trips to the Dominican Republic, St. Barth or Miami and I'd go alone with my kids. Anyone I met there always asked me, "How can a husband refuse to come on vacation with a wife like you?"

In Punta Cana, when Savanah was 11 months old, I met my friend Trevor, a dashing hokey player hunk from Toronto and almost had an idyllic affair with him. Instead, we stayed friends all these years, and still are... All this to say, I had so much temptation with extra marital affairs but never really went there till Gil.

My friendship with Gil and his mom really filled a void in my life. I sometimes felt I belonged more with them than with Joe's family. My own family was in Miami, and somewhat estranged because Joe didn't get along with them. To be honest, he acted so odd around them I preferred to keep them at bay.

Gil never really tried anything with me, and I can't say I fantasized about him either. I was too preoccupied with Joe changing his ways. We had three kids together and it had to work. I hoped for more than 13 years, but it never happened.

I had my dream home, on the beach, and with one hop over the BQE, I was in Manhattan in 20 minutes to my amazing job. I just had a beautiful baby girl— Dakota, who was just a few months old, and I had my body back. I worked out every day. At the time, I was already doing what became my patented THE METHOD protocol six years later...But I was unhappy. Joe was verbally abusive to me, which was endurable, but the worst was he was verbally abusive to Dylan. He called him "retarded" and "dumb" a lot, and that made me hate him. I loved him and I loathed him. I spend most of the little time we had together protecting Dylan from his verbal abuse. He was never physically abusive; he was traumatized from watching his monstrous father nearly beat his mother to death when he was growing up, but the verbal abuse was bad. He would call me a cunt if he found crumbs under the table or if a jar of hunts

74

tomato sauce was not marked kosher. He would call Dylan retarded when he would repeat the same things over and over or would not make eye contact when he spoke to him.

The kids were stressed around food a lot. Joe had a fucked-up relationship with food. One of his older sisters was obese he said, and his older brother Ralph had weight issues. Plus, his two younger brothers always had to watch their weight. Joe was obsessed with being skinny. He ate two meals a day, and while he loved my food and only my food, he refused to eat out, which was weird as fuck if you ask me. He was obsessed with his weight. He insisted I teach him my Pilates method, and once he learnt it by heart, he would do it on his own to exhaustion; sometimes I would find him asleep on his mat in the living room at 11pm.

His obsession with weight-loss made him tyrannical with the kids. Dylan gained weight, and the issue is mostly (I knew this since his cognitive specialist taught me about it) all due to gut issues that go with autism. He gained a lot of weight; he was almost obese. My cute boy, on top of being different in his head, was becoming an easy target for bullies because of weight-gain I could barely control because of all the GMO shit in the United States. One of his brilliant pathologists, a professor at NY Presbyterian Hospital, explained when a person with autism suffers from a casein or dairy allergy, often times, autism symptoms are exacerbated. Although its effectiveness is still contested by some, many parents opt to place their children on a Gluten-Free Casein Free (GFCF) diet to help eliminate or curb the autism symptoms caused by milk and dairy.

Dylan became intolerant to dairy, so then I became aware of the Brain to Gut Axis I speak about so much today with my clients and my audience. Everything I did to alleviate his autism symptoms would cause weight gain. He got bullied a lot for his weight, more than for being different. But his biggest bully was Joe. He would come home while I was having dinner with the kids, God forbid that asshole would even bother having dinner with us, and ask about our day... and as he would walk into the kitchen he would say, "You fat tubba waba, stop eating."

Dylan didn't understand insults. I think his clean soul and heart still don't understand insults today, so he kept eating, unbothered. But the little girl with the wits and the quick brain next to him was listening to everything... Savannah became scared of eating when her father was around. The minute she heard his car in the driveway, she would shove the last bite so fast in her little mouth she almost gagged. I would reassure her and tell her to eat, but she didn't want to disappoint him. She was his favorite. Yes, the motherfucker had a favorite! Is that even possible for a parent? YES, it is. My mother has favorites too and it ain't me. Actually, sometimes my mother reminds me of Joe. When I married Joe, the masochist in me married my mother (more later on how life turned shit around for me in that aspect today). Savannah started eating emotionally and on the sneak. She went from being this little shrimp to rapidly gaining weight, too. Dakota was a few months old, so she wasn't overweight. She was a cute happy baby with baby rolls and pudgy cheeks I would bite all day. At some point Joe called all three kids fat, though. He called Dylan retarded; he called Savannah a liar; and he called me a snake or a cunt, depending on his mood.

He had to have loved me. Today, I know he did. He actually called me and told me he has never had a love like me in his life, in his own dysfunctional way. He made sure we had food on the table; he made sure I always had a newer and better car than him. He worked hard and got me the house of my dreams. He commissioned insane renovations to build me a walk-in closet and fixed the house and our backyard to my liking. He was a master of confusion. I still think today he was fucked in his head by his abusive father, which left him to struggle with knowing how to love, so he loved the only way he thought he knew.

But I didn't see it that way then, and even if part of me did, it wasn't enough to forgive him for all the mental abuse he put us through. Joe liked me, but he didn't like the kids. He would devote his Sundays to making me happy, walking around Soho and shopping, but he was happier if I decided to keep the kids home with their nanny. He made a bigger deal about my happiness than theirs. He did make forced efforts to be a better father, each time I threatened to leave him. He would take them to mini golf (in his navy-blue suit, that was awkward) and always made it sound like "okay, mission complete, I hope they are happy." He lost his mind if I decided to have one of the kids sleep with us because they had a nightmare, so I had to make sure the kid slept on my side of the bed, not between us.

He imposed his religious rituals on us; he smothered us in a religion I grew up with but didn't recognize in the hands of Joe. He turned a religion I loved into a sect I hated and feared, and I still do. He lived for Shabbat* (I dreaded Shabbat). During my childhood, Shabbat was the most fun time of the week. It was a festive family gathering with delicious food, conversation and love. Joe turned the 24 hours of Shabbat into a prison and a time of submission. I had to cook Shabbat dinner every Friday, like my mother and my grandmother did before me, but it was not with pleasure. It was forced. Starting at 2 pm on Fridays, Joe would start calling me a "Goy" (a non-Jew in urban offensive language). It's actually Yiddish for "gentile" but in Joe's mouth it was an insult. "I'm more fucking Jewish than that asshole ever will be," is what I mumbled when he would say that.

Why did he call me a goy? Because sundown (which was hours later) was getting close, and he was upset I was still working and may not make it on time to light my candles. Seriously, he terrorized me with Shabbat. We had Shabbat dinner, and I always had his younger, unmarried brothers over. I loved them like my own brothers but at times one of them would get on my nerves. He was so self-righteous and such an asshole.

Bobby, the other brother, the sergeant in the NYPD, was a sweetheart. I've always loved and respected him. When I'd invite my brother over, Joe and his obnoxious little brother would be so rude. They would make fun of my brother and disrespect him, calling him a French frog. The funny thing is, right now reading this I'm sure you're wondering, why didn't you just leave? Well, where exactly did you want me to go? Divorce was not a trend yet back then; it was looked down on, and a divorced woman was as good as a hooker in the Jewish community. I had a child with special needs, who couldn't possibly endure the change of life that comes with a divorce, and I had a mother who refused to help me or welcome me in her nice condo in Miami with open arms. She literally always said, "We leave it in God's hands." I fucking hate her for that and I don't forgive her.

I called her after Dylan was born, begging her to let me come home. She said, "NO! Who is gonna take you with one kid?"

76

I called her after Savannah was born, and she said, "HECK, NO. I don't have any money to help you, let alone welcome you and your special needs son." (That was a crack of shit, she could have sold one of her Bvlgari or Diamond Rolex watches alone, and it would have helped me leave him and start a new life).

I never called her for help ever again since then. My mom did a lot for me by educating me the way she did, teaching me about multi-faceted cultures and French etiquette. She curated my education and transmitted her values to me. She raised me to become a well-traveled woman, a prima ballerina, and a talented pianist. She had me take art classes at Les Beaux Arts, learn six languages, and sent me to Cambridge University in the UK on an exchange program. She inspired me and gave me the tools to become an independent woman and to go to law school. She helped create what I am today. But a loving, warm, life-saving mother she was not then and is not now.

So, where the fuck was I supposed to go if I left Joe? And truth be told I loved him. He was the only man I had ever slept with and had been with my entire life. I still had high hopes that one day he would become normal. I'm talking about Joe, not Dylan. To me, Dylan was more normal than Joe ever was.

As I started to make more money in the fashion industry and Dylan was finally showing signs of improvement, I truly fantasized about leaving Joe. I think Gil (my neighbor) was the catalyst for my divorce. We were friends, so he shared with me how he would surprise his wife with a weekend to Miami, or how he bought her a pair of Jimmy Choo boots on his business trip, or how he planned on throwing her a birthday party, and how she didn't appreciate any of it and treated him like shit. He was literally doing everything for her that Joe never did for me. And that hurt. I started to feel I deserved better. After all, Gil's wife didn't work; she was awful to him. She was lazy, complained all day, and wasn't fit, he said. Yet, she had it all. I started looking to get divorced. Yup a few months after moving into our dream home, I wanted to get divorced and rock the boat.

I told Gil, I'm going to see a lawyer, and if he tells me I can have full-custody, I will get divorced. Joe was too bad a father to have shared custody. He would fuck Dylan's brain up for good if he ever was to have custody. He probably wouldn't want it anyway.

I went to see a lawyer. Joe had no history of physical abuse. He provided. He didn't have a criminal record. He was a respected member of his community. If he wanted shared custody, he could have it. I kept hoping something would change, either Joe or the standards for shared custody.

Gil was getting increasingly unhappy in his marriage, but his biggest fear about leaving her was facing his parents. I know, lame. He told me he started sleeping in the guest room and was starting to hint to his wife that they should try separating (today I know he was lying to me about that) I believed him then, but today, I don't believe for a second he slept in the guest room once.

So... it's summer. I take my kids to the beach. He brings his to the beach. His mom joins in and brings cold beer (she was cool I'm telling you). Him and I start flirting on with BBMs (it was the WhatsApp of blackberries back then) and Facebook messenger, but when we would see each other, we would just smile at each other and chicken out.

At that point, I finally decided to have a crush on him. The more I spent time speaking to him, the more we had in common. Some people who saw us with his mom sometimes thought we looked alike and were brother and sister. He was starting to get seriously into body building. He started speaking all that body builder language. I knew so much about all this because, if you know anything about what I do today, you know my profession is Fitness and Health, and I'm certified in the Physiology, Anatomy, and Hormonal response to fitness activities.

He is built, and like me, works out every day. We are both passionate about living a healthy lifestyle, which 13 years ago wasn't trending like today, and we both were ripped and very fit. That summer, we fell in each other's arms. We were scared, clumsy and awkward about it. We both felt adultery wasn't for us.

Today, I'm not so sure this was true for him. When the whole thing crumbled and exploded (as most affairs do) I found out he had other affairs before me. But at the time, it felt like he was as scared as I was, and guilt ate at us more times than not. After our first time, we were consumed with each other, but it didn't happen again. I didn't want to disappoint or hurt his mom. He didn't want to lose his kids or hurt his parents.

I started to sleep further and further away from Joe, at the edge of the bed, and it's funny he didn't notice it because he wasn't affectionate to start with, but still he would mention it. "You are sleeping so far away."

I would make a snarky comment like, "You don't mind treating me like I'm dirty when I have my period and I'm Niddah*, now do you? So, what is it to you?"

Fuck him for the way he treated me each time I had my period, like I was impure and unclean. I couldn't even pass him food at the table. I had to put it down so he could then grab it, like I was some fucking leper. I should have shoved a SUPER PLUS tampon up his ass at the time, that's how angry that made me.

Gil and I didn't sleep together again for weeks, but our relationship and bond definitely progressed deeper and became stronger.

We would see each other at the synagogue, at his parent's house for dinner parties, at functions and weddings. It was painful and exciting at the same time.

He made me feel loved, beautiful, and like I was the only woman for him. He called me Succubus (a demon in female form, or supernatural entity in folklore that appears in dreams and takes the form of a woman in order to seduce men). The truth is he was mystified, intrigued, smitten, and intimidated by me. He made it sound a lot more romantic. He said he was in love, and that I was his best buddy because I had the mind of a man in the body of a goddess. I don't even know if any that is true today. Men will say anything to get into your pants.

Each time he would speak about his wife and how she would treat him, I felt pity for him. I wanted to rescue him from the monstrous human he made her out to be (Today I'm not so sure it was all true, although I do know she is an asshole).

Then, the FBI came to my house, I got indicted, and my whole case started unraveling into my conviction which led to my incarceration. I didn't tell him anything. No one except for family knew anyway. I became distant and tried to avoid seeing him. I didn't want my relationship with him to come out in the open at my trial (it didn't).

Joe and I were going through the motions, trying to figure out life for the kids when I would go away during the last days leading to me turning myself in.

The day before surrounding to FCI DANBURY, I sent Gil a FB message, telling him my mom was very sick, and I need to take her back to France where she will undergo a treatment. It could be two days or one month, I didn't know. (This much was true, I thought I may be in prison for two days or one month. I never imagined I'd spend a year).

He was panicked, devastated, got clingy, and asked if I'll call him, or if he could call me, and if we can be in touch. I said no, not for now, that I'd be in touch when I can.

I left my Facebook account open and went to jail.

*Shabbat observance entails refraining from work activities, often with great rigor, and engaging in restful activities to honor the day. Judaism's traditional position is that unbroken seventh-day Shabbat originated among the Jewish people, as their first and most sacred institution, though some suggest other origins. Variations upon Shabbat are widespread in Judaism and, with adaptations, throughout the Abrahamic and many other religions.

According to halakha (Jewish religious law), Shabbat is observed from a few minutes before sunset on Friday evening until the appearance of three stars in the sky on Saturday night. [1] Shabbat is ushered in by lighting candles and reciting a blessing. Traditionally, three festive meals are eaten: in the evening, in the early afternoon, and late in the afternoon. The evening meal and the early afternoon meal typically begin with a blessing called Kiddush and another blessing recited over two loaves of challah. Shabbat is closed the following evening with a Havdalah blessing.

Shabbat is a festive day when Jews exercise their freedom from the regular labors of everyday life. It offers an opportunity to contemplate the spiritual aspects of life and to spend time with family.

*Niddah Literally, the feminine noun niddah means moved (i.e. separated), and generally refers to separation due to the Jewish ritual of impurity. A woman on her period is considered impure and thus should sleep in a separate bed from her spouse. The Biblical regulations of Leviticus specify that a menstruating woman must "separate" for seven days (Leviticus 15:19). Any object she sits on or lies upon during this period is becomes a 'carrier of Tomah' (madras uncleanness). One who comes into contact with her madras, or her, during this period becomes tame (ritually impure).

Chapter 9: Not Your Typical Princess

My dream house In Neponsit, NY (FAR ROCKAWAY), On the Beach Block

Leaving Brooklyn to live in the Rockaways was a dream come true. I remember watching Dylan as a toddler, in our house on McDonald avenue, Brooklyn (the house under the railroad tracks), looking out the window all day, like this was a prison. The concrete streets out there, the dirt, the pollution, that was my reality back then. I used to wipe his nose and find black dust on the tissue. It would break my heart. It was ridiculous that we lived in that house that cost something like $800,000 at the time, with two mortgages on it, but literally a dump.

The house was actually cute. It had been remodeled by the Italian wise guy we bought it from. We referred to him as Uncle Mikey. When Joe moved us from Miami to Brooklyn (remember we lived in his father's basement), he introduced me to Mike M. and his new wife, Eileen. Mike was a modern version of Frank Sinatra, probably from the same era, too, and Joe would insist we go visit him in the gingerbread house on McDonald Avenue and get really friendly to convince him to sell us his property. Mike was a "retired" made man, a gangster, an ex-mobster (some general of an Italian Crime family), and he made you feel it. He had big blue eyes, sleek grey hair, and a very built body you could catch a glimpse of because he wore the cliché wife-beater white tank tops with designer jeans, sitting on his Italian leather couch each time we visited.

My job was to impress them with my culture, my class, and my academic prowess as a law graduate. It wasn't hard to be friends with him and Eileen. They were good looking, well-travelled, and intriguing. Joe was in awe of Micky's blue-eyes. If he could kiss his ass deeper, he would reach his colon. Eventually, Mike agreed to sell us his cute house, with new parquet floors, a fancy runner on the stairs, a brand new surround system like they made them in 1999, and a spanking new white Formica kitchen with Kitchen Aid stainless steel appliances. Joe was over the moon, and I, not so much.

Like who in their right mind wants to live in the only cute little house on an industrial zone   boulevard in Brooklyn, overlooking the Pakistani 24/7 convenience shop, with a neon light so bright it would wake me between each F train that would make its way over my head and shake the fuck out of my bed every night? Joe was happy like a pig in shit, not just because he got to live the life of a mobster (remind me to tell you how every dinner reservation we made all over the city wasn't under our beautiful Jewish last name but under a notorious crime family name), but he was happy because he landed the real estate deal of a lifetime. See, Joe was good at real estate, and if he taught me anything about it, it is that investing into a R zone makes you a fucking idiot (it's residential zoning, and no one should invest in residential). Okay, but we bought a fucking residence, no? It is a house with fucking new cherry wood parquet floors no?

Wrong, it is a C zone (yeah, real estate zoning is my shtick now, did you notice?). It turns out, Joe moved me and my newborn baby not into the perfect family home but into what he planned on turning into a huge commercial building someday. But we couldn't tell Mickey or he would literally kill us since that house was his baby. We even bought his ugly white with gold fucking awnings Jeep Wrangler he parked like a prize in the garage, just to show him how much we loved everything about his house and prized possessions. Joe said we can't demolish the house till the day he dies or he will put a bullet between our eyes.

When I think about it today, it is so ridiculous. We had to keep the friendship going for a few years, as we continued living in the damn house, till eventually we were able to create some distance, but we still couldn't turn the house into the investment it was and finally move into a normal street. Don't get me wrong, it was a premium piece of property. Anyone who knew anything about real estate knew that we were sitting on potentially six figures worth of land. But we weren't seeing it in our bank account or in our backyard.

We did live in the richest neighborhood in Brooklyn. If you know anything about anything, you know living right off Kings Highway and East 5th street made you Jewish Syrian Community Royalty. My nice car was always parked in the pretty driveway right on the ugly rat infested boulevard, and everyone from the community who drove by daily knew I changed cars the minute I drove a brand new one.

So, from the outside looking in that life we had looked like an enviable one. We were the young good looking couple, with the nice expensive cars, jewelry, clothes, the newborn baby, and I was the girl that worked on the hottest cable TV show of the moment, slowly becoming the "it girl" in the NYC fashion scene.

On the inside of that little gingerbread house, it was not like that. Joe grew more religious and strange by the day. He slowly started wearing white and navy only, but I didn't notice it immediately. He then added on the Tzitzit, the specially knotted ritual fringes or tassels, worn under his shirts. He adopted strange rituals of prayers throughout the day, and we grew apart. He harassed me about money a lot. He reminded me he thought he married a rich girl, and he thought my family would buy us a house. He often brainwashed me to resent my family for not helping us at all.

Joe's relationship with money, as I explained earlier, was strange. His motto was "We don't have any money" even if we kind of did. I mean we owned our home (sure, he mortgaged the fuck out of it so he could use equity to buy more properties). We had nice cars. I went from having a BMW convertible to a Porsche convertible (yes, with the baby car seat and all), to having a Range Rover. I had a nice diamond eternity band and engagement ring. For Savannah's birth, he gave me an all diamond Rolex as a push-present. How the heck did we not have any money? But the constant anxiety about it was looming over our heads. Joe claimed everything was from credit lines and mortgages he took. He truly made me believe we were broke for the 17 years we were married.

His relationship with money made me uneasy. I left him to pay the mortgage, the car payments, and utilities, and I kept my money separate. Not that I made a ton at first, but enough to pay for preschool, for my live-in nanny so I could work, for my babies' clothes, and everything else he refused to buy because I wanted nice designer things for them. He kept saying, "Oh, yeah, la French bourgeoisie of my ass with all the fancy schmancy for babies."

Joe resented my French-ness a lot. Today, I realize he was intimidated by all the culture, the savior-vivre, the etiquette I emulated from my up-bringing. Recently, in the wake of his second divorce, he called me and he said he was wrong and simply never felt worthy. But more on that later.

Joe kept us in that damn house for a long time. I hated it so much. The train vibrations that shook the house day and night, the sounds of fights and broken glass from the bums hanging out by the 24/7 convenience shop, the weirdos that parked in front of my driveway every day. I simply couldn't wait for Mickey blue eyes to drop dead, so we could demolish this piece of shit house, turn it into a goldmine commercial building, and enjoy the royalties in a mini-mansion somewhere by ocean.

Savannah was born there too, in 2001. Here I was, 23 years old, holding my one-week-old baby girl, on our very Mickey Blue Eyes Italian Leather. I look at this picture and see I already didn't smile with my teeth because my asshole ex-husband thought my high and baby fat plump cheekbones made my face look like a fridge. I wasn't happy. It was not a happy life. I was only happy because I was once again the mother of yet another perfect child, and I was happy I got into my size 23 jeans, thanks to my mother who, following the tradition of her mother before her, banded the shit out of my mid-section with a Velcro band, till I literally threw my guts up.

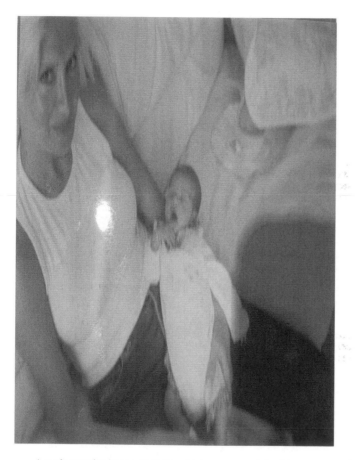

I can't say the house of McDonald Avenue was full of happy memories, but all three of my kids were born in that house. We had a good life for part of the time we lived there. I went from working at Silvercup studios during the day, to being a piano teacher in Brooklyn during hiatuses and days off and selling my shit on eBay at night. Dylan got diagnosed with being on the spectrum. But then, my career flourished, and I went from being an assistant costumes designer on *Sex and the City* to *Gossip Girl* and being a fashion stylist and prop stylist for fashion magazines like *Vogue*, to dressing celebrities for the red carpet. I made good money. I was front and center at Fashion Weeks. I enjoyed all the advantages but skipped the booze and drugs at the parties which I often left early to be with my babies.

Joe and I would go out dressed to the nines every Saturday night. We were regulars at Downtown Cipriani, the Rainbow Room, STK in the meatpacking district, MPD, Tao, you name it. We always had a table waiting for us and just the two of us had a great time, religiously every Saturday night. We were glamorous and young. I ate and he drank... Yup, don't forget Mr. Very religious didn't eat non-kosher, but he knew it wasn't the lifestyle I chose and not the one we had when we got married so he let me. I would order my food and he would order his Johnny Walker Black straight up with Diet Coke on the side, and would have many, many of them while I enjoyed my tuna tartare and my margarita.

Joe was such a fucking confusing guy. When I married him, he was this rugged very cool guy, then he turned into a bit of a super conservative religious man. But not on Saturday nights, no. On those nights he would become the same wild guy I met in South Beach, and more and more so as he downed his many whisky cups.

We wouldn't make it out too early either because Saturdays were for observing Shabbat. And that meant Joe going to the synagogue twice that day, once in the morning to come back at 1pm to have Shabbat lunch, and then again in the afternoon, to come back after sundown. That aspect of my Saturday was like being imprisoned. No going out, no touching the phone, no watching TV. He made it into such a solemn day that I came to hate my own religion, one I once cherished and enjoyed, especially the traditional family gatherings that honored it. Once Joe came back from the synagogue after Shabbat, the kids and I had to be like good little soldiers, gathering around the kitchen table to he could make Havdalah, the Jewish religious ceremony that marks the symbolic end of Shabbat and ushers in the new week.

The ritual involves lighting a special Havdalah candle with several wicks, blessing a cup of wine, and smelling sweet spices. Shabbat ends on Saturday night after the appearance of three stars in the sky. It was not something unfamiliar to me. My grandfather always made a beautiful Havdalah and so did my father. I remember having to smell tiny rose buds in a silver cup my grandmother and mother always kept for the occasion. The same rose buds from Morocco, used to make my Fucking Beautiful Rose Oil that I put on the market in 2019. The smell is so reminiscent of these good childhood memories for me.

Joe ruined Havdalah for me and so many other Jewish traditions. He turned everything about religious tradition into sheer torture, an array of restrictions and compulsions. The prayer and ritual that my grandfather and dad made so fun and short, Joe turned it into a 50 minute-long weird as fuck ritual, with added prayers, and weird voodoo shit. Some rabbis insisted on bringing him Parnasah (income for livelihood aka wealth). Ironically, I often compared this life of religiousness with Joe to being incarcerated.

Was it God's way of punishing me? Sending me to prison for real to really make me feel what incarceration was like? I thought so while I was behind bars because all these religious assholes Joe would bring around, filling you with fear of God and guilt. But today I can tell you, ABSOLUTELY THE FUCK NOT. Living this religious life with Joe that I didn't chose and going to jail have nothing to do with one another and both were fucking shit.

I feel like between this life of religiousness, the not so good marriage, and prison, half my life passed me by, and the only element that made the first quarter of my life worth it was having my kids. That first part of my life was not easy from the instant my dad passed. I went from being this spoiled daddy's girl, to having a mother who wanted me to marry my young cute ass to the first rich balding man that lived in Star Island, Miami. Eventually, I totally rejected that and had to struggle to keep living the lifestyle of the fortunate, with a lot less help and support. My older brother, Gilbert, gave me tough love, with a lot of tough and very little love.

I don't think he realized how much love my father had given me. None of them did. My mom is a selfish woman. She went into survival mode. Sure she had money, and it was hers to have. She and my dad worked hard for it, but she was out of the husband she travelled the world with, and went to formal galas with, enjoying the fruit of their hard labor. She couldn't be bothered with the youngest of her children she was left with: me. She felt I was nearing adulthood anyway and might as well marry rich and live the life my sister-in-law (who married my brother Gilbert) lived. She often compared me to her. But France was 8 years older than me, and I was still a teenager.

Two months after my dad passed, my brother Gilbert summoned me to his house (this was in Miami), I was emancipated and already lived alone at the time, and my dad paid my bills and school. When I arrived, my brother was sitting at the head of his dining room table and ordered me to sit. He pulled out checkbooks. He said, "I have been put in charge of mom's accounts, and of the bills, including yours. This is mom's checkbook. I will pay your rent, your utility bills, and tuition with it. This little booklet is your car payment; you will pay it monthly with your allowance. We are cutting your allowance by half, since dad is dead." I can still hear all of this in my head...It was hard, and it was harsh. Here was my rich brother, with his Bentleys, Rolexes, and his mansion, telling me my little allowance was being cut in half because my DAD IS DEAD.

I remember playing tough because Gilbert was not nice to me. Since I became a teenager and grew a huge pair of tits, I seemed to make him uneasy. I wasn't the little sister anymore. In his eyes, I had become this nuisance he had to take care of. I held back my tears and asked so innocently, "But dad gave me the Jeep for my birthday. It was my gift. Why do I have to pay for it?" He didn't flinch and explained it was a lease, and after three years, I would have to give it back. My whole little girl's world went spinning. I remember on my 16th birthday my parents and I lived in the gated community of Williams Island, the "IT" luxury condos of the late '90s in North Miami Beach. I was comping back from school, and my childhood friend Laetitia was visiting me from Toulouse. She had come to class with me because, like most French kids who grew up watching Beverly Hills 90210, she was so intrigued with the American way of life. When I arrived home, my dad said to come with him downstairs. We all went down, and as he waved the valet parking, a spanking shiny brand-new Jeep with a huge red bow on it pulled up in front of me, and my whole family screamed, "Happy birthday!" One of the happiest days of my life, just like in the movies. The last time I had felt this way was when my dad bought me Elton John's Yamaha CFX 9 foot long grand Piano and surprised me with it for my 10th birthday.

Finding out the car didn't really belong to me, shattered me. It was like part of my dad, and my happy memories, were going with the car.

I always had part-time jobs after school in Miami, but nothing significant enough really. It used to be extra money to buy some crop tops at Wet Seal, the latest candy-colored reeboks, and the new Bobby Brown lip glosses at Saks in Bal Harbor Mall. My meeting with my brother rocked my world. Since that day I've never stopped worrying about paying my bills, that knot in my stomach I still have today when bills arrive has been a permanent resident in my gut since that dreadful day I found out MY DAD WAS DEAD for real, and now in retrospect, I realize I have been on my own ever since, sort of.

I was not even an adult yet, living in my tiny studio in Williams Island (four floors under my parents' apartment), my mom mourning the death of my father in France, while I became my brother's responsibility. I took a second part-time job to make this car payment. I kept my job at Bisou Bisou, in Bal Harbor Mall, selling cutesy luxury clothing to the glamorous Latinas who came in with their fat ugly boyfriends, and I took a second job working the night shift as a waitress at the Cheesecake Factory. I was told I would get better tips at Hooters, but when I went for the interview, the manager told me I couldn't get upset if my ass got slapped a few times by optimistic patrons... (Yeah, sexual harassment today wasn't as refined as it was back then.) I went to school every day, changed into my fancy clothes for my job at the luxury mall in BAL Harbor, and then drove myself to Aventura mall for my shift at the restaurant. I remember feeling so tired, so stressed, and so bitter when my paychecks would reflect all types of deductions I hadn't seen coming.

I made my car payment the first month, the second month, and then I missed the third. Irresponsibly, I didn't even think about collectors calling my brother. I figured that since my dad passed they wouldn't reach him, and the following month when my sales commission check would kick in, I would make both my late payment and current one. Except my boss, Dahlia, and her husband Edmond never paid on time; they always found reasons or errors why I shouldn't get paid my due. And that was fucking shitty because I was their best salesgirl. I could sale a fucking plastic bag and convince them they looked great and oh so chic! I played up the French flair and it worked. My bosses at Bisou Bisou were friends with my brother, and as a matter of fact, that's how I got the job. So whenever I complained to him that they didn't pay me or they cut my pay unfairly, he would remind me what a burden I am in his life and how I need to shut the fuck up because those are his friends and I won't ruin the friendship.

Edmond and Dahlia paid me late, or didn't pay me for a whole month sometimes, and so my car payments were late... I also didn't know quite yet how to be a "poor girl"... I always had nice things, an allowance, and a bit of money to go to PF Chang's with my friends on Saturday nights. So it was getting tough to budget. I still was involved with friends who could go buy the latest Danskin sports bra and shorts before dance practice, and it took me a while to realize I couldn't. On campus, they offered you the new MasterCard, and you could apply and be approved instantly. So since my Visa from Citibank I got from my dad was always maxed out, well, I got the MasterCard too. And I would make late payments or just pay the fee and let the bill go forever. My childhood was over. I had worries and anxiety about paying my bills... I didn't feel close to my mother. She wasn't nurturing or concerned about me. Did she even know about these new financial restrictions my brother imposed on me? So, when Joe proposed, we got married just 6 months after my dad passed, and I fucking jumped at the occasion of not fending for myself on my own. We could be poor together.

Once I married Joe, I didn't last more than 10 months in Miami. Living the life I grew up in there requires a bit more money that Joe and I didn't have, and my family was not willing to help. So pregnant with Dylan, we filled up a U-Haul and he drove it back to NY. I kept waiting for my mom to shed a tear at seeing her youngest daughter carrying her grandchild leaving and perhaps propose to help us a bit and hold me back. But she didn't; she helped me with all her might, filling up the U-Haul truck as fast as she could. My mom lives by this rule: what she doesn't see can't hurt her, or rather what her friends don't see can't embarrass her. The minute I landed in NY she told her friends I married a real estate tycoon, and I was about to become a judge (no joke).

I flew into New York a few days later. Joe had set up his small basement for my arrival. Young, broke, pregnant, and in love, I started this new life in the big Apple, where I had been accepted to NYU LAW. My whole life in New York was like a double life, part of it made me tremendously happy and the other not so much. I thrived going to law school in the West Village every day. Manhattan was my playground, and the second I would get off the Brooklyn Bridge onto the streets of NYC, it was like a fucking breath of FRESH BADASS air. I was me again, the well-traveled chic and stylish Franco-American girl. Then, at day's end, I would go back to this weird inferior life I shared with my new husband, next door to his dysfunctional family, in our Brooklyn basement on Avenue V, to a life that was not really mine, with people who I didn't know and weren't really like me, looking out tiny little windows, where only ankles walked by.

Joe made me resent my family a lot. He kept saying Syrian Jews (unlike Moroccan Jews like my family) buy houses for their daughters when they marry, that they don't let a new couple struggle. But I think my family felt like I made my bed and I needed to lay in it. I should have married rich. Fuck them; I didn't like bald men, with hairy backs, and small penises that drove Ferraris, so I ate shit.

I learned early on to screw my head on right. I put it in my head that my family owed me nothing, and no matter how fortunate their life was, they weren't responsible for how shitty mine was. I loved Joe for most of our marriage, almost until the end, and I tried really hard to be happy just with our love. But he was mentally abusive (never physically). He could call me a cunt because there were crumbs on the floor. I spent our marriage building up resentment towards him so it would never be fear. I was not scared of him but much of our marriage I had apprehensions. I told him a lot of white lies to avoid fights, not because I was scared, but because he was violent with words and raised his voice so loud it would scare the kids. Then, like most abusive men, he would come and apologize, asking me if I still loved him.

Of course, I did. He got me away from my family and helped me build my own, and for that, still today, I love him. It was hard to love him then. He was a shitty dad; he hasn't got a paternal bone in him, and he admits it himself. Today I don't blame him though. His father was a fucking monster. He watched him beat his mother to

87

death and break every bone. When she died of cancer, her kids were relieved she would never catch a beating ever again. Considering this is what Joe grew up with, I don't fucking blame him for lacking the paternal chip. I always knew I would write this book, and Joe would be a big part of it. I mean I spent 17 years of my life with him. He turned me into an adult; he undid a lot of the bad traits my mom had instilled in me, like ego, pride and telling lies. Part of the realness you know me for today I learned from Joe. He always used to say, "Don't be like your mother, ashamed of the truth," or "Call a spade a spade."

It wasn't easy at first. I was taught the French way of pretending for the sake of appearances, but eventually I became a Brooklynite: I called a spade a spade. I smelled bullshit from a mile away, and I became all about putting your money where your mouth is. And that made me put more and more distance between myself and my mother. I also wanted to stay as far away from Gilbert as possible. After all, he thought I caused him problems with his friends; he saw me as a burden in his perfect life, and he often reminded me, "I didn't ask for the responsibility Dad bestowed on me to take care of you and Roger."

It was also easier to be angry with them so that you don't have to see them. When you live in a basement, in Brooklyn, pregnant, with so very little money that the occasional piece of meat you get to eat is for Shabbat on Fridays, you kind of don't want to go back to Miami and see your family bask in wealth.

My mom came to visit. She has that sense of maternal duty like that. Imagine bringing Coco Chanel with her pearl necklace, Bvlgari watch, and fancy Bouclette jacket to a basement apartment in Flatbush Brooklyn. I remember her looking around the studio a bit appalled and quietly sitting on the couch saying it's cute. Joe and I gave her the bedroom, and we slept on a mattress we borrowed for the occasion. My father-in-law had proposed she sleeps at his house, but she declined. On that trip she had taken me to Zara to buy me bigger clothing. I was not big enough to need maternity clothing, but my jeans and shirts weren't fitting anymore. She took me to La Goulue for lunch (it has always been my favorite place) and then she took me shopping for baby clothes. Walking on Madison Avenue, she said, "Let's go to Cartier! I need to get my watch battery changed."

On the walk there, she asked me what I had done with the Panthére watch she had given me for my 18th birthday...it was her watch. I looked down and lied that it was in the safe. I had pawned it because Joe and I needed the money to live. Throughout the following 13 years, I sold almost all the jewelry my mom would ever give me. I have had so many ups and downs financially in my life that I built no attachment to jewelry. I saw it as a survival tool. Anything and everything I ever owned, whether gifts from my mom or bought by me, have paid Dylan's therapies, our rent, and bills for the past 20 years.

We walked into Cartier, and she was wearing the watch (mental note—she bought two watches on this trip, the Cartier and Bvlgari, part of me was hoping one of them was a push present- It was not). I proceeded to one of the displays and fell in love instantly with the newest model "LA BALLON BLEU." I will never forget that day. I was hormonal, emotionally beaten by my riches to rags sob story of a girl who was a Jewish American princess, with a French upbringing, who got a Dior bag for her 15th birthday (which Savannah still wears today), a Brand New souped-up Jeep for her

16th, and her mother's Cartier watch for her 18th. And here I was living in a nasty basement in Brooklyn, with a husband who was disappointed he married a girl who wasn't as rich as he hoped, and was struggling financially so much that the time my mom visited felt like Christmas.

My mom was not always cold. Throughout my childhood, teenage years and even now in my adult life, she could be sweet, affectionate, fun and kind, while other times she can be cold, detached, egoistic, and egocentric. So, when she came next to me, and touched my arm softly as I was admiring "Ballon Bleu", I only felt warmth and happiness for a moment.

"What are you looking at?" she asks.

"Ballon Bleu, she just came out. I saw it in magazines. Isn't she beautiful?" She asked the salesman to take it out so I could try it on. I tried it on, and for a minute, I felt like a princess again. I thought that while maybe Joe and I can't afford much, if mom bought me this watch, I would shine and feel like the girl I was before. My mom grabs her cellphone and says, "Can you call France for me?"

France is my sister-in-law (married to my wealthy brother), so I start dialing and pass her the phone.

"Hallo, France, tu m'entends?" The rest of the conversation still resonates in my head today, alongside a sort of siren, the kind you hear when you're about to faint. "I found the perfect watch for you, for your birthday! You know you were wondering what to ask Gilbert; it is called Ballon Blue. Ingrid says this is the new 'It' watch, and you know how Ingrid knows style. Yes, yes. I'll get you the catalog. We can pick the gold and diamonds together."

I stood there, dumbfounded, fighting the tears in my throat, and told my mom nothing. She looked at me and said, "Et oui! With God's help your loser husband will one day make enough money to get that for you." And he did, eventually, but she still thought he was a loser.

I hated her. My husband was never a loser. Even now that he is my ex-husband I will never call him that. He was an asshole but a loser he never was.

I ripped the watch off my wrist, threw it at the salesman, and ran outside, suffocating and crying, probably more than I should because I was hormonal, swollen, and pregnant. I will never forgive her for this. Finding favor in my mother's eyes has never been easy. You did have to be beautiful, so I found favor in her eyes for most of my childhood and teens, but once an adult, the only way to truly be a favorite was determined by your lifestyle and wealth. She liked money, and she liked Gilbert's lifestyle: the yachts, the parties, the friends with the expensive condos and the art, the outrageous donations to the synagogue. I was fucked and will be fucked until the day she deemed me rich enough to be impressed with me.

I spent my whole childhood and teens thriving to satisfy her. From the day I grew hair, it had to be long, smooth, and curled perfectly (she would spend a great deal of time smoothing my curls around her fingers to create the perfect Shirley Temple hairdo, "les anglaises" English curls). I was this gorgeous toddler; her friends would marvel over and she would beam of pride. I then turned into "The Body", around age 10. Dancing Ballet and shooting for the "prima ballerina" status... She often bragged that I had the body of a goddess. She took so much pride in that, the long legs, the long arms, the perfect posture, she claimed was hers. The truth is I have my father's long, lean legs, and the reason I know that is because my dad was a comic. When my parents entertained, he would often wear disguises and crack the whole room up with impersonations. Whenever he impersonated a woman, all women in the room would scream how jealous they were of his long (hairy) legs.

Mom even took me to some fucking etiquette sessions where I had to walk with a heavy book on my head around an austere room. I started playing the piano at age 5 and took intensive lessons for hours after school. Whatever I did, I had to excel at, and I wanted to because I wanted her to love me. She was a mathematician, a forensic accountant, gifted with numbers. I was not. I felt each time I did math I disappointed her, and she loved me less. So, I had to excel at something else to impress her and deserve her love. I took up not two foreign languages but 5 in school. I added classes to my long days and studied till the wee hours of the morning so I could be good at something she wasn't: languages. I even took up German to taunt her because I knew how much that language intimidated her. I wanted to become a fashion stylist. I would draw the most insane figurines. Beautiful fashion creations of my own she would hang in her office, so she signed me up for summer classes at "Les Beaux Arts" in Toulouse, France. But she made it very clear, art is not a respectable career; it shall be a hobby. I was the perfect child, and if I was not, she lied about it. When my very blonde hair turned a color she didn't fancy, she bought bottle of hair color and colored my hair auburn. It was as if I was this real life doll that spoke for her perfect brain and incredible genetics. She always encouraged me to love my body and show it. She got me the most colorful tanga bikinis when she travelled to South Africa and would be so proud on the beach when I would run into the water with all eyes on my perfect, sculpted curves.

It seems she invested so much into making me the perfect creature with the perfect brain and skills that she was upset it got wasted on a "low-life" like Joe. He often sensed it and said it, "To your French bourgeoisie fucking family, I'm just a low-life". I always denied it and reminded him how smart and ambitious he was and that he was very much like my dad, who came from a very hard-working humble family, and like him was self-made.

When we moved into the Gingerbread house on McDonald Avenue (did I tell you why I called it that? It's because it looked so pretty it looked like the ginger bread house in Hansel and Gretel's story, but the irony was it was in such an ugly place), my mom came to visit (the maternal duty always made her do it). At first she tried to like the house; it was super nice on the inside. But the first morning, she came to the kitchen as I served her coffee, and I asked if she slept well. She replied, "Of course not!!! The train woke me every 10 minutes, Oh la la quelle horror!"

I replied, "Beggars can't be choosers". Her friend called her, and she as always lied right through her teeth: "I'm in New York, yes Ingrid's house is magnifique! You know Brooklyn is the up and coming neighborhood. She lives in the very rich Syrian community. Her husband is a real estate tycoon, and she is about to become one of the most powerful lawyers. We are looking at judgeship here."

I gagged, this bitch! No matter what I accomplished it was never enough. It was always sugar-coated by a bigger-than-life lie. Then, my brother Gilbert calls (her favorite child) and I'm upstairs taking care of my baby and I hear her whispering, "They live like peasants, oh la la I can't begin to tell you. Ils vivant dans un trou (they live in a hole)."

I have taken a lot of slaps in my face throughout my life. The reason why I handled most of them so well is because my mother's behavior prepared me for the worst of them.

But I loved her then and respected her and I do now... She had a good side; she taught me excellence; she taught me sense of duty, strength, etiquette, culture, health, and hard work. My mom is the most resilient, hard-working, devoted woman I have ever met, and all these qualities I owe to her.

When Savannah was born, Joe made me believe he was working on behalf of an old Chinese guy and buying a property on 34th street in Manhattan. He took me to the building a few times and showed me around. He had to renovate it. We were doing significantly better. I worked UNION for HBO and on the side for magazines and celebs. Savannah was a beautiful healthy baby girl and brought me so much joy.

As a matter of fact, the reason I kept having children with a man that didn't know how to be a father is because each birth brought tremendous joy into my life and seemed to be the only thing that truly made me happy. I didn't care that Joe sucked at being a parent or didn't necessarily care to have a child. I felt complete; I felt like I had my own family and didn't need my mother or my siblings. So, we are doing much better financially, and Joe says the Chinese man pays him a good salary.

I found out soon after that he lied, and we owned the building on 34th street. Joe was the most honest man ever, except when it came to admiting we had money. He wanted my paychecks, so he could invest my money in real estate, but he didn't ever want me to know what he had. I never cared. I never asked him for money, and he never gave me any. I bought my own clothes, bags, shoes, and the kids... and once in a while he would arrive home like Tony Montana after a big drug deal and throw a MAJESTIC chinchilla coat on the bed, saying he saw it in a store and thought it would look good on me...naked. Or he would bring home an Orthodox Jew, a jeweler from the diamond district, with a case handcuffed to his wrist, and have me pick an obnoxiously clean and big loose diamond for my next ring or earrings. But the following week, he would say we are in debt and swear up and down that we have no money.

I didn't really care. I made my own money, which I refused to give him (he harassed me for years to give him the money I made). He also harassed me for years about the fact that I didn't become a practicing lawyer that could've brought home enough money for him to invest in real estate. He felt I had let him marry me under false pretenses 1) coming from a rich family 2) becoming a highly paid lawyer. The joke was on me though.

While I was pregnant with Dakota, Joe got hit with an IRS audit, and it was bad. He got scared shitless. He had done a lot of real estate deals, bought, sold, borrowed. He needed my help. I was good with computers and administrative shit. I took a leave from work, and dove into his bank statements, to provide everything the inspector was asking for. The IRS kept going back in time and expending the scope of the audit. Joe was a small fish, but he was scared. He kept me home all day, sitting in the kitchen on my dell computer and re-doing all his books, while he paced back and forth.

Only, what was truly wrong was that I found out he lied through his teeth. He

91

owned so many properties and made me believe we were broke. It isn't that he was afraid I would take any of it from him if he got divorced. He had his father's house under my name and trusted me blindly to never take it from him. Joe just had this old-fashioned mentality of not sharing with the wife... throw a fur or a diamond necklace at her once in a while and keep her quiet this way.

Chapter 10: No Dirty Divorce

I owe it to my kids. I owe it to myself and to Joe to talk about my divorce. I truly think this will help some women, and perhaps some men too, remove the hate and drama out of the divorce equation.

My marriage sucked. It sucked for me, and it sucked for Joe... It also sucked for the kids. But we were a family for 17 years, Joe and I, and that counts for something. We had happy times, but it's true they were lesser than the unhappy times. We weren't compatible. We weren't raised the same. We did share some of the same wants, and we did like a lot of the same things, but there was more we didn't have in common than we did. Joe misunderstood me, and I misunderstood him.

We were kids. He was my first love. He took me out of a family I didn't always feel I belonged with, especially after my father died, and he gave me a home, a family to call my own. He stood by me when I was in prison. He built me up for that whole year in the kids' eyes. He prayed hard. He loved hard, and as much as he was rough and mean to me, he stood by me like a motherfucker. In hindsight, I think I was Joe's greatest love after his mother Esther (Savannah is named after her; it's her Hebrew name).

Of course, the fights leading to our separation weren't pretty at all, but they never involved tearing each other apart, being disgusting about money, or involved threats about the kids' custody. In our minds, it was simple: Joe could keep the house, and everything he had worked for, including his properties, and I could have the kids. Some people saw it as I bought my kids' custody, but knowing Joe, he believed strongly kids belong to their mother. He never even spoke of shared custody and promised that they would always sleep under my roof, even if it meant he picked them up every morning and drop them off every night on his days.

Of course, things never got to that point because I moved to Monaco, and I moved to Monaco with his support.

Funny enough, Joe never called me Ingrid. He thought the name didn't suit me, so he called me "honey," and he still called me "honey" through our separation and our divorce. Hell, he still calls me "honey" now. Here is a concept I don't understand. How can you be married to someone for over a decade, have fond memories together, a wedding, and when comes time to divorce, you tear each other part and use your kids to do so? Joe and I always promised we wouldn't do that, and we did not. He does not get the prize for father of the year. He just misses that paternal chip, and I think it is because of Tony, Mimon, or whatever the fuck his father's name was.

When I moved to Monaco with the kids, Joe acted like he did not care to see the kids much. He did not want to come see them, and I had to beg him to take them for a few weeks in NY over the summer. It is like he was deeply hurt by our divorce and saw the kids as an extension of me. It was complicated, of course. I had cheated on him with Gil (not to be confused with Gil my husband today) towards the end of our marriage, and that definitely brought on some hostility. But I do see that affair as the only way Joe and I could legitimately end our relationship. We had a hard time enforcing our separation at first. We even tried to get back together a few times. Sometimes, we didn't even try. We would force the separation and get back together against our better judgement.

So, I feel like my affair with Gil broke that bond forever, and it was necessary. Joe and I did not make each other happy. There was love, and there was respect, to a point. There was a large amount of care, there was attraction, but happiness there was not enough of.

Joe was mean with his words, verbally abusive, not affectionate, and not loving. He was reassuring, a caregiver, and a provider, and that was his way of showing love. He was a rock in adversity. But, paternal he was not. He was a bad father. Actually, he was not a father at all. It was hard for him to show up for the kids' birthday parties. He had to be begged, threatened, and shunned to show up to Dylan's little league games. I had to wear his hat during most of the kids' childhoods.

I had to learn how to pitch and bat, so I could play baseball with Dylan. I had to install the basketball hoop in our backyard. I had to set up the new PlayStation. Joe just didn't show up for that stuff. He only showed up to pay the bills and for the religious stuff he imposed on us. For Dylan and Savannah, it was their only way of bonding with him, so they would indulge him with the religious rituals and hours of studying Torah, even though they would much rather be outside playing with the kids up our street.

Since my divorce from Joe, I've watched other couples get divorced, and tear each other apart. They go to court to take the children's custody from one another. I have watched women destroy their ex-husband's reputations and brainwash their kids to hate the other parent. Joe just thought and still does that I am the better parent, and for him, he shows them love by letting them be with the parent most fit to give them the education and the life they deserve. That's Joe in a nutshell. Is he a bad father? No... he is not a father at all.

Does he love the kids? Yes, there is no doubt in my mind that his greatest gesture of love is to have let the kids leave the US and be raised by me. He has since given up his parental rights and has approved of Gil (my husband) adopting them.

When Dylan turned 18, the legal age of adulthood in Monaco, he went to Miami to spend the high holidays Rosh Hashana with my family. On his way to meet my brother at the synagogue, he was sure he saw Joe (he had not seen him in 4 years...that was Joe's choice). When my panicked boy called me to tell me this, I decided it was time for them to meet and for Dylan to have some closure. Dylan was an angry and hurt boy. He had been abandoned by his biological father at the age of 12.

Joe never showed up for his bar mitzvah, never called him for his birthdays, and in the last four years, he never sent him a ticket to come visit him in NY. As a matter of fact, four years before Miami, Joe still accepted having the kids for three weeks during the summer at our Home in Belle Harbor, NY, but that was the last time he would ever see them.

See, everyone bet I would be the first to swing back into dating, getting engaged, and probably married. Everyone, I included, though Joe would be a miserable single fuck forever...

Well, the irony was I was very unhappily dating and living with Dario that summer when I sent the kids to NY to be with Joe. Upon arriving at their childhood home, I got a frantic FaceTime from Savannah in what you used to be my custom walk-in closet, and there was a woman's wardrobe in there. Savannah was devastated.

"Mom, some woman has some ugly thongs in your pretty lingerie baskets, all our picture frames are still here but the photos have been replaced with pictures of Joe and some dark-haired woman."

That was a slap in my face. It hurt for so many reasons, and most I can't even explain to myself.

I had been warned by my best friend Valerie in NY, that Joe was courting Aliza, some Syrian Jew divorcée from Brooklyn. It was apparently the talk of the town, especially because Aliza's ex-husband was best friends with Valerie and her husband...

When Valerie heard I was flying the kids to NY, she called me and warned me an engagement was imminent, and maybe I should warn the kids. But I didn't take it seriously. I couldn't imagine Joe buying a ring for another woman. When we got divorced, he said he would never get married again. He would never ever have kids again (he claimed his three children were all he has and all he wants) and he would never ever buy jewelry for a woman again. Granted, those were the words of a wounded man who had been cheated on. I did not warn the kids because, when I asked Joe, he denied even dating anyone. Little did I know, there was a woman living in my house (the house I didn't claim my half from, even though I was entitled to it). This was my dream house that I raised my children in and picked every piece of furniture for. My house that still had the piano my father bought me for my 10th birthday, and my mother's Bernardeau china and Cartier silverware.

Savannah's call was more than a pinch to my heart. It was like a truck running me over. My own romantic life was in shambles; my career in fashion had gone to shit; and I was living with a clinically diagnosed (but I didn't know) bipolar perverted narcissist named Dario (more on him later), who made sure I lost every cent I ever earned and my dignity. I was stuck living with him, my three kids, and his sweet daughter (who was so fucked up from her parents 10 year constant custody battle), in Monaco.

The kids' stay with Joe lasted three weeks, and the visit went from bad to worse.

Turns out, Joe had gotten engaged to Aliza the day before the kids arrived, which was Savannah's birthday, July 14th. Savannah was such a smart cookie that she realized he stopped her from arriving on her birthday so he would not have to invite them to his engagement. That threw her emotions into a tailspin, and my little girl was badly hurt and felt betrayed.

I was badly hurt as well. My ego was bruised. My emotions also went into a downward spiral. I was jealous, desperate, and re-thinking my life choices. I was sick to my stomach. Thankfully, his fiancée, Aliza was not in the house, and even though her belongings looked like they were there to stay, she did not show the first few days.

We found out my kids' very first nanny, Araceli, was back to working for Joe, and had given Aliza all of my Shabbat dinner recipes. When Shabbat came around that week, Joe took the kids to play mini golf, and when they got back, all of my recipes had been prepared for their Shabbat dinner, with Araceli's help. Stephanie, my goddaughter and Araceli's daughter, had come to visit Savannah (they were the same age) and spilled the beans.

"Mi mama ayuda a la mujer los iviernes y le maestro Como cocina tu mama," (*My mom (Araceli) shows the woman how to cook all of your mother's recipes*). Savannah said it was like we had never left the house, except for Aliza's presence. Everything else was the same: the furniture, the pans, the pots, the food, except the main protagonist "wife" was simply removed and replaced.

Then came another devastating FaceTime call from Savannah. As if finding thongs in my closet was not enough! Joe and I had been divorced for less than two years... and I felt worse at that point than the day we divorced. I never had had the urge to ask for my piano back or my mother's silverware or my kids' photo albums. I left like he still lived in our home and all of it was where it had belonged and was safe. All of the sudden, I wanted it all back. I was angry. I felt violated.

Dylan during that visit was unhappy. Joe had changed ...maybe that woman had changed him, not that he was great before but still. Dylan discovered that his room had been changed. His Yankees baseball memorabilia that took us years to collect had disappeared. Joe claimed they had been damaged in Hurricane Sandy...but only the basement had had damage during that hurricane. Joe explained that he had moved everything to make room for Aliza's boys.

It was like Joe had erased us from our house and replaced us with new "better" players. That caused serious emotional damage to Dylan. He didn't recover for the following four years. He became angry with Joe. He would search him on Google. He would get information from our neighbors.

He would find out Joe drove a Ferrari and a Bentley while he didn't pay for anything for us. Dylan would get so angry. He would often say he wants to go to NY just to spy on him and see how rich he really is. He wanted to slash his Ferrari's tires and spit in his face for how little he did for us. But that anger built up after that trip to NY, which ended so badly.

Savannah would FaceTime me all day. I would be confined to my room in Monaco, away from Dario who I lived with at that point against my will, and crying over the upcoming nuptials of my ex-husband whom I left, whom I cheated on, and was relieved to live away from for the past year and a half. Joe got angry that Savannah would FaceTime me and show me the house. He would start yelling that she is just like me.

"You're just like your mother!" he told her. "She is a hacker and a spy. I don't trust you, so stop showing her my house and my life!"

He confiscated her phone. She had an iPod that he didn't know about because he is so technology impaired and challenged, and she would FaceTime me on the sneak. He was such a liar at the time, hiding his fiancée, hiding his money. He felt the kids were no longer to be trusted. I don't really know what the fuck got into him at that time. He called me after less than a week.

"Tell your fucking French Fry brother to send tickets to your kids and get them out of my house today. They aren't my kids. They are your kids. It is my time to be happy now and they don't want me to be happy."

I tried to reason with him. We never fought through our divorce ever, but this was a whole other level. I started to cry. I told him I never raised the kids with lies, so why is he lying to them?

"Just admit you have a new love," I say. "You got engaged on Savannah's birthday, and the woman is now living with her kids in the house where we raised them."

But, he would not budge. He told me to go fuck myself and get the kids out of the house.

I called my brother Gilbert in Miami. I told him the story, sobbing from my misery at home, and my distress from knowing my kids are being thrown out of the home where they grew up, and I explained I didn't have the money to buy tickets for the same day or the next in the midst of summer vacation's high rates, and also did not have the heart to bring them back to Monaco, to be with miserable me and Dario, who I hoped would die of a lethal accident by the time they would be back.

Gilbert has not always been the kindest to me, but in extreme situations and, especially if it comes to my children, he pulls through and protects them like his own. And he did. After confirming my story with Joe (God forbid I should be telling the truth, and God forbid I should actually not be the one in the wrong here), he called me.

"Okay, I now believe you; your ex-husband is monstrous. I got tickets for the kids to come to Miami tonight and stay with Maman (our mom)," I said.

I announced to Savannah (who was Dylan's guardian angel through those times because he was still genuinely fragile from his pathology) that they were leaving to Miami that night. She was so relieved. Araceli, the kids' old nanny, packed them up, and Joe drove them to the airport as fast as he could. He called me and said, "I cannot wait to have my life back." That hurt so much.

While on the ride to airport, Savannah asked to speak to me so he passed her his phone, and as she was dialing me, a text from Aliza popped up: "Did you drop them off yet? I'm so happy. I can't wait to see you."

To this day, Savannah has not forgotten, but I worked hard on her to forgive him and I think she has. I worked hard on myself all these years and on my kids so that they would never hate him. And they don't. But they never saw him again. I begged them and I begged him, but neither wanted to see each other again.

Joe married Aliza that September. He did not invite the kids. Of course, pictures of the wedding popped up quietly on social media. I saw them but did not show the kids.

It was hard for me that Joe bounced back sooner than I did, that he lived in my home with his new bride and her kids, while I was living one of the unhappiest times in my life.

Chapter 11: Sleeping with the Enemy

Dating after 17 years of marriage is a major life-fucker. You are used to the person you are with calling you back, giving you a minimum of respect, show up when they are supposed to and all that. So dating for the first time at the age of 33, in a place like Monaco, is actually terrifying and mortifying. The first year after the kids and I moved to Monaco, it was not so bad. There was the whole novelty and freedom of being single. Doing things on my own was a breath of fresh air. I got the apartment I wanted. I cooked and ate what I wanted (not drastically kosher), and I got to do what I felt like on weekends. Life with Joe was so fucking restrictive and add to that the year I spent in federal prison... Needless to say, I absolutely loved being alone with my children and having no man to be the boss of me.

I had a nice, fun, and short relationship with Joseph. He lived in NY and flew often to Monaco to be with me. That was my safe choice after my divorce. Not only was he also called "Joe" but, like my ex-husband, he is an American Syrian Jew with strong religious beliefs. But, he and Joe weren't the same. New Joe is more outgoing, less rigid, and more well-travelled. The relationship was short and sweet. He was kind to me and to the kids. I admired him, as he was an accomplished businessman and respected politician in New York City. Ultimately, it was not going to last. He was running to be the president of his Jewish congregation (and they did not approve of my divorcée status). He was in public office in New York City, and an ex-convict, divorced girlfriend was not going to help his political aspirations (although he never ever complained about my past nor found it to be embarrassing). His divorce was so nasty, and I couldn't help but find myself in the middle of it.

His daughter hated me, although she had never met me. His future ex-wife went to great lengths to trash me all she could, and he was literally afraid to book flights for us to travel because she would find out and ask the judge for more money.

But, to be honest, my biggest problem with this relationship? As much as Joseph's personality was charming and attractive, the sex was horrible—for me that is. And that did not match his cocky personality. He was so cocky. He liked to remind me he had a younger Russian girlfriend right before me that he would fly to St. Barth and Israel with in business class. He was still friends with her and insisted I meet the weirdo through FaceTime.

I genuinely cared for him. He was so good to my kids and so sweet and respectful to me. He often spoke of getting us a bigger condo in Monaco, so he could live with us part-time, but that was all a pipedream. I recently found out he may still not be divorced, and it's been seven years for fuck's sake.

I almost want to spare you the time he booked flights for us to St. Barth's, and he used his miles to put himself in first class, but thought I should be in economy unless I too had miles to spare to sit with him. I kid you not... That was the end of us.

Funny enough, many years later, I went to St. Barth with Gil (not NY Gil), now my husband, and saw Joseph with the Russian at Nikki Beach. Joseph was not an unpleasant period in my life. Anytime I hear Joseph's name I smile... He got my toes wet with dating and he definitely was one of the better experiences. We are still on speaking terms, although after reading how bad I thought sex was and how his penis was way smaller than his personality, we may not be talking at all anymore or ever again.

*

Monaco is a beautiful place. Life is beautiful here. The city is beautiful. The cars are beautiful and so are the people, at least on the outside. After some useless dates that had me lose my confidence completely, I met Dario.

His daughter was friends with my daughters, and her mom (a retired prostitute according to Dario) and I would often grab coffee while our girls were playing together. I got friendly with his mom. I didn't think she was a hooker (although I had my doubts and I know today many women in Monaco are or were until they met their rich Swiss husband in the line of duty and turned into good citizens wearing Chanel suits and Hermes Birkin bags). So, I met Dario, who was 20 years older than me. He was a charming (I thought then) Italian, with lots of style and savior-vivre. He was an ex-millionaire who made a few million in a Monaco Hedge Fund, got out right before everyone in the firm got arrested for fraud, and lost most of his money living the life for the next decade. By the time I met him, he had just enough left to afford a nice condo in Monaco, but he definitely was no longer driving a Bentley, nor did he get to keep his 50-foot yacht. I truly have a knack for ending up with guys who absolutely don't spoil me, nor take care of me!

He kept the attitude of a rich man though and all the charming skills that come with it. He touched my heart with his kindness to my kids. He took Savannah with his daughter to Lake Garda in Italy. He taught her how to ride a bike, and back in Monaco, he often took the kids to the fair for hours. He did all that before we even started dating. I guess being married for so long, I didn't like being a single mom. I had a need to exist as a wife, mother, and be part of a functional family. Dario gave me that optic, and so I fell for his courtship. I ignored every red flag and every single warning his ex had disclosed in our conversations when she and I were friends.

He wanted to move in together, and he wanted my kids to have more space. It is true that the kids were sharing one bedroom, and as nice as our condo was, it was tight. Dylan was already a teenager and sharing rooms with his baby sisters after literally growing up in a mini-mansion wasn't easy. But it built character for each and every single one of us.

The kids accepted and liked Dario because he treated them right, and they jumped at the idea of a huge apartment in the heart of Monaco. We found a huge one. He could afford the rent he said, and we all moved in together as a blended family. This new family setting helped convince the judge to give Dario shared custody of his daughter, and we submitted the apartment plans to show that we had more than enough room for her.

Needless to say, his ex hated me for the relationship and even more for the custody win. I took care of her daughter like my own during our weeks of custody, but this woman hated me even more for it, and she still does. Last time I saw her in Monaco, she was being all chummy with one of Gil's ex-booty calls. Next thing I knew, the two witches threw a handful of sea salt on me at the Met Café in Monaco's Fancy Metropole shopping center.

The minute we moved in with Dario, he changed. He became verbally abusive to Dylan, very tough on Savannah, and even meaner to my little Dakota, not to mention plain disgusting to his daughter. I found myself often protecting the kids, his included, from him. I later found out he was clinically diagnosed with bipolar syndrome and is a pervert narcissist. This guy that had been a millionaire, literally lived off of the very last bits of his fortune. It became clear he counted on my job to pay the bills, but he was also sick with jealousy.

If I even looked at a guy in the supermarket, he would accuse me of knowing him and having had an affair with him. At the time, I worked for Fashion TV, and I had to travel to Sweden for an event. Dario said only hookers do events. I called my producer and said I could not make it. Then came the Monaco Television Awards. I brought him along. I interviewed a few celebrities, and then he had a shit fit about one of the producers leading me to my next interview while holding my elbow. He stormed out and I was left totally disoriented and doing my job poorly. He then threatened to put my kids in boarding school if I had to go to Ibiza or Sardinia to interview Roberto Cavalli.

"If you can't take care of your kids, then why should I?" he said.

I had a nanny for them, but he chased her away. Ultimately, I had to quit my position before they fired me for turning down so many jobs. He insisted I sell my Range Rover (the one I brought back with me from New York), my watches, and even my jewelry to help him pay the bills, even though he literally stopped me from doing the very job that paid my bills.

He would ruin birthdays, Mother's Day, friends get-togethers with unexplained mood swings, and would disappear in the den for days. I would look out for the den's door for up to 48 hours, and he would never come out—not even to shower. From the day we moved in together, we never slept in the same bed. He always blamed his bad mood on my kids or his. He literally brought me to my feet financially, till I sold everything I owned and was so broke, without a car or money, and incapable of moving out financially. I stayed in that apartment for one year, dreaming of escaping. I called my mother for help, but she once again declined. My older brother Gilbert towards the end said he would help me with buying a new car, and he did... I got a Mini Cooper.

I finally got myself together and found an incredible head-hunter, who helped me compose a badass resume. Within days, I got an insane job offer from an American businessman in Vietnam. I signed an NDA, so I can't go too much into it, but let's just say my law degree, my experience in the entertainment industry, and my stint in federal prison earned me more money than I had ever earned in my whole life. This was my way out.

I waited for my first paycheck to come in, and when it did, I rented my kids and me a gorgeous little villa overlooking Monaco and the dreamy Mediterranean Sea. I could see Le Corbusier's Cabanon from my terrace. I didn't tell Dario a thing. I planned on moving out while he would be away or out for a few hours.

Our last week in that apartment, he had Monaco Marshall's coming to our door to seize his furniture and valuables for unpaid debts, our rent included. I didn't feel bad for him. This guy took everything I owned and had worked so hard for and fucking sold it, and he treated my kids like shit. We were moving Monday. I knew he was due in Monaco court for a few hours, and I had agreed with my concierge that I would move a few of my things on the down low.

That Sunday was solemn. It felt like my last day in prison. That's when you keep your head down so no-one fucks with you and with your release date. I was in my room when I heard Dario yelling at Dylan in the kitchen. I ran like a mad woman through the long corridor, to find this fucking monster (who by the way had been repulsing me for the past year) yelling at my boy because he made too much noise cutting through a slice of pizza with his knife. He grabbed Dylan's iPad that was on the table and threw it on the stove, where it broke into pieces. Dylan's face was white with fear.

I analyzed Dario's behavior really quickly (you learn that in prison) and anticipated his next move to be a violent one. I was right. He was about to lunge at Dylan and hit him, but I grabbed Dylan, who was taller than me already, and pushed him out of Dario's way, only to find that fucking asshole was throwing the kitchen table on me. I moved quickly and grabbed the knife Dylan used to cut his pizza, and somehow as I screamed for all the kids to lock themselves in the room, I lunged at him and put the knife to his throat. He kept saying, "Do it. I dare you!"

Motherfucker!

"I went to jail for less, and I will go back to jail for this, you piece of shit." I cut him, not deep enough to kill him, but deep enough to make him bleed. I don't regret it. I remember the rage that took over, and I felt I couldn't control what I would do next. But once I saw him bleeding, I wasn't backing out. He did. I am glad he did, or I think I would have killed him. He stepped away and left. I called the police.

The police don't take child abuse well in Monaco. I moved out the next day, and after almost two years of financial struggles, deprivation, and a pretty shitty life, the kids and I started living a beautiful life in our beautiful new home.

I felt bad for Dario after we moved out, as he had nowhere to stay. I felt guilty for kicking him while he was down, so I let him use the attached office I had on the new property. I would never see him, and I never charged him rent. But, ultimately, he abused my kindness. My kids disclosed information to me about how abusive he was to them when I was working. I didn't know, and at first, I didn't believe them. But I had to face the truth and my guilt. I had put them in this predicament in the search for my happily ever after. I owed them a better life, and I owed them safety.

Dario got in trouble with the law for all the debts he left behind. I had one of his credit cards still and I purposely left him with the bills. After realizing how much he had truly scared and mentally fucked my kids up, I wanted to destroy him. I threw him out of my small studio office. I pinned bills on him, and I fucking destroyed him. No one fucks with my kids. His life has gone to shit since, and I heard he was not allowed back in Monaco. At some point, I even heard he was a janitor in a small motel in Menton. Karma is a bitch.

Chapter 12: Life After Prison

There was no way I was going to make this whole book about prison life. If you are reading this book, it is definitely because you knew me then or you know me now, and you are curious how I ended up there or how I am here now. I have taken you to my childhood, my life in NYC, my time in prison, and my early days in Monaco. And you must wonder, how did I get here really? Me coming to live in Monaco was either premeditation, premonition, or manifestation, depending on how you look at it.

The first few months of my incarceration, I spend most of my time in denial. I thought I would be out the next day and the next day and the next day. The first week I did not even do laundry, what was the point? I'd be out of there by the time I'd need fresh underwear. Denial in prison is a recipe for disaster. I did not eat because I was told the inmates in the kitchen spit in the food, and I figured it's alright, I'll eat when I get home. I did not drink because I was told running water may be infected with AIDS, but it was all fine I may be out the next day.

I had a strong appeal. I had the best attorneys in the country. I had some of Washington D.C.'s most powerful Jewish lobbyists lobbying for the injustice of my case, and I had the French government diplomatically involved too to get me out. Some people called it hope, but I realize now it was denial. Let me tell you something about the American justice system: you are guilty until proven innocent, that is if you have enough money to prove you are innocent, and it is much easier to go into prison than it is to get out. Once you are incarcerated, the chances of getting out before your sentence ends is close to none. I spent six months of my sentence in denial, living life as if it was my first day. Not eating, not drinking, not sleeping, not moving, not brushing my hair and crying a lot. I did this all while still obligated to hold my job as a piano teacher and as a law library clerk.

Turns out in federal prison, if you don't have a high school degree, you are obligated to study and take your SAT, and if you have a law degree, you will most likely have to take a job in the law library and help delusional drug dealers, gang members, and murderers write habeas corpora that no judge will ever bother with.

I walked outside from my unit to the law library, or to visiting and that's all the walking I did, and the only daylight I bothered seeing.

Red Russia would nag me to go in the yard for a jog or speed walk, and I would decline. I couldn't bring myself to doing anything that felt like I was accepting my fate, accepting that this was my life now. I wasted away. When Savannah would come to visiting, she would always squeeze me tight and say, "Mama, I can feel your bones."

She would then stare down at my hands. My fingers were so thin, and my nails were so weak. She would start tearing up. We had this Friday afternoon ritual to go to the nail salon after school ended to get my nails done and often get hers painted too. We both have fond memories of those self-care Fridays. We would first go get our Dunkin' Donuts drinks, a milk shake for her and an ice coffee for me, and get to my

Chinese nail salon I'd been going to for the past 10 years.

Savannah would say, "Mama, I miss your pretty nails."

After visiting, I often leaned a lot on Red Russia to pick up the pieces. Every single visit was a stab in my heart. I was getting worse each time. I cried longer and harder. Those times, Red Russia would give me a good shake.

"Come on, don't be such a pussy. You are a mother. You are strong, and don't let your kids see you like this with ugly puffy face and crazy hair. You scare the kids." She was right... I sucked.

Ultimately, she forced me into accepting my fate. I would agree to speed walk around the yard, and she would brainwash me with words of strength. She would get me to open up, and when I spoke about my kids, I held back tears so she wouldn't scold me. But, often, she would start crying for me. My profound and obsessive love for my children touched her.

The only times I saw Red Russia cry is when I would speak of my visit with my children or when I would explain Dylan's story and when her son Andrew came to visit and she found out his socks had holes which indicated that the family she was paying to take care of him wasn't taking care of him right.

After the six month mark, I almost came to terms with my incarceration. I still did not accept that I still had 36 months to go. My appeal was still pending, and my team of lawyers was starting to feel the hand of corruption in my whole judgment and appeal. My older brother, Roger, had a connection that could get my case on Bill Clinton's desk, and ultimately bring it to Senator Hilary Clinton's attention. And he did. She started to inquire about my appeal with the 4th Circuit Court, normally appeals are heard sooner than six months. Mine sat there, days after days, weeks after weeks, and months after months. My attorney Nat Lewin was no small-time attorney, either. He had won Supreme Court cases, and he was well regarded at Capitol Hill. He was bewildered that this small-time mom selling fucking jeans on eBay from her kitchen was being completely railroaded and this case was muffled in the cracks of the system.

Knowing Senator Clinton was inquiring about my appeal, pushing the 4th Circuit to deliberate, gave me some solace and patience. I slowly started eating the kosher meals. They were very low in calories and definitely deficient in real nutrition, but at least no inmates touched them or could infect them with anything because of the kosher seals they were delivered with. I started showing up at the gym every day at 9 am and doing my own routine, which has become THE METHOD, my patented protocol. I started reading books and studying the Zohar and Kabbalah esoteric teachings meant to explain the relationship between God, the unchanging, eternal, and mysterious Ein Sof (אֵין סוֹף, "The Infinite"), and the mortal and finite universe (God's creation). It forms the foundation of mystical religious interpretations within Judaism that my grandfather (one of the great Kabbalists of his time) had taught me a bit of when I was younger, and I started going for runs with Red Russia.

I finally agreed after six months to smile at things and take pleasure in Chai time (teatime for Russians is sacred) with her. She was generous. She always bought good food from the commissary. She always treated me to cookies and teas. She would say, "Za-hodi na chai." (*Come for some tea.*)

We would redo the world in our heads and our conversations. We would discuss whether she would need botox when she gets out, what color I should color my hair once I got out, what we would do, where we would be. Once we were having Chai, after one of our speed walks, Red Russia said, "You know, I will be deported back to Russia, and I will have them send Andrew back once I arrive, and I will never be allowed back in the USA. I will have to see you somewhere in Europe."

I didn't even think twice. I looked at her and said, "You know, this country betrayed me. I loved it so much. I pledged allegiance to its flag. I trusted it. I no longer do. Eventually someday, after I get my career back on track, and make good money again, I will move to Monaco, and you will come with Andrew to see me. You will be my guest."

Red Russia didn't drink anyone's Kool-Aid. "Ya, ya, they all say that, and then they leave this place and they never even write me," she said. "I had other friends like you here. They all left and I stay and they never do the things they promised, so don't mind me if I don't believe you."

I smiled and shrugged and promised. "You'll see."

I moved to Monaco with my three children in 2012, a few years after I got out of prison. She visited me (with Andrew) exactly six months after I arrived in Monaco. She has since visited the kids and me many times. She has even met my husband Gil a few years later. I will always remember introducing them at the iconic hotel Negresco's bar in Nice. She took one look at Gil and said, "He is a good man. He loves you. I'm so happy for you. You deserve him." And she cried happy emotional tears like a mother would.

I remember the day I arrived in Monaco I called her (we were not technically allowed to speak when I was in the US. You cannot socialize with other convicts when you get out of prison) and I told her, "Remember, I told you someday I would live in Monaco, and you would visit me? Well, I now live in Monaco. I have a small apartment, but Andrew can sleep on the couch and you can sleep with me. You can come visit."

She came for New Year's. The day she arrived, I was late picking her up from the airport. I ran to the gate to find her sitting on a bench with a grown Andrew (he was a little boy the last time I saw him) and she was sobbing.

"Red Russia!" I called out. "I'm here! Why are you crying? Did customs trouble you?" She ran to me and hugged me so tied and sobbed some more.

"No, no, troubles. I thought you would not come for me. I thought I dreamt it."

I'd never do that. Red Russia is still very important in my life, my guardian angel, Red Russia.

During her visit, we had the best time but also a very emotional time. My kids did not know exactly who she was. So after New Year's, we had a big brunch on my terrace, and Red Russia prepared a typical Russian breakfast for us, and we cheered on Bellinis.

"I never told you who Red Russia is," I told my kids, "and why she is so important to us. Do you remember seeing her from afar in visiting and Andrew too, but what you don't know is that she saved my life a few times. She kept me alive, and she got me through it. She is the reason we are here today."

We cried good tears that day.

*

So, while there are a few ways and reasons I ended up in Monaco, living the life I have today, I owe a big part of surviving prison to Red Russia, and perhaps I manifested Monaco. I don't even know why I said Monaco that day in the prison yard. I had only been a few times, a few summers with my parents, who would leave me at the Hotel de Paris, and my parents dressed to the nines, him in a tux and my mom in her most beautiful ball gowns, would go spend the evening at the Casino De Monte-Carlo. Monaco represented so much glamour in my memories, but also the practicability of the culture. The prince, HRH Albert II, is both Monegasque and American. The languages spoken are English and French, which meant that the kids, and more particularly, Dylan would be okay being schooled there. I could not imagine ever moving out of NY for Paris and its rude citizens or for rainy and grey London and its long winters... so, Monaco, it was.

I never thought about Monaco again when I got out of prison. New York welcomed me back with open arms and offered me more professional success than I'd had before. My kids' lives were back on track, and I went back to my dream house in Belle Harbor. I didn't think I would want to leave. Except I lived a very paranoid life. The sight of black sedans and tinted windows SUVs made me think I was being tailed by the FBI. Each time I saw a guy walking by my nail salon more than once, I thought these fuckers were trying to get me again.

It didn't matter than I had paid my so-called debt to society. My bottom line was I didn't really do anything the first-time so what's to stop them from getting me a second time? Fear and paranoia know no reason. The sound of a helicopter over my house would send me into a frantic panic, thinking there was an FBI raid about to happen. Yet, I didn't do anything other than sell fucking jeans on the internet. It was not PTSD*. It was disdain and complete loss of trust in my country and its legal system. I didn't feel safe in the great US of A anymore. I didn't feel safe for three years in NYC after being released, and it took that asshole Gil (the lover) and his delusional wife trying to get me arrested on a false harassment charge for me to literally wake up and smell the coffee, give NY my two middle fingers and say, "Hasta la vista, baby."

You know what is more terrifying than prison? Getting out of prison and spending every single day of your life being so scared of going back...

I mean, the level of anxiety in prison is so high. It goes from being afraid of shake downs** which could go bad if the guard found as much as an apple in your locker. My thought was always that one of those cunts could have planted contraband in my stuff to get me in trouble. And that meant no more visits, phone privileges taken away. As trike added onto another added onto another could even lengthen your sentence. Anxiety flew high daily, for all kinds of reasons. I didn't fuck with the cartels and the gang members, but I was often called on to translate from Spanish to English, or to draft their habeas corpus in exchange for peace or a favor, or protection. Each time I heard Maria Rosa aka Gorda (fatso) calling for me ("Flaquitaaaaa!") I would always feel a knot in my stomach, at least the first few months. Keep in mind addressing a person by referring to their appearance is ubiquitous from Tijuana to Tierra del Fuego: across Latin America, blondes are uniformly called "rubio", portly persons, "gordo", and the vertical-challenged Chico (the endings change to "a" when the subject is feminine, and the use of the diminutive "ito" or "ita" connotes affection). In the Latina community in prison, it is very common.

Gorda read tarot cards, and according to everyone, she was never wrong. She told negrita that someone would come visit her after 5 years in Danbury with no visits. Sure enough, that month Negrita was called to visiting. Her nephew came to visit to announce the death of her son. My suspicious mind kept thinking Gorda would have been a better psychic if she could have predicted the death rather than the visit, no?

But, I got so desperate for good news, for any ray of hope I could find, that eventually I gave in and asked Gorda to read my cards. She had rules about that, not after sundown, not on Wednesdays, not after her work at Unicor.*

By the time she accepted to ready my cards that is all I could think about that day. She took me to the yard out-back during recess and asked me to shield her by sitting in front of her. Apparently, witchcraft is not allowed in prison. What is the American government scared of? Us flying off on broomsticks and escaping? What a joke. She took out some mystical tarot cards, some of them terrifying, even though I don't understand what any of them meant. She asked me to uncross my legs or everything could go wrong. And she started reading my cards.

"Hay mucho celos..." There is a lot of jealousy, she repeated over and over. "There is a lot of jealousy around you; jealousy is the reason you ended up here. Your husband loves you very much, and he is waiting for you. Your kids too, and the kids are going to be okay. You have a good lawyer. One is very strong but the other one is useless. He is wasting precious time.... Pero tu te vas muñequita, tu te vas, y te vas pronto," she said. "But you are leaving. You are leaving, little doll, and you are leaving soon." This was six months into my incarceration. I believed her, and my heart felt lighter for a few days. I would eat a little more, smile a little more, and write happier thoughts in my letters to the kids.

I'm such a cartesian that today in hindsight I realize how delusional you have to be to survive prison. I was delusional most of my incarceration. If you ever go to prison, this is the best advice I have for you: be delusional. It helps you get by. In exchange for the tarot reading, I wrote many letters I translated from Spanish to English for Gorda. I filed her habeas corpus for her serious drug charge. I kept her informed on the new reforms that could possibly help her with an early release. I became her new favorite person and that scared me, knowing who she was and who she fucked with outside. She was part of DDP (Dominicans Don't Play: a Dominican-American street gang started in Manhattan, New York in 1990). They are known for primarily using machetes and knives as weapons. DDP is located across New York City, particularly in The Bronx, Harlem, and The Lower East Side.

I didn't tell Joe, or anyone on the outside that I was "in business" with a DDP member. No one ever visited her, for obvious reasons. That whole family wouldn't step foot near a federal institution.

The intelligence within the federal institution is actually really good. They know what you are up to and they know more than you think they do.

I often got called into my case manager Mr. Nichols' office. What's a case manager? It is someone kind of normal from the outside world, at least in my case it was. You usually see your case manager the first day you arrive at the prison. This person is the key to your release because he performs correctional casework in an institutional setting: evaluates your progress in the institution; coordinates and integrates you in training programs; develops your social histories; evaluates positive and negative aspects in each case situation; and develops release plans.

My case manager clocked me from day one. "I'm not worried what you will do," he said. "I am worried about you. It is rare for me to have someone in my office who I don't think is a criminal at all."

He was in his mid-forties I think; he had kind blue eyes and a shaved head. I used to joke to myself that with a few pounds off he looked like Bruce Willis. He gave me scary survival tips like, "Don't discuss your sentence with anyone. Don't say where you live. Don't discuss your appeal. Don't trust, nor believe what anyone says. You are here with serious offenders, hard-core criminals, and while we have them in custody, we can't stop their criminal impulses. Keep your mouth shut and your head down, and you will finish your sentence without a hitch and go home."

With a case manager, you come to the realization that even once you are released you will still be in custody. You will most likely be released to a half-way house, which is the most terrifying shit ever. And then you will be on probation, under the strict supervision of a probation officer. I'd often remind Mr. Nichols that I had an appeal going, and I was going to win it and would be released an innocent and exonerated woman. He was kind about my delusions (because you have to know that only 1% of federal cases in the district I was appealing ever get overturned), and he often said he truly hoped I would win it. Going into his office was reassuring and made me miss human contact with normal citizens more than ever. He never ever scolded me or treated me like a criminal, although I heard he could be ruthless to those inmates that didn't follow the rules. He carried a gun, and he was imposing, tall, and somewhat intimidating. But not to me. I think to do their job, a lot of the correctional staff (except for most junior correctional officers who are literally degenerate idiots) have to be a good judge of character. Mr. Nichols was a good judge of my character; he is the one who suggested I teach piano. Since I had an ABRSM Diploma certificate for piano teaching, he said it would keep me away from the crazies. He also called me to his office when he found out I was chummy with Maria Rosa aka Gorda. He didn't scold me, but he said, "Do you know who you are fucking with? I'm not supposed to tell you anything." (And it is true, probation reports on inmates were scary confidential, and prison staff could be charged with a felony for sharing.)

"Please, don't put me in a position where I have to look out for you," he said. "Fucking with gang members will get you a longer sentence. I know you feel you need the protection from these thugs but keep to yourself and come to me if you ever feel in danger. You don't need to associate with these criminals. You need to focus and go home to your children and your nice life."

Next time Joe came to visiting, I asked him to Google Maria Rosa and soon found out who she was. I couldn't turn back though. I was her homie. She would holler for me across the unit. When Gorda hollers for you, you don't fucking ignore her. Besides, I became untouchable with the Latinas thanks to that connection. I was untouchable with the Russians and Caucasians thanks to my friendship with Russia, and as a result the African Americans and he-she lesbians didn't touch me because they don't fuck around with the Latina gangs. I'm from Brooklyn so I had a good sense of street rules of loyalty such as returning favors, not ratting, and overall keeping my mouth shut.

None of them believed I was there for selling jeans anyway. Even the dumbest inmate found this hard to believe, so I ended up playing the game, making them believe I was there for a more serious crime. I went from spending the first few months in fear, to building myself a shield of allies. I had something they wanted (my language skills and my legal skills) and in exchange no one would dare fuck with me.

My biggest fear was the night and the shower. I was more afraid of a sexual assault than a fight or an attempt at my life. Don't ask me why the sexual activity in prison is what freaked me out the most. It happened in the shower, it happened at night, and many of the C.O's would keep their mouth shut about it and let it happen. The correctional officers do not offer any sense of safety at all. If anything, one or two being the exception, I felt more in danger with CO's than with inmates. Some of them were sleazy, corrupt, desperate, and vicious.

I have dodged a few sexual attacks at night. I did not sleep for one year straight; I would literally sleep for 10 minutes at a time. I could hear every snore, every heavy breathing, any toilet flushed, and every single time the CO would pass from one unit to the next, opening the heavy metal door, with his noisy set of keys, and walk heavy steps with his ugly steel-toe shoes.

Once I laid in bed, my body would stiffen. I was afraid to breathe loud, move and wake any of these psycho bitches, especially my murderer bunkie sleeping below me. One night, I felt a hand on my mouth, smothering me to keep me quiet, and another going for my underpants... I had been prepared for this. I had been taught and I had followed every bit of instruction I had been given. My weapon was meticulously prepared every night and placed under my pillow. It consisted of a sock (one of those heavy cotton white tennis socks everyone wears in federal prison) and my lock, the very heavy and big lock we used to lock our belongings in our lockers.

The minute I felt those hands on me, it took me less than a second to realize the time I had prepared for had come, and I had to act fast because no one, even if I moved uncontrollably and woke my whole cell unit, no one would move. No one would help. The CO that night had probably been bribed or whatever to stay away. I grabbed my sock and whacked as hard as I could at the head to the right of my upper bunk bed. I kept whacking and whacking as fast and as hard as I could wherever I could aim till it stopped. It was dark, the exit signs and lavatories lights were the only source of light.

I had to see what was happening. As that dark shadow walked out of my cubicle, I looked at the floor in horror to see blood all over... I waited for her to walk away. I was so scared. I was shaking. I peed myself. My bunkie was fast asleep. They were

108

giving her strong pills to keep her aggression down so she could sleep through anything. I ran and awoke one of my allies, who woke another, and while I went to clean myself up, they cleaned the blood, in the dark, without a noise. That night was the last night I ever slept but even for 10 minutes. The next day, I waited to be called to the captain's office. I expected my sentence to be lengthened greatly. I looked around at every single inmate in my cell unit, to see injuries. I didn't know who it was; I had never seen her face. I heard her grunt. I heard her curse, but it was so muffled I couldn't even recognize the voice. Till today, I don't know who it was, but I have my suspicions.

A few inmates were missing the next day... and when a bed goes empty in your unit, you assume that person was sent to the SHU, taken unexpectedly back to court to testify against someone, or was transferred to another prison, and that is never forewarned. I didn't leave the unit that day. I was scared for my life. I was scared of retaliation. I was scared of getting charged with assault or attempted murder. I said I was sick. I went to the medical office and claimed I had a stomachache, so the CO would leave me alone if I sat on my bed all day. I was on the upper level of a bunk bed, and it became my watch tower. Sitting up there during daytime, I could overlook the whole unit and the entrance. I could see if anyone was coming for me. No one did... Russia came hollering my name... I would ignore it. Some of my unit mates would come by and say, "Russia Red is at the door asking for you, she wants you to come down." I would for the first time disobey her.

My attacker never came back, and no one ever came for me on her behalf. I know a lot of the inmates in my cell unit knew what had happened, but it remained unspoken... And over the next few days, it seemed I had gained the respect of the worst of them. All of the sudden, if I walked into the TV room, they'd ask me if I want to watch something in particular. If they prepared a prison meal, one of them would come to my cubicle with a plate for me. I played tough. I hardly smiled, but I also never ever cried again in front of any of them. I still showered with my underwear on, always terrified that one of them would pull that curtain open and molest me. But it never happened ever again.

I never shared any of this with Joe when he visited and always tried to keep a smile on for the kids. My sentence was long... Birthdays passed, holidays passed, my kids school plays, school graduations, dance recitals, all of it passed me by. Dakota took her first steps; she started potty-training and kept the diaper off for hours at a time. I missed it all. When they would tell me about it at visiting, I would cry and couldn't stop crying. My heart was broken, and it still is till today.

I am missing a whole year of photo albums of my children growing up. Missing a year out of each and every one of their lives was traumatic. Dylan went through a domino effect of digressions in his cognitive development, and even his speech was more impaired than ever before. We had come such a long way thanks to therapies, and everything else we had done and been through to conquer his diagnosis. Savannah had to grow up too fast that year. She was robbed of her innocence and nonchalance. She realized what was happening only too well and carried that whole weight on her shoulders. She sensed that I was suicidal and felt responsible for keeping me alive. She would wake up at 5 am every day of her summer vacation to make sure she was brought along to visit me on the two-hour car ride to Connecticut. She never truly went back to being a child after it was all over. As much as I gave her princess themed parties and did everything to make her little girls dreams come true, that innocence was gone. She aged. I still see it in her eyes today at age 18. She is an old soul, who carries the well-being of those she loves heavily on her shoulders, especially mine.

So when you ask what prison was like...that's what it was like. It's shit. It fucks your life up forever; it scares the shit out of you, and it ruins the lives of those you love the most.

*post-traumatic stress disorder
** an emergency command used in prison. Its primary function is to command all of your available guards to search everything in your prison belongings that is capable of carrying contraband to maintain order.
***Federal Prison Industries, Inc. (FPI), doing business as UNICOR (stylized as Unicor) since 1977, is a corporation wholly owned United States government.

Chapter 13: Win-Lose Situation

I spent a whole, very hot summer in prison, and it hurt a lot, knowing I hadn't been home in 10 months. Now the kids were home for two months without someone to take them to the beach, out for ice cream, to the Central Park Zoo or the Victorian Gardens ride. That's what we did every summer, living on the most beautiful beach block in Belle Harbor, NY. We used to start our days by our pool. I'd bring home fresh Dunkin' Donuts munchkins for the kids before they woke up, and we would have breakfast, jump in our pool, and then pack lunch for the beach. We used to bring our cute pink beach chairs, our cooler and umbrella, and meet the kids' friends and mine, our neighbors.

My best friend, Sunny, would meet us on our beach block with her kids. Her and I would talk and laugh for hours while our kids would jump in the waves. We would stay there till 7pm, bringing back home our reluctant kids, sun-kissed, happy, salty, sandy, and exhausted. I'd put the kids to bed after dinner and spend the rest of the night reading outside, listening to the sound of the ocean, or dress up for fun summer night out in the city. I loved New York so much in the summer. All the uptown Stepford wives and Wall Street assholes would be gone to the Hamptons. There was something so amazing about the emptiness of New York City in the summer. The nights out were beautiful; everyone was tanned, gorgeous, happy, and carefree. The New York hustle and bustle vanished.

I always took most of the summers off to be with my kids. We would only travel to Europe in August, but the rest of the summer New York was ours, from the beach in Far Rockaway, to having Ice Cream in Sheepshead Bay Brooklyn, to grabbing pita falafel and shish kebab on kings highway in Flatbush, to shopping for designer clothes for less at Century 21 in Bay Ridge, to having long lazy lunches at downtown Cipriani and cooling off with ice cream at the Mercer Kitchen, and taking them to Serendipity II for the frozen hot chocolate, and ending up at the Central Park Carousel. New York was ours, our playground, and we made some of my kids' most beautiful childhood memories.

That summer in prison was torture. I tortured myself with guilt for my children who were sequestrated at home, and I'm sure not even swimming much in the pool because Berta, their nanny, didn't know how to swim. To be missing those precious moments of pure joy and happiness with them was torture. It was not so much that I was missing out on my life, it was more that I was missing out and messing with theirs. The guilt of their stolen childhood ate at me the most.

I couldn't wait for summer to end. It was hot, so hot. It made everyone in the prison crazy, irritable. More fights broke out, the lesbians were hornier than ever, and the bitches stank to high heaven. Body odor was something that was so terrible in prison and hygiene in general.

September came, and as much as I wanted time to pass faster, it ended up being worse than summer. September was a month of High Jewish Holidays: Rosh Hashana,

Yom Kippur, Succot. One after the other, three full weeks of holidays, which meant I wouldn't see my kids much because Joe was shomer Shabbat which means he observed the rules meticulously and didn't drive during the holidays. It was the worst months of them all; I saw the kids three times. The rest of the time the French Embassy would send one of its social workers to visit me as much as possible to keep me sane and keep me informed by communicating with my attorneys, my brother Gilbert, who was handling the attorneys, and let me know how the kids were.

My appeal still hadn't come through. There was no decision on the docket, no injuries, and it was almost a year. I would call Gilbert, who was probably my biggest support system at the time, and cry on the phone, begging him to inquire to do something. He was a powerful businessman, but his hands were tied. There was nothing he could do that he hadn't done. He literally stopped his life, and he barely worked anymore. He flew to Washington DC countless times to meet with lobbyists, with senators, with congressmen, with well-connected businessmen. He went to political rallies and fundraisers to try and approach someone, anyone that could intervene on my behalf.

When Joe couldn't keep borrowing money towards our house and couldn't keep paying my legal fees, Gilbert forced my mom into helping some more. She reluctantly did because he made her. She felt she had done enough when I first went in. He didn't give up on me. Gilbert became my Messiah, the only one I looked to. He promised me he would get me out. He had five children at the time, a family to take care of. He put his life on standby. He wasn't always nice to me when I was free, but he was there when it counted. In more ways than one.

He went into mourning that year. He grew a beard and swore he would only shave it off when I would be released. He became fervently religious and made a pact with god. He vowed to become extremely observant if I was to be released. He held back from huge celebrations and vacations that whole year. He aged that year. When he came to visit me after the holidays, he walked into the room and my heart sunk. My brother, just 15 years older than me, with his solemn beard, a few more grays than I remembered and tears in his eyes. He looked like he had been sitting Shiva for a year. He touched my face, although he was not allowed to, and he cried and his voice cracked so much as he said, "You are my little sister. I love you like a daughter. I will do anything for you. I eat because I must eat, I breath because I must breath, I smile because I must smile, but I truly do not feel like doing any of it as long as you are here. I am in here with you. I am outside but I am in jail."

He hired lawyer after lawyer, and at some point, I had more lawyers than the US president had advisors. He did not take no for an answer. He fought and fought and fought some more. He picked up my calls at the first ring. I could hear him answering an eager, "Yes" to the recording, "You have received a call from a federal inmate at Danbury Federal Correction Institution, do you wish to accept it?"

Hearing his deep, fatherly voice always filled me with reassurance. He never let down. He said I'd win my appeal, and he told me not to lose hope. He had done everything humanly possible to get me out of there.

So, yes, he was not the kindest to me when I lived in Miami. He didn't always support me, and he often made me feel like a nuisance in his nice life, but when it came to this situation, he pulled through like no one else. He and Joe did. Neither ever blamed me, never accused me of actually committing the crime. Actually, no one ever blamed me. The time didn't fit the crime, even if I had been guilty. This is where the outrage and the fight came from. I was doing the time of a hardcore criminal for a serious crime. There were drug dealers, rapists, and thugs with violent crimes doing less time than me.

It was early December now. I had not been a mother for 13 months, my eight-month-old baby was now 19 months, and Dylan did not come to visit me anymore. He was becoming more introverted, and he regressed tremendously. He had not visited since September. Joe wanted to force him to, but the minute he would arrive, he would complain of stomach pains and spend much of the visiting time in the bathroom. I had to make the right choice for my child. He was on the spectrum, and his sense of cognitive empathy had become close to none. No matter how many therapy treatments we had added to support him during my absence, he was no longer emotionally responsive. The cognitive or "theory of the mind" component of empathy involves the understanding and/or predicting what someone else might think, feel, or do. It is the ability to identify cues that indicate the thoughts and feelings of others and "to put oneself into another person's shoes." It is also referred to as "mentalizing," "mindreading," and "perspective taking." The ability to reflect on one's own and other people's minds (beliefs, desires, intentions, imagination, and emotions) allows us to interact effectively with others in the social world. It may also be thought of existing on a continuum with some individuals able to "mindread" relatively easily and intuitively, while others experience varying degrees of problems interpreting and predicting another person's behavior. Dylan's cognitive empathy had been something we had been working on aggressively to make him more "normal" in a social setting. My absence was a set-back and ripped to shreds every bit of cognitive empathy we had instilled in him. I knew he loved me, but I didn't see it or feel it anymore. Visits with him became painful for me. We were both suffering... so I made the decision to let him skip visiting for as long as he didn't ask Joe to come along. Each visit, from September on (12 months into my incarceration), was ripping my heart to shreds. I would be let into the visiting room, after Joe and the kids were let in, and be instructed to sit, and usually when the door from the inmates' side would open, they would all turn their heads and get up at the sight of me. I would scan the room quickly around them, Joe's tired and grey face, Savannah's warm and emotional smile, and Dakota's cherub cuteness and joy, and behind them ... no Dylan. I would walk to them, hug them and say, "Dylan didn't want to come?"

"No, honey, his stomach hurt," Joe said. It was hard, the hardest part of my incarceration for me. I had given my soul to Dylan's recovery. Yes, I said recovery. Dylan was slowly showing signs of recovery from autism.

Research in the past several years has shown that children can outgrow a diagnosis of autism spectrum disorder (ASD), once considered a lifelong condition. Dylan did, and then with my incarceration, he regressed. I won't wait till the end of the book though to tell you that today Dylan has completely recovered from ASD, and he is one of the rare cases of what researchers call "Optimal Outcome". Sure, he is still very special, extraordinary as I call him. Smarter than the norm, his brain doesn't work like ours. It works optimally like regular brains but on steroids. This boy, who was diagnosed at such a young age, was once not expected to ever be able to speak or make eye contact, let alone live alone or go to law school. Dylan went from an Autism Spectrum disorder diagnosis before I went to prison to regress to a much worse kind of autism diagnosis by the 10th month of my incarceration. Dylan was able before my incarceration to feel and receive love. When he regressed, his emotional attachment became difficult and affected our bond greatly.

Part of my sentence was overturned on the merit of the case (which were invalid and false) but also on the judge's errors in applying the guidelines, mainly because he failed (as mandated by law) to outweigh the gravity of the crime with the serious mental condition of my underage child. The judge had been warned at sentencing, that imposing a long sentence in prison as opposed to house arrest, would cause the child to debilitate. Dylan's new evaluation by Dr. McCarthon was re-submitted to the judge after 10 months. He was asked to re-evaluate the sentence, and he declined. Ultimately, this is what cost this judge the most embarrassing reversed decision of his career.

By the 11th month of my incarceration, I was a broken woman. What the world thought of me, what would be of my career or reputation, and even my marriage once I came out didn't matter to me. I was losing my little boy to the horrible battle that is autism. The hope that was once given to me concerning his recovery was based on the fact that I caught his syndrome so young. Dr. McCarthon always said the longer a parent waits, the less chances for the child of becoming a normal highly functioning adult. Dylan was going into his teen years, and it was over. This made me angry, disheartened, and desperate. I was angry with the United States, so angry my French nationality became my biggest pride. I asked the French Consul that came to visit me on a weekly basis to keep the ambassador and the French government informed on how I was doing and to start the process to get my kids French citizenship. By the 14th month of my incarceration, my mom had come to New York and taken all the administrative steps to get my kids French passports. Sophie, attaché French consul in NY, came to visit and showed me my kids' French passports. I was happy; it felt right.

Fuck being Americans, we didn't have to be anymore.

My appeal was decided in June, nine months into my incarceration, and had it not been for the political pressure applied by my senator and the French Government, these judges would have sat on it even longer because this commonwealth district is not known for handing out overturned decisions.

Does this register with your brain? I won my appeal in June and remained incarcerated ... The appeal I had been dreaming of winning did nothing. No one tells you this, when you mortgage your house, borrow more money than you will ever earn to hire attorneys to appeal your sentence. Lawyers talk to you about winning your appeal, but they don't tell you that even if you win, you don't get to go home just like that. You are remanded to go back in front of the very judge who put you in jail. You are supposed to go back in front of that monster so he can do his due diligence and release you...if he pleases.

Winning my appeal was the worst day of my life behind bars. All my hopes came crashing down because I won my appeal and stayed in jail. It's standard procedure, they said. You have to file motions to be remanded to the judge and wait for your attorney to be back from vacation so he can file the motion.

Because I won my appeal, the original judge must now take a look at it. It's up for the judge to right his wrong. So, I'm remanded to my original judge, who must apply the rules dictated by the appeal, but they took their sweet time.

It was summer... I spent summer having won my appeal but still in prison. Then you wait ... wait to be given a court date, then you wait for that court date to be approved by the bureau of prison, and you wait for the US. Marshals to schedule your transfer. From June to December, I was exonerated, but continued serving time in a medium to high security prison. Actually, come to think of it, the railroading by the American justice system went as far as not publishing the opinion (decision) on my appeal for months.

My attorneys would call the 4th circuit clerk daily... No decision on the docket. It made no sense, and it was getting close to a year since we filed. It took a lot of string pulling to get this decision published. Let me explain.

My dad's oldest friend and confidant was this affluent Rabbi ... people queued outside the doors of Charles Kushner's townhouse on the Upper East Side, just to get this rabbi's blessing. ..

Every year Rabbi D.P. would visit New York and grant visits with hundreds of disciples who would line up to see him for a blessing. Women who couldn't get pregnant, men who lost all their money, grandmothers who were going thru chemo...

all in hopes that his blessings would grant them a miracle. It often did. Rabbi D.P. was known for his powerful prayers and his life changing berachot (blessings). He knew me since I was born, and each time he would visit NY, his secretary would summon me to see him. "Rabbi wants to see you, he wants to bless you, and he misses you." The secretary would always give me this address on the Upper East Side, to an empty posh townhouse, with a discreet plaque that read "Kushner Company". Who is Kushner? It's Charles Kushner, the successful (yet infamous) real estate developer who would not sign one deal without Rabbi D.P.'s blessing. He loved Rabbi so much he would let him use one of his many posh buildings to host the visits with hopeful disciples. Does Charles' name sounds familiar? Well, that's because his son, Jared Kushner, is married to Donald Trump's daughter, Ivanka. Long story short, I always dragged my feet to see Rabbi D.P. and indulge him in giving me his holy blessing, after engaging in an affectionate and warm conversation with me, for old time's sake as he glared at me with his deep piercing yet sweet mystical eyes, smiling from the corner of his lip at my rebellious air. See, he knew that even though I married a religious man, I was a rebel and I believed in none of this stuff. I mean, come on, the man was my dad's bestie, and my dad dropped dead at age 57. No miracle here. My dad's death really confirmed how I felt about this pious aspect of Judaism. It is a crock of shit. You can eat kosher, keep Shabbat, observe every single holiday, go to the mikvah, and yet you can still die of a heart attack, be abused by your husband, be unhappy as fuck, and end up in jail separated from your children for doing absolutely nothing. If you still believe in the holy miracles of a rabbi's blessing after what I've seen and endured, I have a bridge to sell you.

I remember when my dad died. My mom summoned me back to France (where her and my dad had gone back to living), after my dad had a major heart attack. I flew back from Miami, and I remember it was cold in Toulouse. It was December, so I packed the only winter clothes I had, thinking, "Gosh, I'm so somber. Every warm piece of clothing I own is black." I arrived at the hospital after my nine-hour flight, to find my dad laying in intensive care with all these tubes attached to him. The beeping of the machines and the buzzing of the oxygen are sounds that I can still hear in my head now. He laid there on the white sheets, with his thick and shiny raven hair, and beautiful tanned skin. It always shocked me how healthy my dad looked, even when he was flirting with death (This wasn't the first heart attack). I was so happy that intensive care only allowed us to be with him one by one. My family was always suffocating to me. My mom... my sister, Corine ... my brother, Gilbert, they always had this superior air with me because I was the young one, the rebellious one, the spoiled one. I was happy they weren't there while I visited with my dad. My dad and I had secrets and a very privileged relationship. He told me things he told no one else, that I will take to my grave. He revealed things to me about his family, about my mother, about himself, that he had never told anyone. He used to say I was different, open and nonjudgmental. I guess he saw something in me, the public, my audience today sees but no one else but him noticed before now.

The minute the nurse left me with him... I went to touch his hair and slid my fingers thru his beautiful mane. It was so beautiful and youthful, so abundant and rich, just like him. He was a big man, tall and towering over me, strong, slender, with such an allure. I remember bringing my lips to his forehead and holding his face in my hands, while my tears trickled on his face and saying, "Papa, it's me, you're tiggy."

He nicked named me his tiger since before I can remember because he said, I had the eyes and the walk of a feline. "I love you, papa, I'm here can you hear me? Do you remember you always call me tiger?"

He was in an induced coma they said, but he started moving his legs uncontrollably, and for a second I got excited. He heard me; he was waking up. But his legs kept moving and moving. They were convulsing, I guess. In came the nurses, my mom, and my brother screaming, "What did you do?"

I didn't do anything I just whispered to him about our secrets. He was dying, his heart was stopping. My mom started screaming, calling out all the Jewish saints she knew, and praying in Hebrew. I got pushed out of the room... only to see her and my brother come out and tell me to go say goodbye. Goodbye? What do you mean goodbye? I just said hello to him. My older brother Gilbert shook his head, crying, and held me for the first time in a very long time and said, "He is gone. He left us."

I looked at my mother and said to her, "Didn't you say Rabbi D.P. just blessed him? Can't you call him to resuscitate him?"

I wasn't even sarcastic. I guess if he could save him now, I could give this religious bullshit a chance. I went and kissed my dad for the last time... I tried to open his eyes. I still had hope. Then, I remember thinking, he doesn't look dead. He looks like he just got back from the beach. And then I felt despair, that he left me with this family I didn't really have anything in common with. What were they going to do with me?

So you see... while I love Judaism and I love being Jewish, I loathe the institution of the religion because it failed me. It deceived me, and it was weaponized to torture me mentally when I got married to Joe.

Chapter 14: Con Air

There are no fucking miracles … I'll tell you that. I did pray for a miracle for a year, and it's quite fantastic how the power of hope keeps us going. When I missed Dakota's second birthday, my Valentine's Day baby, it was horrible. The lesbian couples were hanging arts and crafts hearts and shit all around their prison wives' bunk beds. It made me throw up in my mouth. My reality had become absurd, like I was on another planet. I wanted to scream, and part of me wanted to die.

Finally, in late September the appeal I won finally would get my case remanded in front of the judge in Virginia. Months after my sentence was overturned, the red tape of the fucking criminal justice system still kept me behind bars, serving a sentence that was technically overturned. Now I needed a sentencing attorney to represent me to make sure the Judge would in fact overturn my sentence. I would have to be transferred back to Virginia to face him once again.

I thought I would be released from Danbury and fly myself to Virginia to receive an apology from this judge. Once again, I was dreaming. It doesn't work like that.

My court date was set for early December, which gave the Bureau of Prison enough time to organize my transfer back to Alexandria, VA county jail, and court.

I was disheartened and giddy at the same time…Could this truly be the end of my sentence?

Russia said, "Now people know you gonna go out; they gonna try to trip you. If you trip, you go to the SHU and they extend your sentence. Walk with your head down. Don't talk to anyone and don't tell anyone you are going home."

I just told a few… to the rest I said I had to go back to court to be heard for my appeal. I didn't tell any of them I won my appeal. I was scared they would trap me and set me up. I kept to myself till my transfer date.

They called me to medical for tests. I asked for my attorney, but they refused. They are entitled to take my blood and keep my DNA. I don't get how that's legal if I won my appeal. Why would they keep my DNA? But when you are in Fed, you don't have rights anymore. They own you. Just like when my kidneys failed and they gave me the antibiotic they gave everyone else for dental infections.

Everything about my departure scared me. I didn't know what a prison transfer was like. That isn't how I imagined leaving this place. I imagined myself so many times going through R & D again, seeing the kind CO who welcomed me the first day. I imagined my family would have come to leave my clothing, I had given Joe a list of what I needed (since the clothes I wore when I went in were shipped back home). I didn't think I would be transferred like a murderer with handcuffs and shackles.

My stress level skyrocketed when they told me they would just wake me up at 4 am someday to report to R&D and that I wouldn't know when. What if it's a visiting day? How will I let my family know? Where am I being transferred to? For how long?

I wasn't entitled to any answers to these questions. Ms. Wilson, my counselor, promised to call my husband and let him know not to show for visiting that day. She wouldn't tell him more.

Could I really trust her though? Over the past 11 months, she had gotten weird with me. She would get really personal and treat me like a normal human being. She would say reassuring and kind words to me when she would catch me in tears, missing my kids or getting bad news about my appeal being delayed. But then sometimes she would freak me out.

Once, I went to her office to talk to my attorney, and she waited outside of her office while I was on the call. When she got back in, she noticed I was smiling.

"So, you are going home, huh?" I nodded. "It's a nice home on the beach, you are very privileged. Will you still live there?"

I panicked; how did she know? "How do you know what my house looks like?"

"I drove by it the other day. I was in the area and I was curious. Nice Range Rover in the driveway, too." My kids live in that house. What's a correctional officer from DANBURY CONNECTICUT doing in Belle Harbor NY, 2 hours away, in a very residential neighborhood she had no business driving through.

I never trusted her ever again. I don't think it's ethical nor legal that she used the privileged information in my sentencing report to go fucking scout my house.

This Federal justice system rips you to shreds, whether you are innocent or guilty. It strips you of every right, your privacy, your sense of self. Once I got out, I was never the same ever, at least not until I left the United States.

It's 5 am, the CO is standing by my bed. He instructs me to get up, get dressed, and follow him. I knew it would be a male CO that would come to get me. Because in prison everything is as fucked as it can be... So, I showered every night and dressed in case it was time for my transfer, although it was three weeks early. Where would they put me for three weeks while I wait for my court date?

He walks me to R&D. It's pitch-black in the yard, and he doesn't talk much. I hate his guts anyways. That guy was a piece of shit.

He says a female CO will arrive at 6 am to have me changed and shackled, ready to transfer with US Marshals. I have never been shackled. Actually, I've never been handcuffed. That seems nuts for someone who has been in prison for 14 months at that point, doesn't it? I self- surrendered, and once I did, I was placed in general population. I had never left Danbury till that day, so I was never arrested prior to going to prison. I was never handcuffed. I didn't even know what that felt like, but I was about to find out.

I was placed in a holding cell in R&D. I know in an hour or two I would see the outside world for the first time in one year. Part of me was excited to be a step closer to my release. Part of me was shitting my pants, thinking anything bad that can happen will happen and this nightmare will not end. The little voice kept saying, "But you won your appeal." The other voice kept screaming louder, "But you weren't guilty in the first place and you still went to prison."

I was given an orange jumpsuit to change into, apparently my ugly khaki uniform was federal property and I had to give it back (could you die at the irony?). I'm given fabric espadrilles... I hadn't rocked the orange jumpsuit yet (that's for those who are sent to the SHU ... segregation, or the hole as some call it). At the eve of my one-year anniversary in jail, I finally was going to feel the full experience. The handcuffs, the shackles, the orange jumpsuit... Orange was finally the new black—ha!

Before I got undressed and dressed again, the female CO made me squat and cough. She looked up my asshole and my vagina, and she looked under my tongue, to make sure I wasn't carrying any weapons. I mean, of course, I sold jeans on the internet. I could be fucking dangerous, you know. I kept thinking: I kept believing they are spending taxpayer dollars on transporting me like a dangerous offender with marshals, and all. The great fucking US of A using major resources to protect the country from very dangerous little me. I'm being sarcastic, can you tell?

I hear the heavy doors of R&D being unlocked and buzzing the US marshals in. They come in and are handed my file. I can see them from the holding cell (the door to the cell remained open the whole time. I guess that was nice enough on the CO's part to realize I wasn't going to escape as I'm being transferred to Virginia to be handed my release papers. They are two U.S. Marshals, one small lady with a short-haired perm (she looked like a slightly tougher version of Alice the housekeeper in the Brady Bunch), and a man who looked like a buff look alike of JR played by Larry Hagman in 1980s TV series *Dallas* (cowboy boots, the chunky silver cowboy belt, big gold sunglasses, and a heavy Southern accent). I figured he was from Texas. I wasn't far off. The man turned around to size me up and flashed a very white smile. "Big ol' me for this little lady?" *I feel you buddy*, I thought. This fucking convoy just for me. They both carried a gun and wore bulletproof vests and windbreakers that said "U.S. Marshal" on them. The woman comes to me and tells me, "Sorry, honey. I'm going to have to shackle you. Make sure you pull those socks up or your ankles are going to get sore and bloody from the long trip."

She put the shackles on tight, and they hurt. I didn't want to be a sissy, but then she asked me to try walking and I couldn't, so she decided to give me an extra notch for comfort. Then she tells me to position myself to be handcuffed. At that point, I hand her my wrists, putting both my arms in front of her.

"You're kidding, right? You know we ain't gonna handcuff you this way," She says.

I look her dead in the eye, and I say, "This is my first time being handcuffed. I don't know handcuffing etiquette, sorry." I proceed to explain my journey and how I've was never formally arrested, or taken to central booking, that I just drove myself to the FCI on the day of my prescribed surrender. She was shocked. She softened up a little and made me put my arms behind me, placing my wrists in the way that would hurt less, and she commented on my bony tiny wrists, saying she had to make it tight because I could get myself out of them easily otherwise. I almost argued that they could trust me, but I knew better. They don't trust felons, whether they sold jeans on eBay or microwaved their baby for dinner like one of my roommates did.

120

The handcuffs hurt, but the shackles hurt even more. I thought of peeing before all of this happened but the metal toilet in the cell was in the direct field of vision of the male CO, so I held it. We were buzzed out of three vault doors. I can still hear the buzzing and the sound of the metal slamming behind me after each door. You have to wait once you get through one door, in the corridor, till the door behind you closes and they buzz open the next one. Everything echoes: JR's heavy breathing, their boots, and the chains of my shackles dragging on the floor. And then we were outside, I took a quick look around. It still didn't feel like freedom. I wanted to cry. I never thought I would leave this place as a prisoner. I imagined myself being picked up by Joe, the kids, my sister, Corine... I imagined myself wearing my cute David Lerner leggings, my Moncler puff jacket as I got buzzed out, to fall into my family's warm embrace and cry happy tears of relief. I never thought I would come out shackled, handcuffed, wearing an orange jumpsuit, thick white socks with holes in them, and cotton espadrilles on a cold crisp December day.

Outside, a white van marked, "Bureau of Federal Prison - Inmate Transport", with bars on the windows was waiting for us. The female marshal sat me in the back and used the loose chain from the shackles to attach me to a hook on the car floor. I asked her if I had to stay handcuffed with the hands in my back during the ride. They looked at each other and opted to handcuff me in the front. "Don't do anything stupid."

Yeah, don't worry, Karen. I'm not going to slit your throat. I fucking sold Juicy Couture tracksuits and jeans from my kitchen, that's why I'm here.

We start getting out of FCI Danbury grounds, and in a few minutes, I will see civilization as I once knew it... I was nervous. I almost felt like I would see cars flying and all kinds of new inventions like in *Back to the Future*. Because one year behind bars felt like 2000.

We venture onto Connecticut's roads, with lots of foliage, state roads, and expressways I've never seen before... a small town. We stop at the light. I look into the other cars, ashamed to be looked at... I used to be afraid to look inside prisoner transport vans. I see a CVS and Dunkin' Donuts. I miss Dunkin' Donuts in Brooklyn so much, going there after school with my babies, eating munchkins with them, letting the kids run around while I grabbed an iced Hazelnut latte with my best friends, Julie and Valerie. I missed my life. It felt so far away, so surreal then.

We stop at another light, and I see a TGI Fridays, a 7-11, a Burger King, a steakhouse... I miss life. I look at the car next to us. The mom is driving, and the baby sitting in his car seat in the back, his older brother licks the window and waves at me. I can't wave back he will see the handcuffs. I smile, and tears come rolling down. This ride is a tough for me. I didn't feel like it was the highway to freedom because I didn't feel any kind of optimism. After all, I haven't had much luck thus far. I'm uncomfortable. I feel blisters forming on my ankles, and the shackle is painfully tight on my ankle bone. My wrists throb, too. I wiggle my tiny right wrist and hand out of the handcuff, just for a few seconds. It came right off; I just wanted some relief. Then I would put it back on. I finally ask them, "Where are we going?"

"Honey, right now we are taking you to Maryland, to a federal airport strip. From there we cannot tell you were you will be flown." Wait, we are taking a plane from Maryland to go to Virginia? This doesn't make sense. So, I engage conversation again.

"I'm worried. My court date is in 22 days in Alexandria, Virginia. Is that where I am going?" They were kind and patient.

"Hon, if that is where your court date is that is where you will end up. The DOC will often send you to a transfer center somewhere in the US and then to Virginia a few days before court."

I'm freaking out. I'm so scared. I don't know when I will see my family next. I learned my attorney's phone number by heart. I guess wherever I will go I will be allowed one phone call, right? They always do on TV.

The ride is five hours or so. The marshals talk to me a little, and they ask about my kids. Southerners love kids. They have a way of softening up when you mention children. "I bet you are excited to see them," she said.

Yeah, I'm excited, but not really, because between now and my court date, I could die. I could be found guilty of another crime. I could get gang banged... so much shit could happen. My life is disposable at this point. I have no control over anything that happens to me. I'm scared. I'm actually more scared than I was in Danbury Prison. My heart had been pounding since 4 am that morning. They gave me a stale prison sandwich when we stopped for gas, and I politely took three bites and told them I didn't want anymore. They kept offering water. I tried drinking.

I was already losing one of my kidneys, so I did try to survive to see another day of this shit my life had become. FUCK MY LIFE. I often wondered if this was all happening to me to punish me for using non-kosher tomato sauce to make Joe's Moroccan fish dish for Shabbat dinner... Or was it retribution for having an affair with Gil? But, wait, people cheat every day. They don't go to jail and get taken away from their children.

We arrived at what looked like an army base. I could see large metal gates and barb wires, and a huge landing strip, a control tower, and police checkpoints. We arrive at the first check point, and it's like in the movies. JR opens his window and hands the agent my file. We got going on the 4 pm aircraft. I'm trying to hear the destination, but they know better than to mention it.

He looks at me, looks at my federal ID badge on my orange jumpsuit, uses a mirror detector thing under the van, and looks at us suspiciously again. I notice he is a sheriff. I'm so confused by the chain of command in these states. I feel like my life doesn't even belong to me anymore. I want to pee so badly, but I don't say anything. I start smelling my own body odor. I've been nervously sweating. The smell is horrid. I've never smelled myself this way before. Till today, I can still smell that strange sweaty smell. I guess when you are shitting yourself scared, your body releases a fear hormone that smells like a dead skunk.

"Now, we wait," JR says. We wait for what, I don't know. The lady opens her door, another sheriff comes up to her. "How many more are we waiting for?" He says something like 12... then she asks, "How many we got on the aircraft?" He mumbles a number like 26. I'm scared. I don't know what any of this means. Who are these 26 people? Where are they going? Where am I going? Are they dangerous? I had done some investigating before leaving the FCI, and I found out transfers are rarely for successful appeals and releases. They are usually for court dates, inmates who decide to rat against a co-conspirator for a shorter sentence, or to be judged for another crime they committed after the one they are serving for. What that meant was that 26 inmates I'd be flying first class with would possibly be gang members, murderers, and the worst scum of the earth you can find in federal prisons across America. Many of these 26 don't have much to lose. Except for me.

We start watching orange jumpsuits come off the big aircraft. This plane is huge. It looks like a military aircraft. Is this like a red eye: passengers get off and others get in? I see all male prisoners ... and to my horror, they are all going down the aircraft on the tarmac, shackled and handcuffed to one another on a chain. Some of them have tattooed faces, others have huge scary scars that tell stories I don't want to hear. JR turns around and takes off his gold Elvis sunglasses and says, "Sweetie, you are going to have to brace yourself. On this flight today, there are 22 males and four females including you. Some of them haven't seen a woman in decades. Look down at the pavement and don't engage with them. Don't cry, don't show fear. If anything happens, we are here to protect you, but it's intimidating and not pleasant. Alright, sweetheart, are you ready? I can tell you aren't made for this shit, but you're gonna be alright. Susan and I are federal marshals. We are trained and able to handle any kind of situation. Don't mess with us and we got your back." I nod. I'm scared. I don't know what I'm scared of, but I'm scared.

My marshals escort me to the tarmac and tell me to stand there. From three other vans, come three female inmates to line up next to me. I'm first in line. I'm scared. The men who were chained to one another are turning their backs to us and instructed not to turn around. JR comes with a heavy chain and proceeds to chain me to the inmate behind me. At this point, my shackles are chained to a chain belt around my waist and to my handcuffs and between my legs is the heavy chain that connects me to the 3 other female prisoners. We will go first on the aircraft, they say. But not before they bring out more male inmates from a prisoner transport bus. So far, none of the male inmates get a clear look at us until six marshals escort what looks like a stand-up, pope-mobile glass box, transporting an inmate in standing position, with his face plastered against the wall of this weird glass trolley. He was chained all over and wearing a Hannibal Lecter cannibal mask. I kid you not.

I'm going to shit myself at this point. I look at my female marshal for help, but she is too preoccupied with securing this convoy. There is chatter behind me. They are told to shut their traps. Finally, the men inmates, all 22 of them, are instructed to slowly turn around and they do so carefully, as like me, they are chained from shackles to belt to handcuffs to each other. They make eye contact and start hollering at us, disgusting words. Some of them lick their lips and mimic fellatio with their disgusting tongues. They scream how they are going to have their way with us by violently raping us. I know they are chained. I know the marshals are armed, but I'm scared as shit still. I'm cold. I'm shaking. I peed in my pants a little. I am holding back tears. I'm still feeling that nasty sweat trickle down under my breasts and my armpits. I'm feeling all kinds of gross and discomfort. This category of fear is physically painful and excruciating.

The three other females and I are lined up and led up to the aircraft under the disgusting, degrading, violating scrutiny of the male inmates. We are led to the front of the aircraft, unchained from one another, but still handcuffed and shackled, and we sit, chained to a hook on the aircraft's floor. The other women are going to the same facility and sitting together. I'm sitting alone with my female marshal and JR in front of me. My lady marshal says, "Listen, sweetheart, the cannibal guy in the box is placed in the back in a separate section of the plane, so you needn't worry about him, but if you need to go to the bathroom, you will have to do the walk of shame and possibly face very degrading and scary behavior from these male inmates, especially the lifers."

I already had started to wet myself on the tarmac. It was a matter of time before I stained my orange jumpsuit with pee.

As the aircraft took off, I shyly looked around, but never behind me for fear of meeting the stare of a male inmate. I could hear them catcalling us:

"Hey, sweet pussy."

"Mamacita!"

"I can smell some fresh cunt all the way back here." It was sickening.

I quietly started to cry, at the surreal life I was living, not sure it wasn't about to get worst, if that was even possible, sitting in an aircraft with a seven-foot tall JR meet Elvis marshal who said he is from Oklahoma and a little lady carrying a serious weapon whose name was Susan from Texas. The aircraft looked exactly like the one in the movie with Nicholas Cage and John Cusack in *Con Air*. A military aircraft with metal chairs and metal floors. I mean the amount of times I've referred to movies writing this story, indicates just how terrifyingly fictional this whole period of my life felt.

JR said once the wheels go up, he will be able to tell me where we are going. But not before. He tells me about his adventures as a federal marshal. He also tells me on this aircraft there's a serial killer and a mass murder being transferred to another supermax prison. I could only speculate on what Hannibal Lecter was in for... Apparently, he tends to bite prison guards' ears off. This is not fictional at all; it is not even slightly changed for your reading pleasure. I wish it was.

I'm at the point again that I can feel urine drizzling down my leg. I am terrified to ask Susan to take me to the restroom in the back of the aircraft. But, I work up some nerve and ask her. She says, "If you gotta go, you gotta go. Come on. Get up. Walk in front of me."

She unfastens her gun, puts her right hand on it, and we start walking. I look right in front of me all the way in the back of the aircraft, and I see Hannibal Lector in a huge cage still chained and pinned to the back of his box. It's scary and surreal; he is still wearing the cannibal mask. She whispers to keep my head down and keep walking. The male prisoners start chanting, whistling, clicking their tongues, and sticking their elbows out to touch me. She kicks a few out of the way, and tells their marshals to look out, but a few of them manage to touch my butt, and I feel paralyzed and electrocuted by sheer panic. I already think of the way back. I can't walk faster because I'm in shackles, and they are heavy, and they are noisy dragging on the aircraft floor.

Susan comes inside the small bathroom with me and removes my shackle chain around my waist. She helps me bring my jumpsuit down to my knee and asks if I'll be okay with my underwear. She says she can go out. I ask her to stay. I'm scared to be handcuffed, shackled and butt naked, having to open the door back up to ask her for help. She tells me she will stay as long as I don't have to take a dump. I'm embarrassed that my white prison panties are wet with some urine. I don't know if she notices, but I apologize to her because it's gross. I can smell the stench of my body odor and my urine mixing together. I'm dying to ask her to let me wash my arm pits in the aircraft restroom, but I don't. She dresses me, and chains me back up at the waist. And tells me to take a deep breath.

"If you walk fast, I'll walk fast behind you. Try not to trip, and not to worry too much." Bizarrely, because I was coming from behind them, that ordeal went by a lot faster. I can still feel the sight of relief I felt finding the safety of my cold metal airplane seat. I could hear the other female inmates chatting about FTC (Federal Transfer Center) in Oklahoma and how they had friends there and couldn't wait to see them. These women are fucking sick in the head. This is what they look forward to? Like it's another frat house?

That flight felt like it was taking me far away from the life I had known and from my children forever. At that moment, I felt I would never see anyone I knew or loved ever again. It was the last ride to hell. I ask JR, "Am I going to Oklahoma?"

He nodded. Panic took over my whole being. Why would they fly me all the way to the south of the United States when my court date was all the way up in Virginia? This made no sense. Geographically, it made no sense. My court date was in 22 days, so why was I going to Oklahoma? Maybe there was another stop. Maybe we were dropping off some inmate there and then they would fly me back up closer to Virginia. My mind was going 1,000 miles a minute, my heart was racing, and my sanity was rapidly dissolving from every pore in my body.

We landed. Tears kept trickling down my cheeks. I didn't have it in me to believe in any god anymore. I had given up on praying a long while ago (can you blame me?). I gave myself a pep talk and convinced myself to hold off a little while longer. I said to myself, "Ingrid, go into survivor mode until your court date. If you still don't get out, you are free then to give up on life. Until then stop thinking about your life outside, stop thinking about the kids, and just survive."

I was first out from the front of the aircraft. I got to hear the pigs holler more disgusting shit at me, for the last time I hoped. Then I realized I would have to fly back to Virginia and go through the same shit again.

Off the aircraft, I was picked up by two sheriffs and taken to Pottawatomie County Jail. It was my first time riding in a sheriff's car. The female sheriff explained that the Federal Transfer Center didn't have room for me, so instead I will stay in county jail until my next transfer. I arrived at the county jail at midnight. They processed me, took my mug shot, then put me in a cold holding cell with no chair and no bed for hours, till they took me to get fingerprinted, and then put me back in another holding cell with a crack addict in withdrawal, having bouts of seizures and foaming from the mouth.

They came at 5 am for a medical visit. One more degrading ordeal of getting naked again for a pervert male doctor who wanted nothing more than sticking a fucking thermometer up my ass. I argued butt-naked, requesting my attorney or having one appointed for me. I knew I didn't need anything stuck up my ass to be deemed healthy enough to be housed at the county jail. No self-respect is left in my being at that point, I feel numb to the level of legal, mental, and physical abuse the federal government put me through for selling jeans on eBay.

The worst part of this whole incarceration was this transfer, to be remanded back in front of the judge of put me behind bars.

I was given a basic hygiene kit, two disposable panties, one disposable bra, and a spork (a fork spoon that cannot be turned into a lethal weapon) and 18 hours later, I was let into the county jail cell where I would spend the next few days. I didn't know for how long. They buzzed me into this cold concrete big ascetic cell that looked like a big glass room, containing 40 metal bunk beds of three levels each. This room looked like a spaceship dorm. It had a common bathroom, a corner with tables (I assumed we would use to eat), and a wall with lined up benches with pay phones. That is all I saw: the pay phones that was my only focus. This cell was a state of the art cell. You never saw a guard. Food was sandwiches at every meal, delivered through weird electronically actioned elevator boxes that delivered your tray when you entered your inmate card into the slot.

Inmates there were welcoming. They weren't all doing hard time because it was a county jail. Some were there for not paying child support, others for minor drug possession, but a few like me were going back to court. The inmates speculated that the walls were glass, and the prison guards could see us through the walls. We never saw them, and they hardly ever saw us. One of the inmates was this compelling older woman with a message for the outside world that she was hoping I would tell when I got out. Turns out, she was a notorious criminal and was in county jail awaiting her next Federal Court date. Her name was Elaine Brown, a New Hampshire woman who gained national attention with her husband as tax protesters in early 2007 for refusing to pay the U.S. federal income tax and subsequently refusing to surrender to federal government agents after having been convicted of tax crimes. After the conviction

126

and sentencing, a long, armed standoff with federal law enforcement authorities at their New Hampshire residence ended with the arrest of Edward and Elaine Brown.

In July 2009, while serving their sentences for the tax crimes, the Browns were found guilty by a federal district court jury of additional criminal charges arising from their conduct during the standoff. This woman had made the news big time and listening to her story while we stayed in county jail together only fueled my hate for the justice system. She was nuts though, almost possessed. If you spend enough time with these neurotic inmates, you tend to go bonkers yourself. The best thing that happened to me in that jail was the shower. It was so clean, such a luxury, and I felt so safe since we were in a digitally guarded box. Peeing and pooping was nerve-racking because you knew the guards were watching out there. I remember trying to go while keeping all of my garments on and basically moving my underwear to the side so that my no-one would be jerking off to my naked butt on the other side of those walls.

I still couldn't call my family. My attorney, I was told, would not be alerted for up to a week as to my whereabouts for security reasons. As long as my attorney didn't know where I was, my jail account would have zero dollars and I couldn't make phone calls. I went six days without knowing if my family knew where I was or if I was going to make my court date in Virginia. Everyday inmates would transfer out, but I wouldn't. I would spend my time doing abdominal crunches and power yoga head stands on the floor by my bed, to avoid Elaine's conspiracy theory stories. I fucking couldn't give a shit that she didn't want to pay taxes, and that she held a fed at gunpoint outside of her house because Americans, in fact, do not have to pay taxes she would say.

Deep down, I thought she looked like a murderer. She had darkness in her eyes. But she was also classy, well-spoken, and reminded me of one of the Golden Girls. I couldn't wait to get out and Google her to see if she was telling me the truth: she was.

On Day 15, I was freaking out. I had been without news from my children, and it was my birthday. I asked for my attorney every day at the window (there was a bank teller like aquarium window we could ring at in case of emergency). I didn't know if my family and my lawyer knew where I was. I was going to miss my court date and stay here forever.

The next day, I finally got a phone call from my attorney.

"Ingrid, I don't want you to panic, but the feds lost you in the system to try to make you miss your court date." My world collapsed. I realized I was still holding on to some hope until that phone call. I didn't feel in danger in that prison. I was left alone most of the time, and all I had to do was kill time and try to keep my mind from thinking of the children until my court date. I was afraid the feds would forget to transfer me. But I still hoped everyday my transfer was coming. Weirdly, I preferred the matrix-like jail cell to the big correctional facility in Danbury. I guess the fact that many inmates around me kept leaving gave me hope that this wasn't a place where people stayed forever.

Turns out only 1% of federal appeals result in an overturned sentence. And turns out the Feds are sore losers. So, as the full-fledged railroading effort that my whole criminal case had been to them, they had to try and sabotage my court appearance and keep me serving the time they had spent serious tax dollars on prosecuting me for. My sentencing attorney was notoriously known for his last straw legal victories. He was to fly from California to Virginia for my court appearance and release. He told me that he was doing all he could so I would be transferred on time for my court date. He was reassuring but also skeptical.

"I don't know why they want you behind bars so bad, Ingrid. I've never seen this before." He said he had to call in favors in high places to find me in the system. Finally, he was able to fund my jail account, and I got to call home on my birthday. I hadn't seen, nor spoken to my kids in days. They didn't know where I was. Savannah picked up and cried when she heard the prison recording. I could hear her pressing "one" to accept the call from Pottawatomie county jail. She sang, "Happy birthday to you, Mama! You are going to come home" in her soft, shaky voice. There were no phone minutes limitations in county like there were in fed so I called a few times a day for the next few days. I didn't sleep. I didn't eat. If I missed my court date, my case could be adjourned for months. I could stay in county jail for months, doing time served, if I fell into the cracks of this fucked up warped system they like to call a justice system. I had seen it happen to others. Mostly people of color, minorities who didn't have the same access to legal counsel as I did. The unfairness I've suffered is nothing compare to the African American female population in the federal system. I saw it with my own eyes. I wiped tears off some beautiful black faces during my time with them behind bars.

My court date was in nine days. I got picked up for transfer 72 1/2 hours from my court hearing. I thought I would have a heart attack, worrying about making it in front of the judge in Alexandria, VA at 9 am in early December.

I ask the officers who pick me up how they plan on getting me to Virginia in 72 1/2 hours. They don't know.

Chapter 15: Fuck My Life

My shackles, handcuffs, waist chain game is fucking strong at this point. I know exactly how it goes. I'm sitting in a prisoner transport bus (you know the kind that looks like a yellow school bus that was painted white). I assume we will be picking up others. I don't know how long a bus ride would take from Oklahoma to Virginia, but from my geographic memory, that would be something like 20 hours. I look at the bus, and I don't think I see a bathroom. I see a cage in the back.

There is one marshal, one driver, and one police officer. I'm scared. I'm thinking if we pick up dangerous male offenders they won't be enough to overpower them if needed.

We drive for several hours, and I'm trying to figure out where we are. We go through some states. I'm starting to feel relief, as we are going back up north. We pick up inmates, male and female, who get seated, scattered and far away from one another on the large bus. We are all chained to a hook in front of us on the bus floor. The ride was maybe 14 hours long.

We arrive in North Carolina and drop off some inmates at a county jail. We go again... I'm starting to breathe a little easier, thinking, *okay, we are going to Virginia.* Yes, we are. I'm delirious. I'm singing in my head, "The wheels on the bus go round and round, round and round, round and round. The wheels on the bus go round and round all through the town, and to Virginia." I used to sing it for the kids... now, I'm singing it in my head. I do believe I reached a state of delirium during that time. I do believe like many inmates I had gone cuckoo. I wondered if I would ever be normal again after I went home.

I fucking hated Virginia. I still do, but I was dreaming of seeing that sign: "Welcome to VIRGINIA, the state of the motherfuckers who send mothers to Federal Prison for selling jeans on the internet." After my release, and for years after that, each time I saw a Virginia license plate in NY or in Miami, I would freak out and think I'm being followed by the FBI. Even 10 years ago when I moved to Monaco, there was a Cadillac Escalade with VA license plates that crossed my path twice and I shat myself (Paranoia was my illness for more than 10 years after my incarceration).

Next stop is mine, but we are still in North Carolina when the bus stops for good. I look at the marshal and tell him it can't be right. I need to be in court in 57 hours in VA. He says they have to stop driving before sundown, and that is where my journey ends with this bus, and they will probably have me spend the night at this county jail and send for me tomorrow with another prisoner convoy.

I'm dropped off at the R&D of this North Carolina county jail. I'm nervous. My anxiety is running high. My heart is beating so fast I can hear it pounding in my head. I know I'm going to have to be processed again. Yup, first I'm sitting on a metal bench in a holding cell and some hick officer comes to get me after hours of sitting there, still shackled and handcuffed. I'm walking slow because my shackles hurt my ankles so bad. He turns around and tells me to make less noise. It's past 11pm and inmates are sleeping. I lose track of time during these transfers. We get picked up at 4 am and end up arriving at the next county jails and waiting to be processed in cold concrete cells with metal doors and no sight of daylight or even artificial lights.

Each time you hear their steel toes approaching and the keys clanking, you feel hope this is for you, to advance in the process. Not sure what process though.

The hick gets annoyed with me. My shackles are noisy. I can't help it they are so heavy and long how am I supposed to do this?

He fingerprints me, and he gets annoyed again. His digital system is glitchy and he can't get my thumb print. Each time each print is green and then the thumb is red and the whole hand comes out red, and says "Failed, try again." He grabs my finger and crushes it hard on the reader and he hurts me. I'm in a foul mood. I'm thinking of saying something, but then I remember what Russia said: "Dis people, they all want to trip you so you don't go home."

She often said to me, don't forget you are doing time but you are gonna go home. The officers they do time with us, but they never go home until they retire. That's why they are motherfuckers and jealous of you.

A female CO comes to get me to get disinfected. Excuse me? What the fuck does that mean?

"Take off your clothes and put it in the garbage bag here." I take off my clothes and I keep my disposable bra and panties on and cross my arms in front of my chest. I'm cold. I'm so tired. I'm not hungry but I know I should eat because I feel like I could faint. I feel dizzy.

"Take off your clothes, I said."

I look at her and I ask, "Why? Why do you need me to take off my panties? I won my appeal I'm going to Virginia to be released, technically I shouldn't even be an inmate right now."

She gets angry. She grabs a sort of hose and tells me she will put me in the hole and I'll miss my transfer if I don't comply. I take off my panties and my bra, and I put one hand in front of my privates and my other arm across my chest.

"Spread your legs wide open and your arms!"

God, if you exist: FUCK YOU!

She sprays me with something that smells like pesticide and tells me to close my eyes and my mouth. She says we don't need your lice and your bacteria here. She wets me with that cold smelly spray from head to toe, including my hair, and has me bend over to spray me between my legs. I feel the liquid enter my vaginal labia, and it burns. My eyes are burning, too.

"You will shower tomorrow. There is no shower at this time. Its' lights out for inmates." She gives me this county jail's uniform and tells me to reuse the disposable panties and bra I came with. She doesn't hand me a towel or anything. I have to let that horrible liquid dry off of me. The uniform is one FUCKING BIG JOKE! It's the cliché of prison wear, a Halloween costume: an oversized pants and blouse set with black and white stripes. Is this a joke? I put it on and feel relief for the rough fabric drying the pesticide off my skin. I start feeling rashes all over my face, my neck, and other parts of my body.

I'm wearing a huge, stripped prison uniform. I feel like a holocaust prisoner. I'm thinking, "So this is what they felt like?" Then, I shake it off and think I'm lucky I'm not being beat up or killed. Although, I did get gassed with a toxic spray.

She leads me to my cell, six bunk beds in one tiny cell, and five inmates in bed, none of which turn around to look at me. She tells me to take the top bunk in the middle, and sleep on the naked mattress because there was no laundry services to give me a sheet at this time.

I climb on the bed and the woman next to me on the next bunk turns around to look at me. "Hablas Español?" I nod. She tells me my face is on fire, that I look very red. She goes down her bed's ladder, quietly rummages through some belongings and comes back on her bed with a small bottle that looks like hand sanitizer. "Ponte lo ahora es aloe," she said. It's aloe vera. She said many of them got the rashes, too, when they arrived from the "pinche docha" (the fucking shower is how they referred to the disinfecting spray).

I felt all kinds of disgusting, the pesticide dripping from my wet curly hair mixed with the stench of my body from the day's travels, that weird sweat smell I got during these transfers that I had never smelled before, not on me and not on anybody else. The fear hormone sweat. It smells so bad, and I can still smell it as I write about it now.

The big artificial blinding lights are turned on at 5 am. I may have dosed off for 20 minutes in all. We have to get up and come to the cell's door for breakfast. They give us a sandwich and apple sauce. I don't eat the sandwich. I eat the apple sauce to avoid fainting.

I don't know what time it is, but I'm scared. No one is coming for me yet, and time is passing. It feels like hours, and no one in the cell knows what time it is. One of the inmates thinks it's noon. From my calculations, North Carolina to Virginia shouldn't take more than 4 hours. The day passed, as I sat on my bare, disgusting mattress, probably infested with bed bugs, and waited. I passed the time talking to the inmates who would talk to me. They were nice. One of the women on a lower bunk was rumored to be from one of Los Angeles' most dangerous gangs and going back to court to testify against her boyfriend, the head of the gang, In exchange, she will be deported back to a Dominican jail where she would probably be killed for being a rat.

The Dominicana telling me this swears she recognizes her and knows exactly why she is being transferred. My bunkie is waiting in this county jail to be deported back to Peru, after serving a nine-year sentence for conspiracy and a gun charge. So this county jail was also a deportation center. This all sounded so scary to me. Was I lied to? Maybe I wasn't going back to be released. No one seemed to be in this county jail or the one before to be released. Maybe I'm just delusional and like the rest of them my next stop is another hell hole.

Dinner is served. I'm crying my eyes out. They haven't come for me with less than 48 hours to my court date. Sun is going to go down, and they don't transport prisoners after sunset. They served dinner at 5pm.

Ten minutes later, they come to the door and call my name. I'm escorted out and processed out. They tell me to change into a new orange jumpsuit that says DOC on the back, and Federal Inmate on the right chest pocket. They put my federal ID in that pocket, the only belonging that I have had with me since I left Danbury. I'm still wearing the espadrilles. They shackle me, handcuff me, chain me, and take me out of the facility. I hear that buzzing sound of the doors again, and heavy lock sounds behind me.

"Are we going to Virginia?" I ask the marshal.

"I'm not your tour guide," he replies. "I'm just following orders." I wish JR had come for me, at least he treated me like a human being, and he was kind. I tell the marshal, "I'm supposed to go to Virginia to be released. I'm remanded to my judge after winning my appeal." He says, "Sure, you are, but here, you are an inmate."

I am alone with him and a female marshal who doesn't talk to me once in the van. My shackles hurt. I notice my socks lost their elasticity and keep sliding down, letting the shackle press against my skin and my ankle bone. My ankles are black and blue, and the blisters started popping out again. I was still full of rashes all over my body and my face, even my scalp from the "pinch docha" the pesticide shower. The ride feels long, but it takes about three hours. It's dark out when we pass state lines and I see the "Welcome to Virginia" sign. My heart feels so happy. I start crying, tears of relief, tears of hope. I thank the God I don't believe in anymore. I whisper to my kids, "Mama is coming home, babies" as I feel my salty tears on my lips. Through the blur of the tears, I see us pulling up in front of a huge super modern building "ALEXANDRIA CITY JAIL". I'm exactly where I'm supposed to be, near the US District Court for the Eastern District of VA, where the judge who sent me to prison for four years will officially overturn my sentence and release me after one year in federal custody.

The marshals bring me and my file to the front desk. They remove my shackles and chains, and once again, I'm put in a holding cell. It's a cold concrete cell, but it looks brand new. The doors open electronically. This building is state of the art.

An officer comes in and throws a green plastic mattress on the floor, telling me it's for spending the night. I'm wondering if they are going to let me go in front of the judge smelling like sweat and pesticide. He comes back and takes me to be processed. Once again, he takes my mug shot, he too struggles with my fingerprints on his state of art reader. Each time their computers read my finger prints, they all do the same thing: stare blankly at their screen, which probably delivers my rap sheet in disbelief (because they realize the dangerous offender in front of them is a mom who sold jeans from her suburban kitchen in NY). They stare at me and smile. He is nice, so I ask him if I can speak to my lawyer. He hands me the phone and dials the number for my lawyer. "Ingrid? Are you in Alexandria?"

"Alan, it's so good to hear you. I got so scared. Yes, I'm here in Alexandria."

Alan is charismatic, strong, and reassuring. I have never met him in person, but I know all about him. He was a sort of superhero inmates talked about in Danbury. My friend, Jessica, used him for her sentencing and she only got one year. He says, "Your sister, Corine, flew in from France, your brother Gilbert flew in from Miami, and Joe is arriving tomorrow morning for court. Do you need me to tell Corine anything? We are going to try and get her and Gilbert in to see you after you and I meet and prep for court."

I was crying tears of hope and relief. "Thank you, Alan. Thank you. Please, can you ask the jail to get me lotion? I have a very red and painful rash all over my body and face from being sprayed with pesticide in North Carolina."

Silence...he says nothing, but I can hear him breathing heavy. "What? You were sprayed with pesticide? Kid, I'm so sorry for everything you are going through. This is so fucking unbelievable. What lotion do you want? Corine will drop it off for you, and I'm going to try and get it in there for you."

I asked him when I could see my big sister (Corine, my angel on earth, 17 years older than me). My mother figure even though I do have a mother. Corine was the soft and kind love and care in my life since I was born. My mom was colder. I longed to see her, and I wanted to see Gilbert too. The man who sacrificed his whole year to finding ways to get me out. They made me feel safe.

I spent the night alone in the dark, empty cell. I laid all night on the green plastic mat ... counting the hours. Waiting for footsteps and keys to walk by. My back was hurting so bad from these past three weeks in transfer, in concrete cells, laying on hard floors, sitting in beat up buses and vans, shackled and chained with heavy chains. My skin was burning, all over. I didn't know what it looked like because it was too dark and I hadn't seen my own face in three weeks. There are no mirrors in county. It smelled like urine since I laid next to the nasty metal toilet bowl that never gets cleaned.

Finally, a guard came for me and took me to an official's office. I guess that was the city jail counselor. I had to go through the whole processing all over, discuss my crime, my procedure etc. How many fucking times do federal facilities have to put all this shit into their system? Don't they have better things to do to keep the country safe?

"Alright, I'm going to put you into Unit B. It's a good unit, and you will get a cell to yourself there. You can shower. Here are some toiletries, and tomorrow morning the marshal will come to get you to bring you to court."

Well, HALLE-FUCKING-LUYAH !

This facility is very state of the art: secure elevators, electronically activated doors, computerized walls on the corridors. I get to my unit (it's all indoors in the building I arrived at the day before). There is a common room, and it's so far nicer and cleaner than any jail and prison I've been at in the past year. I'm a little scared. It's always scary to be the new kid, but these county jail settings are actually safer than federal prison or holding cells.

Alexandria City Jail (my unit looked exactly like this one)

Photo credits: BOP

Everyone here is waiting for their arraignment or their trial. I hate to notice that I'm basically the one of two white females. Every single other inmate is black or Hispanic. This speaks to how people of color are not given a chance at justice. Their attorneys are court appointed (Get this: Court appointed that basically means they work for the court). These attorneys are pro-bono; they don't have time or money to invest in going to trial, and they encourage all of them to plead guilty for a shorter sentence. They are told that, because of their socio-economic profile and race, a jury is more likely to come back with a guilty verdict and automatically a maximum sentence. All these black and Hispanic women in this unit are most likely going to do time, some of them for crimes they didn't commit. Others are going to do hard time for a crime that didn't fit the time. One of the inmates is told to show me to my cell, on the top floor of this unit.

She explains that I have to be in there at 9:30 pm and at 10 pm the door will lock automatically. The officer already instructed me about the next day. At 6 am my door (and only my door) will open. I should get out and wait downstairs in front of the general armed door to be transferred to the courthouse.

I was almost home, I hoped. I prayed to no particular god. My own god wasn't my god anymore. I didn't believe in him anymore.

I asked my chaperon if I could shower because I felt filthy and smelly. She said yes. I asked if I could get a razor to shave my legs. She said only in the morning before court the officer will give you a razor, and after the shower, you will have to return it.

I went to shower. It had been days since I was able to shower. I still smelled like pesticide, and my rash wasn't better. I washed my hair. I scrubbed my burning body, and I changed into the beige DOC uniform. I went into the common room, where inmates were playing cards. No one was scary. No one bothered me. I grabbed a book, and I sat. It was the first time in a long time I didn't feel scared.

They came to get me. My lawyer was here to prep me for court... I was going to see a non-law enforcement human for the first time. They brought me to the visiting area, all still very clean modern and state of the art, and took me to a private room. He was there, Alan, with his eccentric cowboy hat. Chubby, charismatic, and warm, he embraced me softly. "Hi, kid, how are you? You've been through a lot, but hopefully it all ends tomorrow."

He explains that we will be given the choice to get a re-trial. Wait ... why? My sentence was overturned and remanded to the judge. Why can't he just let me go?

"It doesn't work like that," he says. "You won your appeal because the judge violated your rights and made erroneous instructions to the jury. He also didn't apply the adequate guidelines according to your circumstances when he sentenced you. But you know the government, they don't like to admit they are wrong. So we asked for a re-sentencing instead of a re-trial." It made no sense. I was exonerated and remanded... Well, federal procedure makes no sense. Let's leave it at that. So what Allan was prepping me for was to tell the judge how I was a mother of 3 children, one of which had a severe disability that worsened as a result of my incarceration. He wanted me to say I did not belong in prison for four years and this is why the circuit court overturned my sentence. Now we had to convince the judge to honor the circuit court recommendation and give me time served. He said my judge was appointed by Reagan. He was 80 years old and had been on the bench for decades, and I was the first overturned case he ever had. His career was taking a hit. We didn't want him to be overzealous and revengeful. We had to be humble and plead for mercy.

I was so confused. This was a punch in the face. I had to plead for mercy from a judge who erroneously sent me to prison for 4 years, after winning my appeal? He won't apologize even? NO. The federal government is never wrong; they never apologize.

Alan coached me and helped me prepare my statement. I had to address the monster who separated me from my children for a crime I didn't commit. I made mistakes in that business I will always own up to that, but none of that should be prosecuted to the full extent of the law, and beyond.

I want you to understand I was sentenced to 48 months in prison, and that is more than a child rapist gets in the same district. I sold jeans... denim pants (and they were

135

determined even by the feds as being authentic not counterfeit as they had hoped).

Alan made me feel almost confident that nothing will go wrong, and as agreed with the prosecutor who lost my appeal, I would be released with time served.

I took my statement with me, and Dylan's latest medical file and cognitive assessment so I could read it in my cell that night. Alan said he was working on getting Corine and Gilbert approved on my visitor's list so I could see them that afternoon.

He did, and later that day I was escorted to visiting. The guard was kind, she said, "Your beautiful family is here for you, and they are very excited to see you. They told me you haven't seen each other in a long time. You have 30 minutes because visiting is already closed, but we heard your sister came from Paris, so you got a special authorization. Paris… Wow—it's so fancy. Is that where you are from?" From this day, I never ever felt American ever again and felt proudly French in my core.

"Yes, I am French."

I got into the visiting area and it wasn't how I expected. I expected to sit at a table with them. Instead, it was a booth with a huge glass partition and a phone to talk to my visitors. They weren't on the other side, yet. The guard said, "I'm going to go let them in, wait here and when you see them, pick up the phone to talk to them."

I started crying. I was nervous. I didn't know how much I had changed. I weighted 75 lbs. I had cut my light blonde hair in a short bob, and I had cried every tear in my body, so much so that I had lost most of my lashes. I had a rash all over. I was 32 years old and I felt 100.

The door on the other side of the glass window opened, and I first saw Corine, her beautiful face, her petite frame, her luscious auburn hair. She looked me straight in the eyes with her tired worried eyes as I cried and cried. I could see she was holding back tears and trying to be strong. Then I looked behind her at Gilbert. He had grown a beard that had become grey. His hair had, too. He looked smaller and older than I remembered him. I aged him… my sentence aged him. He used to tell me on the phone, "You are inside doing time and I'm outside doing time with you. You don't eat, I don't eat. You don't smile, I don't smile. I will not be free until you are home."

He wasn't lying. I saw it in his face. He wore the whole past year on his face and carried the weight on his shoulders. They stood across from me…and before we picked up the phones, they both tried to calm me down with soft eyes and whispers I could make out by reading their lips. My sister put her hand on the window… her beautiful hand. I remember looking at her nails. She had a beautiful French manicure that was the prettiest thing I had seen in a long time. I put my hand against hers on the window. We have the same hands exactly. It fit perfectly. I cried some more. We spoke on the phone: my brother first because he was in charge of my whole legal team. Alan was not all … there was my appellate attorney, my Virginia attorney, and a few others.

"I spoke to Alan, and he says you should be out after the hearing tomorrow. Do what he says, and it will be fine. We are taking you home. Hold on just one more day."

He started to cry. There is nothing worse than to see a grown man, a father figure cry. My sister then took the phone. I heard her melodious voice for the first time in a while. "You look so young. You look like you are 16 years old. I feel like I'm seeing you again when you were a teenager. Prison preserved you," she jokes.

She was concerned about my rash. I explained what happened with the pesticide shower in North Carolina. She was alarmed. She said she brought me lotion, but they aren't allowing it. She also tells me she brought me a bag for tomorrow which she will bring to court. She smiled as she said she got me my favorite La Mer Creme, my perfume. She bought me nice lingerie, jBrand jeans, two cashmere sweaters and Chanel flats so I could change when I'm released. That sounded surreal and like it wouldn't happen. Thirty minutes flew by. They said they were staying at the hotel, near where I stayed at when I came for my trial, and that they would see me in court tomorrow. I cried when they left. I watched them being taken out of their side of the visiting area and waited for the guard to come get me.

The guard came for me 15 minutes later, and she was the one who escorted them out. She takes me back to my unit.

"You look like your sister. Was that your husband? He is handsome and your sister is beautiful." I told her that was my brother. She wished me good luck for tomorrow. I went to my cell and sat on the bed. My cell was so modern and clean; it was almost nice. I even had a window (it was on a high floor of that huge building). That window was a long thin rectangle a body couldn't fit through (well, I had lost so much weight my body probably could), with a skyline view of Alexandria. You could even see the roof of the courthouse I would be released from the next day. I looked at that roof all night. I couldn't sleep.

At 9:30 pm, I pulled the heavy door of my cell and waited to hear it lock electronically at 10 pm.

I grabbed Dylan's medical file and psychological evaluation Alan had left with me and I started to read it. My whole world collapsed. Dylan's evaluations had never been worst. Dr. Sissy McCarton, the woman who ultimately believed she could cure autism and did for Dylan, conducted the evaluation, as well as another two cognitive specialists and his child psychologist, Dr. Stephen Billick. They all agreed Dylan was on the worst debilitative state of the spectrum, and in the past year, the behavioral, special education, occupational therapies that once helped and improved his disorder have become useless. He has gone into a regressive state, with impairments more severe and extensive. The report stated that this childhood disintegrative disorder will generally have the worst outcome possible for a child with ASD like Dylan. Everything we had done to heal him had been undone and worsened. Dylan could no longer go to the bathroom independently as he had before, his motor skills for tasks as simple as going up and down the stairs had worsened into full-fledged impairment. His chronic stomach pains were more pronounced than ever. Dylan was 10 years old at that time. The report assessed that he had the developmental cognitive behavior and mental development of a four-year-old child. After eight years of intensive therapies and incredibly promising progress that enabled Dylan to go to a regular school in a smaller special education setting, Dylan was back to having the mind of a child, and it was all my fault. I blamed myself... The 4th district judges blamed the judge who sent me to prison for his complete disregard of Dylan's condition when setting my sentencing guidelines.

I collapsed and cried, alone in my cell. My beautiful little boy was hurting; he will never be normal and will never grow into a normal functioning adult. I spent the night crying and hoping. I kept looking at the Alexandria skyline, the lights and the roofs. It was the first time in a year I had a view of civilization, of city lights and buildings. It was nice. I learned my statement by heart. I threw Dylan's evaluation in the small bin, and I waited for the sun to come up. It was a new day. I hoped for the best but prepared for the worst.

The same cell as my cell at Virginia City Jail (with that window view on the city)

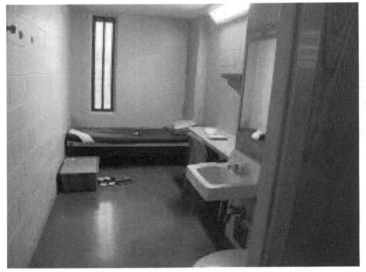

Photo credits: BOP

Chapter 16: Tell the World I'm Coming Home

It's D-Day. Today is the day. I hear my automatic door buzz open. They open it from a distance. I follow the instruction I was given. I got dressed quickly, used the disposable comb, brushed my hair, and brushed my teeth at the sink in my cell. I looked behind once and whispered, "I hope I never see this place again." I let myself out and went to wait by the general secured door. I'm led through the corridor, into the secured elevator, down to a secured parking lot, into an unmarked black SUV with federal government plates with two mean marshals. I didn't get to wear my own clothes or presentable clothing. I'm wearing an orange DOC jumpsuit. I look like a convict. I'm handcuffed shackled and chained still. I try to resist this.

"Officer, sir?" I ask. "I'm remanded back in front of the judge because my sentence was overturned, so why am I still shackled?"

He looks at me sternly. "You are still in federal custody as far as we are concerned. You are still a prisoner. When the judge says so, we will remove the chains and shackles."

We arrive at Alexandria's Southern District Courthouse. I don't recognize it because we go from a service parking lot in the back into the detention area. They bring me to yet another holding cell. This time it's a cell with bars. I can see the corridor that leads defendants into the courtroom.

The marshal tells me he will come to get me when it's my turn. I ask for my attorney, and he tells me I'll see him in the courtroom.

I'm nervous. My legs hurt. They feel like cotton, almost paralyzed. I'm afraid when they come for me I won't be able to walk.

He comes for me, removes my shackles and the chain around my waist, but he leaves the handcuffs on. My hands are sweaty and cold at the same time. My stomach hurts. I don't know for sure what is going to happen. He holds me by my elbow down the corridor. We wait in front of a door and wait till the door opens. The bailiff lets us into the huge courtroom, right behind the judge, to his right. There are people in the courtroom, probably waiting for their family member's case to be heard, their own arraignment, and on the side, there are inmates lined up in orange jumpsuits like mine and handcuffed, too. I see my attorneys sitting at the defense table. I look to the audience and find my sister, my brother, and Joe. I put my head down. I feel ashamed they get to see me handcuffed in an orange jumpsuit. My brother nods his head to tell me everything is going to be okay.

The marshal leads me to my attorneys and removes my handcuffs. He orders me to sit between my attorneys. I look over my shoulder and see the marshal is standing right behind me with his hand on his clog. Does this asshole really think I'm going to fucking murder everyone? I sold fucking jeans online!!!

My attorney leans over. "We have a victory," he says. "Your original prosecutor just stepped down. He accepted the defeat of your appeal. They sent a substitute who just told us he won't oppose your release. Make your statement, sound sorry, and you are going home."

I look over at the new prosecutor on the opposing table. I was terrified to see the horrible prosecutor who railroaded me and sent me to jail. To find out he stepped down from the district attorney's office because of my appeal was insanely reassuring and satisfying.

139

The bailiff finally called my docket number and name. The judge looked up from his file and stared at me as I got up on the lawyer's instructions. He read the appeal, the decision, and admitted his decision was overturned. He listed his judicial errors.

"This court erred in finding the defendant guilty on the count of [...]. This court erred in miscalculating the sentencing guideline range [...]. This court exercised a blatant disregard for the defendant's extenuating circumstances and the heavy burden carried by the defendant, mother of Dylan, a child with a debilitating aggravated disorder and her crucial role in the child's welfare. This court erred in admitting hearsay as evidence..."

My head was pounding, and the judge's voice that had been echoing in my head for the past 14 months was cradling me into a weird out of body experience. I felt like I was floating over my own orange draped body. His words sounded far away.

"Will the defendant address the court?"

My attorney gets up. "Yes, your honor, she will," he replies. I pray to no god in particular that my legs carry me through. I was led to the reading desk at the center of the courtroom in front of the microphone. I cleared my throat and addressed the court. I apologized for my lack of morals and diligence that led to victims not receiving their goods. I explained my motivation for conducting business with the desperation of a mother who acted with the sole purpose of funding her son's medical treatment.

"I understand the end didn't justify the means, and, for that, I am sorry," I said.

Dylan's doctors were in the courtroom (my legal team flew them in from New York) to speak to my moral character and deep devotion to my son's welfare and recovery, and to testify on the seriousness of Dylan's condition and the irreparable impact my absence has caused and will cause if I were to remain incarcerated.

Each doctor's testimony described their encounters with me since my early 20s, when I first found out Dylan's diagnosis. Dr. Billick said, "I've never seen a mother more in pain from her son's afflictions. I've never seen a mother more devoted than her. I've never met a mother more determined to help her child and alleviate his struggle. I have never seen a mother more desperate to find the treatment to fix him."

I cried through the testimonies. I cried through the enumeration of his pathology, his regressive behaviors and symptoms.

The judge mentioned he received hundreds of letters from my community and my peers speaking to my moral character. He is convinced he said that he erred in his judgment, and he then elaborated with a bunch of technical legal terms that were unbeknownst to me. So much so that when he finished, I had to turn to one of my lawyers and ask, "What did he decide? I didn't get that?"

"You are going home. You got time served with probation, on that one count of non-delivery of goods. You're going home, kiddo! Congratulations!"

The judge addressed me in a kind manner. He said he was sorry for the hurt this has caused my family, and he is convinced he will never see me in his courtroom again. He said I am to be processed and released from custody immediately. I cried, and my lawyers hugged me. I asked if I can go see my family and hug them and I could.

I turned around to meet Gilbert and Corine's eyes. They were crying too. The marshal only lets them come close to the front bench and touch my hands before he handcuffs me again to take me away. I rip my arm away from him and say, "Are you deaf? Didn't you hear the judge? I'm free."

He grabbed my arm violently, my sister watching in horror, and handcuffs me. "Until you are processed out, you are still in custody. I don't make the rules I enforce them."

My attorney tells me he is going to the clerk on the other side, to process me out and will meet me there. He will bring me my change of clothes. I'm brought back to the holding cell, and the marshal leaves me, saying someone will come get me when my discharge papers are completed. I could see through the opaque window/wall some shadows. I could hear my attorney's voice. But then, nothing. I'm looking at the time on the wall clock in the corridor: 45 minutes, then, 60 minutes.

"Excuse me! Anybody there?" I call out. An officer comes to see me. I ask him why I'm still here. He says my attorney is still there sorting things out. They will come see me with more information.

I started to freak out. Were other charges filed against me? What could they be? I had heard that sometimes after you serve a federal sentence, state charges are filed for the same crime and you need to serve state time. My anxiety got so bad I started to cry hysterically.

Three hours later, I'm still in custody in the courthouse's basement holding cell. A marshal comes in.

"Come on, give me your wrists. I need to cuff you," he says

"What? Why? What's going on? The judge released me, and my attorney is waiting for me, my sister, my husband."

"I'm following instructions. I'm taking you back to Alexandria City Jail, and your attorney will come and see you there."

I knew it! I knew this was too good to be true. I'm never ever going home.

*

We got back to Alexandria City Jail, and the front desk officer sees me.

"I thought you were being released today," he says. "I look at him.

"Me, too. Can I speak to my attorney?"

The marshal interrupts us and gives him my file open on a certain page, and the officer looks down at it.

"Okay, let me process you back in and then you can call your attorney."

Why aren't they telling me anything?

You know what's worse than doing four years in prison? Thinking you are being released in the next few minutes to find out you aren't.

The officer brings me to the phone booth near the holding cells and dials my

141

attorney's number. I'm dictating to him.

"Ingrid? Are you okay?"

"Alan, no. I'm not okay. What is going on?"

"Don't panic. I'm outside with your sister and your brother. We are still here. We encountered an issue with Homeland Security."

"What the fuck is Homeland Security?"

"It's ICE, Ingrid. They say they have an executive order to take you into custody because you have a French passport. They want you to accept being deported because the French government intervened diplomatically when you were first found guilty. There is a homeland security officer here to take you. Let them take you from federal custody, and we will figure it out when you get to the field office. Your brother is calling the French ambassador in Washington."

"But I'm American. My children are American, and we have never lived in France. They can't deport us just because I'm also French."

"Let me get off and call a friend of mine who is an immigration lawyer and knows people in Washington. I think we are caught up in a diplomatic conflict."

I am devastated. Anything bad that could happen will happen and does happen. How can an American be deported? And my sentence was overturned... I spent the night on the floor in the cold, dark concrete holding cell.

Homeland Security came for me the next morning, with two officers wearing those official wind breakers. One of them says he is my case officer. They handcuffed me this time but didn't shackle me. The Homeland Security SUV was taking us to the Virginia field office. He tells me not to worry and he would explain it all when we got there. We get to an office that looks like a Bob-the-Builder built in office. Men in uniforms sit at their desks, with some boardrooms with long tables and chairs. Everything is white and brand new. He sits me across from him at his desk and removes my handcuffs.

"Are you hungry? Thirsty?"

I shake my head. I need a shower. I stink again, and I haven't showered in 24 hours. I slept on a roach-infested floor, with my head near a toilet bowl that never gets cleaned. He asks me basic questions: date of birth, place of birth, mother's maiden name, children, and last addresses in the past seven years, known or unknown aliases. He takes my fingerprints. He tells me he has to make sure I am who they think I am.

"Who do you think I am?"

"Well, you tell me...we heard you are a French national with a recent French passport. We heard the French government got involved in your case, and the embassy intervened on a diplomatic level. We also heard that you got recurrent visits from the French consulate and embassies while in custody at FCI DANBURY."

"Do you think I am a spy?"

He laughs. "No, not at all. We are friends with France. But we know France tried to extradite you and executed a remote judgment that went against the judgement here in the US. We also have reports that France attempted to petition for a prisoner exchange in your behalf and would release you once you arrived in France if successful."

"This still doesn't entitle the USA to deport an American, does it?"

"Well, it could. Or you could just agree to be deported, and I would release you on your own recognizance, and you would self-deport to France within the next three months?"

So, if I agreed to self-deport, this asshole would let me out and give me three months to get out of this fucking country? Sign me up. Who the fuck wants to pledge alliance to this fucking hell hole after what they put me through. I knew better. I had to worry about my American children. I had to worry about Dylan's treatments and therapy. The children didn't speak French, and Dylan would never speak any other languages, according to his doctors' predictions.

He gets a phone call, and he hangs up and tells me, "Look, I am going to put you in that glass holding cell there. I'm going to move the other detainee to another area so you can be alone. I can't talk to you anymore because the ambassador of France is arriving here for you from Washington. We have to wait for our diplomatic team to arrive and for him, so you all can meet."

He puts me in the cell. It's all glass. He tells me I'm not really imprisoned. I can call him and he will come see me if I need anything. I sure felt imprisoned.

There is a phone in there I'm free to use. I call Gilbert.

"Hi. Call your lawyer. He will explain. I don't know what to say. Don't worry. The French government is looking into it."

I call home, and Joe picked up. "Joe? Why are you home? Aren't you waiting for my release?"

A cold silence greets me. "I had to come home to the kids, honey. I couldn't stay in Virginia; we didn't even know where they were taking you. It's classified information."

I cry. He cries. "Sorry, honey. I don't know what to say."   ·

"Joe, if I don't get released today, I'm going to accept the self-deport. I can't stay in custody anymore. I've suffered too much. I miss the kids. You will just bring them to France. We will move there."

He says, "Yes, of course."

I see a huge official commotion in the office, people standing up, and a group of suits walking through the office and into a board room. I'm trying to see if I recognize a French man. Richard, my case officer, comes to see me.

"Okay, so the officials are here," he whispers. "The ambassador of France just arrived from Washington, and he is asking to see you alone. Okay?"

But I smell so bad, I tell him. I am not presentable. Richard looks at me warmly. "I think this can actually help you," he says. "Don't worry."

He takes me into one of the empty board rooms, offers me some water and installs me at the table. He lets in this charismatic older French man in a suit, with a briefcase. I try to get up to greet him, but he holds my shoulder kindly.

"Please, sit down. You are exhausted," he says. "Do you speak French?"

"Oui," I say.

He waits for the officer to leave and to close the door. "Are you okay? Are they treating you well here? I want you to understand you are not their prisoner, if I wish, I can take you with me today."

I nod. He explains that I'm in a diplomatic pickle, and that the US is angry that the French government countered their executive muscles when I was first sentenced.

"Basically, they are saying, 'Since she claimed she was French to get out of doing the time, she can now go to France.' It's a spiteful diplomatic stunt. I am personally here today on President Sarkozy's behalf to negotiate your release with Homeland Security with diplomacy. Do you allow me to do this on your behalf?"

I say yes.

He asks that they not put me in a holding cell anymore and leave me in an office instead while he speaks to the officials. He leaves to go into that boardroom full of suits and emerges again 30 minutes later. He comes back to see me.

"Okay, I negotiated your release. They will release you as soon as I am back in Washington and have our Paris Foreign Affairs department send a diplomatic seal. It was nighttime in Paris already, so they would send it at 9 am Paris time (3 am here). They cannot keep you here. It is a field office, so they will arrange for you to spend the night and will release you as soon as they open in the morning."

He says, "Allez courage, c'est bientôt fini." Be brave; it's almost over.

The field office was closing at 6 pm, and my case Officer Richard explains, "There is no overnight holding cell here, so I have to drop you at the county jail that houses our temporary deportees. I will ask them to not put you in a cell and let you stay in a visitor waiting area overnight. There is no bed, but at least you will feel free. Or do you prefer a bed in a cell? Don't worry. You will still be released tomorrow." I shake my head. I prefer to sleep in the visitor's waiting room of the county jail.

He drops me off there, and he explains that I'm not really in custody, but that they have to keep an eye on me overnight until he gets the document from the embassy. He walks me into the visitor's area we got buzzed into. He apologizes I can't shower. He tells me I've free to wander around that large room. I can lay on the lined-up chairs to sleep. There are no visitors at night. He asks me if I want him to go get me Subway for dinner or KFC. I feel bad and I shake my head. He gives me 10 bucks and says I can use the vending machines. He will be back tomorrow. He turned out to be an angel, and I wanted to hug him. No one had been this nice to me in a long time.

I sat there on visitor's chairs, watching the TV screens hanging high up on the walls. I couldn't change the channels, but it will do. I went to the bathroom, washed my armpits with soap and water and dried off with toilet paper. I was afraid to be caught half-naked by a janitor or something. But I still washed myself as much as I could. I smelled so bad. Sleeping on the gross holding cells piss-infested floors, wearing polyester jumpsuits, going days without showering, and feeling extreme fear causes the smelliest body odor to erupt.

I felt better, and I went to the vending machines. I got M&MS, Twix, chips, and coffee. I had my feast, watched TV, and tried to sleep on the chairs. It was uncomfortable. I sat on the floor and tried to sleep sitting against the wall, but I couldn't. My back had been hurting for weeks since the first transfer. I felt the old aches of my corrected scoliosis creeping back up on me. Eventually, I dozed off, with the bright lights on and the 4 or 5 TVs at every corner of this large waiting area. The next day, he came to get me before the county jail opened to visitors. He stopped at Dunkin' Donuts and got me coffee and a donut. I ate it in grateful silence.

He put me in the holding cell, but he left the door open and told me I could get out. At 10 am, he came to see me, and asked if I can call my husband to see if he is here. Joe had flown in to bring me home. Richard insisted Joe come on in and bring me a change of clothes. Joe was outside, and he said, "Sign your discharge papers and come out. I'm in the taxi and we need to get back to NY immediately. Today is Shabbat."

Was he nuts? I couldn't give a shit about Shabbat. Richard calls him, "Listen, buddy, your wife is wearing an orange jumpsuit. If she comes out of the building this way, she will cause a panic and will probably get arrested on suspicions of being an escaped inmate. For her safety, I cannot release her without her change of clothes."

I'm so grateful for this angel of a man. He comments on my husband being a bit of a dick. I agree.

"It's a big day for you. You are flying home after a year and a long ordeal. Don't let him ruin it for you. When he comes in, I will bring you the bag. You go into the bathroom, change and throw the uniform and espadrilles in the garbage in there. Then, I will walk you out of the building."

They buzzed Joe in. He gave me a weird dismissive pressed embrace and handed me the Sonya Rikyel duffle bag Corine had originally prepared for me.

"Hurry up," he says. "You could change in the taxi." I refused.

I went into the bathroom, got naked, and changed into the clothes Corine has bought for me. I used the deodorant, put my perfume on, and brushed my hair. Joe kept knocking.

"Hurry up, honey. We have a plane to catch. I need to be home for Shabbat." I didn't care. I felt stressed, but I still found the Chanel Glossimer lip gloss she left for me, and I smacked it on my lips. I put the Chanel ballerina shoes on and I opened the door. Joe and Richard were waiting for me.

"Where is the uniform?" Richard asked.

"I threw it out since you told me to. I threw out my inmate federal ID card, too." He smiled and said he would go get it and destroy it. He walked us out of the secure building. I shook his hand and thanked him from the bottom of my heart for his kindness.

Joe didn't even show emotion: no happiness, no hug. He was running on the street, trying to hail a cab and telling me, "Don't you want to get the fuck out here?" I did, but I was 30 lbs underweight, weak and felt like my legs couldn't carry me.

We got into the cab, and I asked if he called the kids. He said he decided not to tell the kids anything because the kids got disappointed and devastated so many times that they stopped believing I was coming home. He said that after court, when he came home without me, Savannah was inconsolable and cried herself to sleep. He said we will call them when the plane lands. His phone kept ringing. He answered and spoke some weird words in Hebrew, like some weird sect-like thing. And he said, "Yes, she is coming home."

He kept saying we need to land before sundown, or it will be Shabbat and he can't drive on Shabbat.

That is not how I imagine my first steps outside as a free woman. I can always count on Joe to make a beautiful moment into a horrible one for the sake of religion.

Before we arrive at the airport, he digs into his pocket and takes out my diamond wedding band, my huge engagement diamond ring, and the diamond Rolex watch he gave me as a push gift when savannah was born. He also brought my Blackberry. He hadn't turned it on in one year. I turned it on and looked at my voicemails. I found voicemails from Savannah from a year ago on the night I turned myself in and the next day. I listened: "Mommy, where are you? Come home! I need you!"

"Mama? Are you coming home? Dad says you will soon, but not now. I don't believe him. I hate him. I love you, Mama! Call me, please!"

I started to cry. It was overwhelming... I didn't feel relief or happiness yet. I felt anxiety.

We arrived at the airport. Joe went to the Jet Blue counter and bought my return ticket (this asshole didn't believe I was coming home until I was in the cab with him). He gave me money to go buy some magazines (I used to love reading tabloids on Shabbat). I bought *Hello, Star,* and *In Touch* magazine, some M&M's, and walked back to the Jet Blue counter. I kept looking over my shoulder, scared. I felt people were staring at me like they knew where I had been. I kept looking at my thin fingers, wearing shiny diamonds that felt so heavy. I kept looking at my legs in those skinny jeans. I was so thin.

We went through security, and I was scared. I knew TSA wasn't law enforcement, but the sight of uniforms petrified me. We boarded the plane. "Welcome onboard Jet Blue flight to NY JFK airport. Please, fasten your seat belts..."

I looked at my phone and called home, but it went to voicemail.

We landed in NY 10 minutes before Shabbat, and Joe was furious. He drove home to Rockaway, furious to be missing candle lighting time. He robbed me of that important moment I was going through called freedom. He pulled up in the driveway of our massive beach home. Everything looked bigger than I remembered. We went to the kitchen back door, a French door. I saw Savannah half-dressed in her hello kitty pajamas. The nanny Bertha came running to the door to let me in. It was like she just saw a ghost, and Savannah ran away.

146

I went into my kitchen and smelled the weird smell of home. Joe called Savannah back. She came back, running, and jumped into my arms, and then she quickly moved away she got scared.

"Mama, you are so thin. I feel like I was going to break you." I reassured her and hugged her so tight. I cried. Bertha brought Dakota. She was still a baby, but she screamed, "Mommmy!" I grabbed her, and I smelled her. I held her. Dylan took longer. He stood in the hallway, watching us. Then finally, he came to hug me. I held him tight. He asked if I brought him gift. I hadn't. I felt bad. I knew Dylan didn't realize the situation.

Joe went to get ready for the synagogue. He said I don't have to do anything, and he cooked dinner and got a cake in case I was coming home. My kids had stopped hoping I would come home. I asked Savannah recently why she ran away when she saw me. She said, "I wasn't ready. I had just hung up with Uncle Gilbert, and he wouldn't confirm that you are coming home. We expected you two days ago, and Dad came back without you. I was yelling at Bertha when you appeared at the door: 'Is she coming or not! I need to know!' I had lost hope, Mom. I had just lost hope."

I looked around my house, like I was a visitor intruding on a family's life. Savannah followed me everywhere. I went up to my room and I saw Dakota's baby crib was still there and messy like she had just slept in it. I went into my custom walk-in closet and saw nothing had moved. My Louboutin collection, my Birkins, my color-coded wardrobe still hung on my satin hangers. My accessories, everything was there exactly as I had left it. I told Savannah I needed to shower because I didn't smell good. She agreed, and till today, she tells me how weird I smelled when she used to visit me in Danbury. Till today, she and I are haunted by certain smells that trigger some bad memories of our time in prison. Savannah, she did jail time with me.

She stood there waiting for me to get undressed. I told her to wait outside. I didn't want her to see my skeletal body, my rib cage protruding drastically, and scare her. I needed to gain weight. I looked awful. She sat outside the bathroom and waited for me patiently. I will never forget this moment in the shower. I cried and I laughed. I couldn't believe what I had been through, and I couldn't believe I was home.

Chapter 17: How to Make Lemonade
When life gives you lemons, you make lemonade...
And life sure gave me a lot of Lemons.
Here is my Lemonade Recipe:

Since my time in prison, I have lived my life by a Murphy's Law thought process: Everything that can go wrong will go wrong. And it did for me for a very long time after I was released from prison. Granted, I didn't make the best choices along the way, but still.

You see winning an appeal and having a federal conviction overturned is not great. You make enemies out of powerful people who aren't used to losing and tarnish their impeccable career with a track record of sending innocent people to jail or handing out long sentences to moms for petty crimes. My case should have been a few small court cases from customers who didn't get their orders. Instead, the Commonwealth state of Virginia decided to make a federal case out of it and make it Internet fraud case law. That didn't turn out too well for them, and they made sure I would eat shit as a result.

The judge didn't just let me walk out a free innocent woman, no. I would have had to accept being remanded to trial and go through the financial burden and ordeal of going through a trial all over again. My house was already mortgaged twice, and Joe had taken a hefty credit line to keep paying my legal fees. When my mom refused to keep contributing to my legal expenses, my brother Gilbert paid some more. This case had been extremely financially and emotionally taxing on all of us. I couldn't put us through that again because we couldn't afford it. That meant accepting the judge's half-assed apology and reversed verdict and ending up with probation. Because I had dual citizenship, this made me a flight risk.

America couldn't fucking make up its mind. They tried to arm-wrestle me into self-deporting my American ass to France, but then they took every single measure to prevent me from leaving the country when I got out of prison. I went home after 14 months of incarceration, and it was a Friday. On Monday, I had to report to my probation officer in Manhattan.

That first night at home was difficult. Joe's brothers came over for Shabbat dinner, and I sat like a guest at my own table. They were great throughout this whole ordeal. They were lovely to the kids. They sheltered them from the harsh truth. Bobby, the sergeant in the NYPD, would go pick them up every Friday afternoon and take them to Toys R Us to pick out a toy. The brother-in-law I liked the least (he was a douchebag to me and my brothers, and he called them "French Frogs") Eyal (we called him Yali, but he also called himself Jimmy because an American name is so much easier when you try to act like a badass in Brooklyn) was good to the kids, though. He picked them up from school and took them for ice cream often. For that one year, these three men raised my children, and they did a great job. They preserved their innocence as much as they could. They reassured them that I would come home soon, and they told the kids I was a wonderful strong woman. I owe them for that.

So we are all sitting at Shabbat dinner, and they were happy to see me, greeting me in the warmest way, but I guess the mantra was not to talk about the pink elephant in the room. Yali was engaged to a girl named Marlene I never met but heard was so pretty and from a good Jewish Syrian family. Bobby was still dating a lovely mom of two, Erika, who I really liked. We talked about nothing in particular. Bertha helped Joe serve the food. It was the first time I sat at my dining room table and didn't get up to serve.

I sat there eating Shabbat food I hadn't eaten in a year. They all said they had missed my cooking and how much they loved it. I smiled a little, but I was in deep shock. It is not a big party when you come home. It's painful in many ways, and it's scary too. You don't really know if any aspects of your life are still the same. All I knew was: I was with my kids, and that is all that mattered.

I made the decision that night to not be a victim. I made the decision to act as though I had never left and not to go to therapy or take meds to sleep.

I hadn't slept in 14 months. That night, I slept on and off, awakened at night count times (when CO's would come into our cell units and count us). I would jump out of my sleep that night, thinking I heard the guard's steel-toed footsteps coming near me. I felt I was awakened by the blinding light of his flashlight, and I heard keys all night. I saw faces from Danbury. I was haunted by that one guard I hated so much. For years to come I saw him in my sleep and I also saw him on the streets. I used to call him the Nazi. C.O Hayden was the one in visiting who heartlessly used to tell Joe to rip Dakota out of my arms and used to get a kick out of terminating my visiting hours 15 minutes before the actual time.

That first night in my bed, in my beautiful house on the Far Rockaway Beach front, I kept waking up thinking I was in my prison bed, in my cubicle, with my murderer bunkie shaking the bed each time she twisted and turned her 400 lbs body in her sleep.

I still hate the night, and to today, I hate sleeping. The nightmares and night sweats continued till I met Gil (my husband today).

I woke up the next day, went down to the kitchen, and made my kids breakfast. I had held myself back from sleeping with them and holding on to them all night. I wanted to give them a sense of normalcy. I went and laid in bed with Savannah while she was my little angel sleeping, and I caressed her hair that smelled like strawberries. I smelled her for a moment. She was sharing the large bedroom with Dylan... I then went and laid down in bed with Dylan. My special beautiful boy. I touched his cheeks. He had my dad's cheeks. I smelled him too; smelling my children had become obsessive for me when they would come and visit me. I closed my eyes and smelled them and smelled them. I kissed him softly and whispered, "I'm sorry, baby. Mommy is going to fix you."

I got up and went to see Dakota in her crib, my toddler. I missed so many

149

important moments of her childhood. In that one year, she learned how to walk, grew teeth, and started to potty train. She always slept in this adorable position, laying on her knees, holding her head down on her right cheek with her butt in the air. I touched her head softly. She woke up. She turned around and looked at me with those big brown beautiful eyes she still has today. "Mama? I want baba."

Baba was her bottle. I took her in my frail arms, and she held on tight like she did in visiting, and we went down to the kitchen. She smelled like baby lotion Mustela, and it brought back a rush of memories, from the day she was born till the day I kissed her goodbye and surrendered to prison. I also whispered in her ear, "I'm sorry, baby. I'm sorry. Mama is here now."

I was so sorry. I am still sorry for what my children endured. I'm still sorry for what they have had to endure since. The judgment of others, the insults of having a mother who is an ex-convict, my own anxieties and neurosis they have had to tolerate...

The next day was Sunday. We went to Soho for our usual Sunday stroll, like a year had not even passed. Like I never left. We went to downtown Cipriani for our usual Sunday brunch. Joe didn't eat; he never did. It wasn't kosher. He just ordered a Diet Coke. I kept looking around, worried that we would see people I knew, and that they knew where I had been. We did meet a few, and I'm sure they knew where I had been. But no one looked at me weird, no one judged me, no one made me feel unwelcome. That was NY! New York is forgiving. NY is all for second chances. NY was my home. We walked around Soho. It was our traditional Sunday stroll, and I went to Sephora on Broadway and bought some makeup. We went to Daffy's (the bargain for millionaires was that store's slogan) and bought some designer clothes at a portion of the price. For a second it felt like I had never left. I felt happy and free... and then within seconds, I would get scared. Scared the feds would change their minds and come for me again. Scared my kids would be taken away. Scared this wasn't going to last. It couldn't be that, just like that, my pain and suffering ended. It couldn't be.

Monday, I took the kids to school. I was nervous I wouldn't know how to drive anymore. I was afraid I would crash my big Range Rover. I didn't. I drove the kids to school as though I had never gone away. They were going to Magen David Yeshiva in Brooklyn. I ventured onto Ocean Parkway, nervously. It is a close-knit Jewish Syrian community we belonged to. People knew my car, and you couldn't miss my platinum blonde hair and dark sunglasses either. Not too many women fit my description in Flatbush back then.

I'm sitting at the light on Ocean Parkway and Avenue Z, and I looked at the car next to me, and I see him. I am slightly behind him, so unless he really turned his head over his shoulder, he wouldn't notice me. I prayed he didn't and I prayed for the light to turn green. It turned green, and my lane was moving faster. I zoomed through really quickly, hiding behind my hair. I was shaking. I wasn't ready to see anyone. I wasn't ready to explain where I had been. My own best friend, Valerie, hadn't been told. Prison was so taboo back then. I was so ashamed and also so sure I would come home within a few days, perhaps no one would have noticed I was gone.

Of course, Valerie did notice. She kept calling Joe and he kept lying to her, telling her I was in France with my mother. She knew better. She knew how I couldn't breathe without my kids. She threatened to go to the police. She knew my relationship with Joe was often strained, and she knew his dad had a history of beating up his mother. She truly believed he had killed me and buried me in our backyard. He told her to fuck off. Then, of course, eventually she found out. That Syrian Jewish community was amazing to my children. The whole school body was aware of where I was. They treated the kids with so much warmth and sheltered them from scrutiny and hurt that whole year. The community can be a real bitch, but in the light of tragedy (and a mother being taken away from the kids is tragic to them) they unite. I've never felt more supported than I did when I came home. I didn't get any dirty looks; I didn't catch any nasty chatters at carpool. As a matter of fact, I was told that that our Jewish congregation prayed for my release every Shabbat without ever gossiping about my situation.

I arrived at Magen David that Monday morning, looking like my old self in my Moncler puff jacket, my Chanel classic flap bag, my cute leggings, my black tall Uggs, wearing my big Tom Ford black sunglasses. I got the kids out of the car and held their hands tight as I did the day I dropped them off and then self-surrendered. Then Al the head of security, a retired NYPD captain who had known my children since first grade, came up to me and hugged me.

"We are all so proud of you! You are so brave! And the kids are fine; we all took care of them. Welcome home, kiddo!" Wow, that was emotional. I didn't expect that. I didn't expect to be welcomed home. I expected to be shunned. Al passed away, a few years ago I heard, and I wish I had had a chance to tell him how he changed the course of my life that day. I had come home, planning to feel ashamed and having to prove myself to society again. He gave me a different perspective, and he was the catalyst to me, "owning my truth." What that community did for my children and I, their level of acceptance, solidarity, and open-mindedness, I will never forget.

Sure, there were naysayers and ugly gossip going around too, but they didn't compare to the amount of respect and support I was getting from that community. They weren't doing it for me, they were doing it for my children. When you belong to this community, your children are protected at all cost.

I dropped Dylan and Savannah off... Dylan went straight to class with a happy smile on his face. Savannah first went and then she ran back to me.

"Mommy, you are going home right? You are going to be here when I come out later, right? Mommy you aren't going back to that place, right? I don't need dad's number anymore; you said I can throw out the post-it you gave me that day."

I wanted to take her home with me, but I grabbed her and hugged her tight. I smelled her hair that smelled like vanilla and cotton candy, and I reassured her.

"I'm not going anywhere. I'm going to go to the nail and the hair salon today. To look all pretty for you when you come home." I went home to my little baby Dakota, and I sat with her at the kitchen table, just staring at her like she was a mirage and drinking my hazelnut coffee ... the coffee I had dreamt of having again when I was in Danbury. That day I had to report to my probation officer, and I would have to do so once a month. I had to wear an electronic bracelet for six months.

He put it on and gave me basically the whole day to come and go. He said I'm required to work. Shit! Did I still have a job? What was my job even? That is when my life as a paranoid woman started. I felt watched, I felt tailed, and I felt like at any time they were going to come back for me. The probation situation was scary. One violation could put me back in prison doing more time. You'll see, it's easy. Don't break the law.

Well, I wish it was that easy. Getting pulled over could be tricky and filling out my expense sheet for the week could be a federal crime. Basically, probation required that I enumerate all our expenses (including Joe's, who was not on probation and was our source of income at that point). If I failed to report even one supermarket purchase or a cleaners' bill, it could be considered a violation. The federal government wants you back in jail at any cost. It makes them money and it shows they were right about you.

Everything I did, everywhere I went, I questioned whether it could be a violation of probation. I knew if the feds wanted it to be, it would be. You know what was a violation? Having probation officers come to my house at any time of the day and night to check how I live. That was a fucking violation. A violation of my privacy, of my life, of my children's and my husband's freedoms. My probation officer was a good guy, and he was doing his job. He often told me he couldn't believe I was even prosecuted. He dealt with real criminals every day; he felt he served society. With me, he shook his head. But he barely cut me any slack. He had to report to the Eastern District of Virginia, and he always reminded me, "They have a hard-on for you. I don't know why."

*

I received a bbm on my blackberry: "Is that you I saw on Ocean Parkway? Are you back?"

I looked down at my phone, read the message and thought twice. I didn't have time for this shit now. I didn't want anything to do with him or anyone. Not yet. I reply, "Yes, I'm home. But I am not ready yet for a conversation or an announcement." The next texts comes in almost immediately (I'm wondering if the feds are reading my texts). "No need for a conversation. I'm just so happy to know you are home. My mom is going to be so happy when I tell her. I told her I thought I saw you this morning. She said I'm crazy."

I smiled. "Yeah, I'm home. Tell her I'll call her soon." And then comes the next text. Isn't that how it all started? Cute texts, rolling in one after the other, smiles, and then ... "[sad face emoji] and me? Aren't you going to call me?" There it was. Think, Ingrid, think very carefully what your next text is going to be. Walking a thin line, on probation, with an electronic ankle bracelet you don't care to explain, and a husband who has been by your side for 14 months. I shake my head.

"It's not a good idea. I'm sure it's best for your marriage if we leave it this way. And it's best for mine. I gotta go." I hope he lets it go, but not really. He does for a while.

I call my agent … ringing … I hang up. I never told anyone I went to prison for 14 months. I lied to all of them and told them I needed time of to go to France and take care of my mother's health. I call again, and she picks up.

"Ingrid, sweetheart, is that you? We were so worried about you. How did you do in there? You know my uncle Al was in fed; he said it's awful. Are you home? When are you coming back to work? I can book you on a job next week."

And she did, she booked me a job. I got it approved by my probation officer. I went back to work, and my agent lined up jobs for me for photoshoots, private clients, and dressing housewives for Bravo TV. I had come home to a brand-new era of socialites, starlets, and reality TV personalities. For months, none of my peers asked me any questions, no one said anything. I wanted to believe no one knew where I had been, until I started to get some press as the up and coming young fashion stylist in New York.

The editor interviewed me, asking about my career in fashion, my big break working for HBO and Patricia, my sense of style, growing up in the fashion industry, and then she says, "And coming back from adversity? From prison to Manolos?"

I looked at her and said, "From Prison to Louboutins rather, Manolos are old news." She glared at me. And I went home, worried sick about what she would write. She wrote it… nothing happened. No one ever said a word. I always disclosed my criminal record when I signed my work contracts, and I still always got hired. The fashion industry is both savage and forgiving like that. Still, I was afraid to go back on the scene. My agent booked me for Mercedes-Benz fashion week, and I got scared. I almost backed out of it. I was sick and tired of camouflaging my electronic ankle bracelets in boots, or ankle straps faking an injury. I had to wear the bracelet as part of my parole, to make sure that I was at home in the evenings. I was sick of worrying about chatter, I was tired of being ashamed of my criminal record, and I was scared of being judged.

I had styling jobs lined up for Fashion Week. My big one and first one on the roadster was Marc Jacobs. I arrived through the back, went through security checkpoints with my backstage pass (I was always so proud of bearing), rolling in two clothing racks with styling assistants in toe, my head down, dressed to kill with high heel over the knee Sergio Rossi suede boots that hid my ankle bracelet, tight Jean Claude Jitrois leather leggings, my JMendel cropped fur jacket, and my large black Tom Ford sunglasses. Hiding behind my big blonde hair, I entered the large backstage room, electrified by the hustle and bustle of the show, and all of the sudden it all got very quiet. I looked up to find so many of my peers I hadn't seen in 14 months (stylists, make-up artists, hairdressers, producers, editors) all of them started applauding. I looked behind me I thought Marc may have entered the room… he didn't. It was for me. It was a warm welcome back that said, "We couldn't give a fuck where you've been."

The only one who gave a fuck where I had been was me, for a really long time. I navigated the next three years with shame and fear that I imposed on myself. My career thrived, and my life was almost back to normal. Dylan started doing better. We went through innovative new therapies and protocols. I changed his diet and focused on his gut health, and we stopped going to Dr. Billick because going to a psychologist made him antsy. Instead, I got him a private special education teacher Morah Nechama (Morah means teacher in Hebrew), and she changed his life. She gave him confidence, and he started reading English and Hebrew so well. She also spoke to him about his feelings. I built a team of incredible therapists around him to help us get him better. We went back to the McCarton Center to evaluate him three years after my incarceration and the miracle happened. Dr. McCarton's evaluation determined that he was no longer on the spectrum of autism. He now had an auditory processing disorder which could be treated with targeted therapies and special education. We never gave him medication, and yet, he got better. So many of the most debilitating symptoms were going away. Dylan was to be mainstreamed into a regular class at age 11. I changed school because Magen David refused to mainstream him. They were making too much money on special education classes and were having a hard time filling them with diagnosed children. The Syrian Jewish community still saw learning disabilities as taboo, and parents often preferred to see their children struggle in regular classes rather than admit they had special needs. Yet, learning disabilities plagued that community severely. I got involved with Bikur Holim to continue to bring awareness, but it was an uphill battle with these elitist mentalities.

*

My marriage was still what it was before prison. It was shit. Joe and I thought we were happy 24 hours out of the week. We basically felt happy going out every single Saturday night, dressing to the nines. We looked like movie stars and would hit the meatpacking district's STK and MPD, or Downtown Cipriani, and occasionally join the mile high club at the Rainbow Room. We had the best nights... those Saturday nights we would be in love. When Joe drank his Johnny Walker Black straight up with Diet Coke on the side, he became the guy I met in Miami all over again. Those are the only happy times in my marriage to him. If you asked him, he would tell you the same. Those nights and the Sunday strolls in Soho were the only times we were happy together and in love.

The rest of the time, I only found happiness with my children. My New York and my babies, we have countless memories of happy times just the four of us, that didn't include Joe. He couldn't be bothered with any of it: Lunches at Sheepshead Bay's El Greco diner, late lunches uptown Manhattan at La Goulue and Fred's at Barneys, afternoon hot frozen chocolates at Serendipity 2, long lunches and mini pizzas at the Mercer Kitchen, going to the ice skating rink at Rockefeller center, seeing Katz and the Rockets Broadway shows... none of this was Jewish enough for him. We had to lie to him and tell him we ate at a random kosher place we never even stepped foot into.

He inquired and investigated on where we ate and if it was kosher. I spent my marriage lying to him and teaching the kids to lie to him so we could keep living the life we loved outside of his sect.

We literally lived a double life: the very religious boring life Joe wanted us to live, and our palpitating, fun, stylish, and cool life in the city he forbid.

I was getting so good at living this double life, except prison had changed me. I didn't want to hide anymore. Prison had turned me into the queen of I DON'T GIVE A FUCK. I would pick fights with him over the religion. I would rebel. He kept on screaming from the top of his lungs: "Who are you? You aren't the same person anymore."

I wasn't the same anymore. I had been prosecuted, persecuted, and imprisoned. I no longer wanted to accept living a life I didn't sign up for and I didn't want.

So eventually, I answered the text... Gil's text. And, slowly but surely, we started our friendship again, and it quickly turned into the affair it once was. Except this time, we weren't sorry; we weren't scared and we were experimenting. We knew how to meet, and where to meet. We got ballsy, too. We saw each other a lot around the kids, at the Aviator sports club almost every day after school.

Joe caught me in my lies. I basically wanted him to. I wanted out of our marriage, but my conscience made it hard to say it to him. How do you tell the man who stood by you for 14 months while you were incarcerated, the man with not a paternal bone in his body who took care of your children, bathed them, cooked for them, went to school plays, and protected their love for their mother, how do you tell the man whose life completely stopped for 14 months that you want out of the marriage?

You don't … you don't tell him. You show him.

So, I subconsciously made mistakes. I would Google the hotel where I was meeting Gil and leave my computer screen open on that page. And he would catch it. We would fight about it. He suspected it was Gi, because he often spoke of how good looking he was and how he looked at me at the synagogue.

Then, Gil announced his wife was pregnant. That was such a blow. Please, explain to me how a guy who is supposedly married to a monster, sleeping in his guest room, gets his wife pregnant?

He justified it, as he justified everything. And as smart as I was, I believed him...

In my marriage, my foot was almost out the door, but Gil's wasn't. He didn't have a prenup. He told me the whole story of how his wife refused to sign it the day before the wedding, but he couldn't cancel the wedding because they had invited hundreds of guests. The company he worked for, the money came from his parents, he couldn't get divorced like that and give her half of his parents' money. He had three kids and one on the way. I should have known better. But somewhere along the way in this affair, I actually fell in love with him. We fell in love. Or at least, I think we did. He was obsessed with me; he would message me all day, think of every way possible to see me, bump into me, and go away with me.

Joe felt I was having an affair. I wouldn't even deny it. Finally, he proposed we get a friendly divorce. I agreed. He got me a lawyer. He hired one, and we dictated the terms to our lawyers. He gets to keep the house, and every piece of property we had, and I got full custody of the kids. He would give me fair child support, but I got no spousal support (that was fine with me, as I could make my own money). He could see them when he wanted to. He also agreed that I could move out of the United States and take the children with me, in which case he would relinquish his parental rights completely and would see the kids with my permission.

That sounded like he was trading the kids off for money... and he did. I took nothing. Didn't I take enough when I went to prison?

He always promised he wouldn't take the kids away from me. He said he watched the federal government rip my babies away from me for 14 months, and no way would he do the same. He kept his promise. He wasn't cut out for parenting anyway. Not a paternal chip in him. His own painful past is definitely to blame, and I don't blame him completely. I have forgiven him since, and I've been working on the kids for years for them to not feel anger or resentment towards him. He has made it hard, but we are getting there.

We signed our divorce papers, but we agreed we would stay under the same roof for some time, that we would even try to reconcile until the divorce was finalized. I didn't really try; I didn't really want to.

He took Dylan and Savannah to his brother's wedding in Montreal. I felt it wasn't right for me to go since we were getting divorced. So, I took Dakota and the Nanny to Miami. We were meeting Gil there. He was down there with his kids and his parents, while his wife was pregnant in NY.

He kept saying, once she has the baby, he will go to a divorce lawyer and see how he can get out of this marriage without too much financial damage to his parents. He kept telling me stories of how unbearable and terrible she was, in contrast to how kind, amazing, and an incredible father he was.

The trip to Miami was such a revelation to me. In over 13 years of marriage, Joe and I had gone away twice. Once to Miami and once to Cabo, and both times were a nightmare. He refused to eat out. I would have to pack kosher meals in our suitcases for every single day. He hated the beach, he hated shopping, and he hated the basic pleasures of life and vacation. Every aspect of life with him was abnormal and out of the ordinary. Not the cool guy I married. I took the kids on vacations by myself three to four times a year, and technically, my first time having a real romantic getaway with a man was with Gil. It showed me what a real relationship was like, even though it was an affair, and our adrenaline was running so high from the fear of being caught. It was also the most normal relationship and the loveliest one I had been in my entire adult life. It's a shame it turned out to be such a lie.

We went to dinner at STK South Beach. We took pictures we would never show anyone. We slept in each other's arms all night and woke up and had breakfast on the beach. We walked on the beach holding hands and kissed with our feet in the water... I had never done that, and I had been married for more than a decade, and I was only

32 years old.

I went home and things were never the same again. Joe had figured out I had been in Miami with Gil. He was furious. I couldn't understand why? We were getting divorced. He couldn't be bothered to show me love, nor kindness let alone the life that I wanted.

I kept yelling back at him, "I've been in prison for 14 months. I don't want to live in your prison any longer."

Joe threatened to go to Gil's wife. I told him, "We are getting divorced, but he is having a baby. Don't do that."

Writing this now I realize how grotesque my thinking was. She was pregnant. What was I thinking?

Each time I tried to walk away from Gil, he made his wife, Copper (I didn't even know a metal type was a first name), so deserving of what he was putting her through. He said each time he tried to leave her, she would seduce him and entrap him with another pregnancy and another child. He would describe her frantic and psychotic behaviors. He convinced me she didn't love him. I came to hate the woman I barely knew. Jaffa, Gil's mother, confirmed a lot of what he would say, in the privacy of our own friendship. She always acted as though she didn't know about my relationship with her son, and she conveniently believed we were still best friends. Gil and I knew she knew.

In a perfect world, my divorce would be finalized, and he would manage to get divorced, and we would blend our families and live happily ever after. Once again, as I write this, I do realize (and have for many years) that it was grotesque.

Gil looked genuinely in love with me. He would travel to Vegas for business and come back to see me first before he went home to his wife and kids. He would buy me the most lavish gifts: a limited-edition Chanel bag from Las Vegas, a pair of Louboutin Boots for Chanukah. He did everything my husband never did... Joe gave me diamonds and furs, but he did it in a way that was always like sticking a pacifier in an annoying, crying baby's mouth.

Ultimately, it all came to be so much to handle, and this affair was getting sloppy. His baby was born, and he came straight from the hospital to see me. I was still living under the same roof as Joe with the kids, in our Belle Harbor house. I'd tell him I'm going out to see friends (I had never done that throughout our whole marriage). That night, he followed me. Gil and I were meeting for dinner at a beachfront hotel two towns away where we didn't know anyone. I walked in with him and felt a hand yanking me back from my chinchilla fur coat. We both turned around to an enraged Joe, calling me a cunt, screaming at Gil how disgusting he is.

"Didn't you just have a baby, you scumbag?" Joe asked for my rings, my watch, and my coat back. That was so ridiculous. I am with another man after so many years of marriage and this is what he comes up with? The expensive shit he got me?

That summed it all up.

After that, my relationship with Gil was strained and often tense. He had started to see a psychologist in the city, to help him sort his feelings out. He was truly tortured between his duty to his parents, his marriage, the burden of 4 children, a money-hungry wife, and our love story. We would often meet after his sessions with her at a hotel on Lexington. He finally went to a divorce lawyer and told his parents he wanted a divorce. Both convinced him it was a bad idea. He reassured me and told me they would come around, and he would find a way. My own divorce was finalized, but Joe and I continued to live this weird cohabitation, and I still cooked for Shabbat. Occasionally, we would still try and be a couple. It was fucked up.

One weekend, Gil said he had to go to Miami, and his mom would watch the kids because Copper was too tired to handle all of them. I saw his mom with the kids that weekend. She was thrilled.

"I'm so happy Gil and Copper get to have this getaway; they really needed it."

I felt nausea come up my throat … I called my best friend, Valerie. She then found out for me they were in South Beach with friends, and bizarrely he had taken Copper on a shopping spree to BAL Harbor and bought her the same shoes and belt as me, and coincidentally, she had died her very dark brown hair a shade of blonde that resembled mine. The friend said, "She is starting to look like Ingrid."

I was livid. Could it be he had been playing me this whole time? He had.

He came back, and once again convinced me to see him. I broke things off and he cried like a child. I felt for him; I loved him. He said he was tortured, confused and pressured from all sides. I fell into his trap again. I continued to be his support system.

He was a weak, egocentric, narcissistic, insecure man.

His wife got a text, telling her about the affair on a Saturday morning. He called me to warn me she may come to my house. She did. Joe got rid of her. Gil called me back to tell me he was going on an emergency session with his psychologist and to not contact him. He would contact me. He contacted me via text on Monday.

"Hi, Tig (that was his nickname for me), sorry but we can't speak anymore. Nothing happened between us, remember that."

We had an affair for almost a year, we made plans, and just like that "nothing happened."

I told Joe. "Leave them alone," he said. "They have to sort it out. You are on probation. She can hurt you and she will. She said she will."

I kept quiet. Gil and I had friends in common; many of them knew what had happened. Many of them were disgusted with him and how he threw me under the bus.

I wouldn't take too long before I started hearing that Copper and him told a story that I was harassing him and following him everywhere, that I imagined we had an affair but in fact I was just a crazy, obsessed convict.

That hurt a lot, and that also was enraging. Until them, no one had used my time in prison to denigrate me. A lot of people stopped talking to me, and I was turned into the bad guy. He was the good guy. The faithful husband who had a "fatal attraction" ex-convict stalker.

That didn't sit well with me... I tried a few times to email him, asking for an explanation. For closure. He ignored me. Next thing I knew...

I was about to pull up at Dunkin' Donuts near my house (and near Gil's since we were neighbors) one morning and my friend Erica whom I met every day called me.

"Ingrid, I don't think you should come. Gil and Copper are outside in their car. They are on the phone with someone, and it looks like they are waiting for you."

What the fuck! I'm still going! I'm not scared of them. I parked. Gil comes to my window and starts taking pictures of me on his phone and ran back to his car. I was fuming! Enraged! What the hell did he want? She was in the car waiting. I got out, went to his car, and knocked on the window screaming, "Why the hell are you here taking pictures of me?"

She took a video or a picture I'm not sure. I could hear someone, a male on the speakerphone. I just understood I was just set up.

My friends, Valerie and Evelyn, were waiting for me. They had something to tell me. Valerie earlier that week got into a fight with Copper at a Chinese auction, and Copper got a restraining order against her. I didn't know why. They were here to tell me why. Copper swore to Valerie that she was going to send me back to jail and away from my kids for a long time. Valerie got mad and threatened her. Copper called the police.

I was about to go back to jail. I felt it... My probation officer called me. I had to report to the nearest precinct. Copper and Gil filed a report against me for harassment and intimidation. Simultaneously Valerie had to report as well to a precinct near her as charges had been filed against her for harassment on my behalf. I remember Valerie's husband sending me a picture of his wife handcuffed and being processed at the precinct. I felt so guilty. Valerie had never even gotten a ticket in her life. She had four small children waiting for her at home, and she was treated like a criminal for defending me.

My nightmare was about to start again. I started shaking uncontrollably. The kids were in school. Dakota was home with me. I was about to be arrested again for something I didn't do, and this would violate my probation and send me back to a federal prison.

Copper won. She was about to separate me from my children because her husband couldn't keep his dick in his pants. I hired Nick Casale, former NYPD First Grade Detective, with a notorious security firm in NYC. To make sure Gil, Copper, and Jaffa didn't trip me any more than they already had. I had 24 hours to report at the closest precinct, and I would do so with my attorney and Nick by my side. The next morning, I took the kids to school, and I was tailed by Jaffa in her Mercedes and Gil in his BMW truck. They were trying to make it look like I was following them. I pulled over and called Nick. He told me to lock the doors, keep my phone video on and wait for him. He understood the whole scope of the issue that they were trying to send me back to jail to avoid the scandal of the affair bringing them shame in the community.

Nick didn't think I would get arrested. We went to the precinct, and I was processed under Nick and my lawyer's eye, and surprise, surprise, because I was on probation, I was arrested, taken to central booking and handcuffed, and spent the night in jail. That night was scarier than any other night I've spent in prisons, jails, or transfers. I thought I would be sent back to jail for good, to finish my original sentence. There was a phone in the cell that I shared with street prostitutes, drag queens, drug addicts, and all kind of street sleaze. All of them got called out except for me. Someone called in a favor.

Gil's brother was an attorney for the NYPD, so he made sure I spent the night in jail. I saw the judge the next day and was released with a restraining order against me. Copper said she was afraid as I drove passed her kids many times and she thought I may run them over. Of course, I drove by often as we were neighbors. My children's school, the supermarket, my son's basketball practice were all on the way.

How could these two parents justify taking me away from my children after the 14 months they had been through? All to make the scandal of an affair go away? To this day I don't know how these individuals could live with themselves. Copper told anyone she could her goal was to send me back to federal prison for a long time.

It didn't work... but this made me realize how vulnerable I was in the United States at that time. That anyone I would piss off, for whatever petty reason, had the power to send me back to prison. After two years of being out of prison, here I was still and more than ever so afraid of being separated from my children. Every night, I went to bed wondering if I would be with them the next day or if I would once again fall into the cracks of the system and end up in a Medium High security prison, missing their birthdays, their milestones, and depriving them of their childhood.

I still saw people from prison in random faces on the street. I saw CO Hayden everywhere, and then I would blink and realize it was a stranger's face. I still couldn't stand the sound of keys. I was scared to death of hard knocks on the door or of doorbells ringing insistently. I was traumatized and paralyzed with fear when someone stayed outside my house for too long, or walked behind me more than a block, or if what looked like an unmarked car or black SUV followed me. It was worse than post-traumatic stress disorder. It was the nightmare I lived inside of me. When someone gets incarcerated, time stops. Life for someone in prison doesn't change day to day. We are stuck doing the same thing every day for the allotted time given to us. But the world outside the prison walls changes daily. Except for me, that didn't change. This couldn't be the life I would live.

One morning, I was out the kitchen door with the kids, putting Dakota in the car seat of my Range Rover parked in my driveway. And as I was getting into the driver seat, I notice four black SUVs parked along my driveway and front yard. One of them looked like it was backing up to block me. I told the kids, "Babies, if men come for Mommy, run inside to get Dad, okay?

All I remember is feeling a warm liquid running down my face and into my eyes and on the back of my heard, it was blood. Joe was holding my head. I was laying on the cement ground, and he was asking me if I could hear him. He said we have to go to the hospital and that I need stitches. I asked about the SUVs, the men in them. He was confused.

"Those are Nakash's drivers; he had a fundraiser for some politicians today they asked if they could park here."

That day I told Joe I needed to leave the US. He agreed. He knew I couldn't keep living in this constant state of paranoia, most of it so justified. He often was afraid for me too. We also realized that we would never be able to properly be divorced and part ways if we stayed in the same city. We had been together since we were kids really, and we didn't even know how to be divorced, since we still lived in the same home. Some days we were a couple and some days we weren't.

I called my mother and told her I need to leave. Perhaps, I would move to Miami with the kids first until I can move out of the US. She panicked. She didn't want me in Miami; she didn't want the financial burden of my kids and myself. She didn't want me to disrupt her lavish life and habits, and she didn't want me to impose on my brother and his family.

I didn't feel welcome. I called Corine. I explained I need to move, that I had a job offer from Fashion TV in Monaco. She offered for the kids and I to stay at her summer home in Cannes, 45 minutes away from Monaco, until we find an apartment and a school for the kids.

I didn't tell any of my friends I was moving. Joe and I explained to the kids the best we could that a new life, a freer and more beautiful life, was waiting for us there. Dakota was too small to understand. Savannah, my trooper, was happy as long as she could be with me. Dylan was more reluctant. Joe promised he would come see us.

One week later, I went down the front steps of my beautiful house in Belle Harbor, waving goodbye at my kids' long-time nanny and crying, knowing I would probably never see that house ever again. The kids and I, along with 12 suitcases, were at JFK boarding a flight to the South of France. Joe hugged all of us goodbye. He has this way of being so unemotional and detached. He walked away before we even passed security.

We landed the next day and settled in my sister's Cannes townhouse, knowing nothing about the French way of life, but excited to learn. I left New York with $5,000 dollars and nothing else. The kids and I settled in Monaco, with some help from Corine and her husband Gilbert (same name as my brother), and finally I took all the lemons life sourly threw at me and turned them into lemonade. It took me a few years to fine tune the recipe.

We had ups and many downs from our little two-bedroom apartment overlooking Monaco where we felt so much happiness. We were free to eat what we wanted and go places that made us happy, even on Saturdays (Shabbat). We made friends and turned them into family. The kids were alright. The disparity between the oppression we felt in the mini-mansion we had left in NY and the exhilarating joy we felt in our tiny apartment was very much along the lines of "Money doesn't buy happiness, freedom does." Freedom from my sect-plagued marriage, from my fears and paranoia, freedom from doing what I was expected to do. The kids and I went from never worrying about the price of meat and poultry to having nothing and eating spaghetti and sandwiches every day.

I was finally in a financially stable situation after living in Monaco for five years. Out of a somewhat abusive relationship that ripped me to shreds financially, I was working for an affluent American Politician in Vietnam who paid me well. The job wasn't without its drawbacks. My boss was powerful, needy, and stressed. I worked remotely from Monaco, as a sort of crisis management covert agent. I slept very little and worked a lot, I and bought my kids everything and anything they had wanted over the past few years and I couldn't afford. I was finally able to give them the life they deserved. We were happy in our big house overlooking the Mediterranean Sea and Monaco.

I was looking back at the past and everything the kids and I had been through, from losing my best friend Brigitte to suicide, losing my job and seeing my ex selling all of my prized possessions including my Range Rover and my jewelry, to moving out like an escapee from Monaco apartment I shared with Dario. These kids had been through so much and I didn't want to bring anyone into their lives anymore. Everyone I brought in seemed to leave.

*

But things were about to change for me. I'd meet my next husband. Gil ... he said his name was Gil Kenny. I thought that was a joke at first. I had never met anyone else with that name before. And now I meet this guy and he spells it exactly the same?

I should have fell immediately for this very tall, bronzed, handsome, charming blue-eyed man when we met in Monaco. We just crossed path and started chatting. He invited me for coffee. He was a movie producer and was on a shoot near the coffee shop. He was so casual, so confident, and so kind too.

I had made a promise to my children, especially to Dylan, that I would not bring another man in their lives. Not after Dario and what he had put them through. So, when Gil kissed me for the first time as I was sitting next to him on the coffee shop's sofa, I decided we would have an affair. I was sure he was married, or from out of town. It couldn't be this exquisite sexy, well-spoken man was actually emotionally available. I wasn't.

"I'm not emotionally available," I told him. "I have three children you will never meet because they have been through a lot, so let's have an affair. Let's have fun together and go to dinner. Let's go to the beach. Let's have sex, but nothing more." He was amused, and I think he loved the challenge, too.

I searched high and low for everything I could find out about him on the internet. I did not trust for a minute that he could be a good guy. I mean his name was GIL, destiny ought to be playing a sick joke on me.

I let him chase me for a few days, and we went on our first official date. He took me to African Queen in Beaulieu-sur-mer overlooking the seaport. By the first course, we realized we had so much in common, and by the main course, we were smitten. This wasn't going to be an affair. My demons were raging inside of me. The thought of having a man I really liked fall for me, think I'm the perfect girl, and then be let down when he finds out I did time... pained me.

I thought, why put ourselves through the idyllic moments if it is all going to come crashing down? I put my fork and knife down, placed strategically at 3 o'clock on my plate, according to the French etiquette my bourgeoise French mother had taught me. I cleared my voice and I blurted it out, "Gil, I did 14 months in Federal Prison in the United States. I'm not that perfect girl you think I am."

My stomach was in knots. This may be our last time seeing each other. But that was okay because I didn't have high hopes. Or did I? Well, looking into his beautiful blue eyes, I kind of did. He took my hand and said, "I'm sorry you went through that."

He held my hand tightly for 20 minutes as I told him the big lines of my story. He cried with me when I told him about Dylan and how it felt to be separated from Dakota when she was a baby. And by dessert, he had a look of awe and respect in his eyes that he still has today. Gil was the first person I ever met who loved me for my past before he loved me for my present.

I still resisted introducing him to my children, especially Dylan, but he wouldn't have it. He asked to speak to Dylan on the phone. I agreed, but I knew Dylan would resist any man coming into my life, so I didn't worry. Next thing I knew, as he and I were sitting at the Club Dauphin Beach Club of the Grand Hotel Du Cap Ferrat, overlooking the magical Mediterranean Sea, I watched Gil wrap up his call with Dylan.

"Okay, then, all of us go to the open-air cinema tonight to watch *Ant-Man*. I will pick you, your sister, and your mom up at eight."

I was in disbelief. My boy had agreed to meet this complete stranger just from a phone call. That was Gil then and that is still Gil now: he leads with kindness and a pure heart.

I fell in love with him first, but he said I love you first. I didn't ask him to move in with us first, my girls did. Three weeks into our relationship, Gil and I had just come back from a lovers trip to Calvi in Corsica. Savannah and Dakota came to greet him with a small gift box, inside was our house key: "This way you don't have to ring the bell anymore. Will you live with us?"

It all seemed so pre-mature, but it wasn't. Gil had his love story with me, and his love story with each and every one of my children. He dealt with Dylan so admirably, with so much love and patience. Dylan no longer had special needs, but he had emotional and social sequels from his past disability, and he had deep hurt from being abandoned by his biological father. Gil healed him a lot. He gave him guidance into entering manhood. He took his hand and showed him how to take a leap into adult life

Two years later, we bought a house together, the house of my dreams, overlooking the iconic French Riviera's Mediterranean coast. Gil took me and the kids back to Corsica, this time to Pinarello, and asked me to marry him overlooking the beautiful Corsican lagoon.

For the first time in my entire life, I felt so much happiness, and I still do. There wasn't a day then nor a day now that I don't wake up looking around each morning and think, "If anyone had told me this would be my life when I was in Danbury Prison, I wouldn't have believed it." This has filled me with such a sense of gratitude in my life, even water tastes good to me.

We were married in St. Barth (French West Indies) on July 7, 2017 with 50 of our closest friends and family members. Dylan walked me down the aisle, on St. Barth's Tom Beach, and led me under the Chuppah that covered our head with Dylan's Talit from his Bar Mitzvah. My brother Roger blessed Gil in Hebrew as he broke the glass. Gil petitioned to adopt the children with Joe's blessing.

*

Today, Joe is back to living in Brooklyn. He sold our beautiful home in Belle Harbor, NY. He sadly got divorced from Aliza, but I'm not worried about him being single for very long, as he is a charmer. I've never truly blamed him for his inability to be a father. Part of me always knew he did it for me. He gave me the children I had been separated from and kept his promise to never separate us again. He sucked at showing love, but I don't believe he sucked at giving it. I do believe that we misunderstood him.

At the end of the day, he preferred to be the bad guy than to hurt me. Could he have been a father to the kids? Not really, he didn't know how. He was afraid of repeating history and being like his own father. He had seen his mother's pain and promised he would never hurt another mother. Today, he is there. If the kids choose to give him a place in their life, he will gladly take it. He recently told me, the kids have a dad in Gil and they have me. At the end of the day we are family. He is right, we are, and the kids are alright. A few years ago, when Joe was at the verge of his divorce from Aliza, he called me and gave me absolution: "I was on my way to the city on Saturday night, you know how we used to do, and that song we loved came on." Gil was sitting downstairs with my mom, and I was curious... What song was it? Seal's "Love Divine."

It was that song we listened to on the Brooklyn Bridge on Saturday nights, with our BMW roadster's top down, music blasting. I got the chills, and I often sang along, hoping someday Joe would ask for similar forgiveness for not giving me the love I needed and wanted from him. Here I was, happily married to the man of my dreams, finally getting the apology and the closure I had once longed for so badly.

"I wanted to tell you, I am sorry," he said. "Tonight, I listened to the song, and I remembered we used to dream we would be driving around on warm nights in Monaco some day in our Ferrari, and we would be happy. I didn't do anything to make that happen. Instead, I ignored you, didn't give you the love. I am so sorry. I now realize you were the perfect wife, and all you wanted was my love and attention. I apologize.

If I had realized then what I realize now, you would have been a very happy woman. I could have made you as happy as you deserved to be. You weren't asking for much. I didn't know. I listened to the wrong people; I took the wrong advice. I don't blame you for cheating on me and lying to me. Oh God, am I sorry. You did nothing wrong. I hope you can accept my apology. You were a wonderful spouse, and I did love you, but I didn't love you right. You can tell the kids I said this."

I was so shaken up by the call, so touched, so relieved. I apologized, too. He said I had nothing to be sorry for. Joe was hurting. His heart was broken again this time by his future ex-wife. My heart ached for him.

We hung up. I went downstairs, sat down with my Mom and Gil, and with tears in my eye, I recounted the conversation. I finally had closure.

Dylan, my labor of love, is now 21, living alone in the UK. He's in his third year of law school, pursuing a career in commercial law. He was accepted to one of the UK's top 20 law schools after he graduated and got the French Baccalaureate with honors. I so wanted to send his diploma to the doctors who said he would never live a normal life. He speaks French, English, and Spanish fluently, and he has friends who love him. He has reconciled with Joe after I arranged for them to meet in Miami a few years ago. He now has a biological father who loves him and a dad who loves him.

Savannah is 19 years old, and she is the light of my life. She is truly that little girl that could and did. She has saved my life and now she is taking on her own. She too lives in the UK, where she is a thriving second-year law student. She is set to devoting her brilliant mind to fighting injustice in the Criminal Justice System. She is pursuing a career in criminal law (both following in my footsteps and honoring my past as a victim of the criminal justice system).

Savannah is Gil's daughter. He is her dad, and he is her father. Their relationship and their love has so much depth and so many layers, it has been beautiful to watch. Gil raised her from her teens into adulthood. He has been there through thick and thin, guiding her into her femininity, self-awareness, and confidence. It was not always easy for either of them because Savannah is the war-wounded character in this story. I should have done a better job at teaching her empathy towards Joe and the sacrifices he made to make sure the kids and I were never separated again. Instead, she has her own vision of things, and while I don't want to speak for her, I hear her often resenting him for being harsh, distant, absent. I gathered this is the result of that fact that Joe has loved me and still did when we got divorced. For a long while, I think Savannah reminded him too much of me. Still, he could have done better.

I hope reading this, she can heal from the sense of abandonment she has felt. She sure deserves to. The love and devotion that child has given me makes me feel extremely guilty that I even allowed myself to ask and take so much from her. Gil becoming her father was the best thing I ever did.

Dakota is 14 years old, and I am still trying to make up for lost time. I may have missed her first steps, but I am here now every step of the way, watching her become a strong, opinionated, brilliant, young woman. She already leads with so much passion for what is fair and what she believes in, with such a free-spirited mind. She reminds me of the person I've become after prison. Physically, she strangely looks so much like Gil, that people notice their resemblance. Dakota remains that wound in my heart. Missing my child's first years of life is one of my greatest pains, the one that is taking longest to heal from. Watching her grow since I've come home has felt like a privilege I have never taken for granted since.

It brings me solace to see how much of a void Gil has filled in this little girl's life and heart. She has embraced him as her father, and she is truly a daddy's girl. I think I've done a good job at explaining Joe's position to her, so much so that she is not resentful, angry, or feels completely estranged from him. She would like to see him someday soon, and she sometimes calls him on his birthdays. I let her decide with compassion and with love.

Last year, I had an epiphany. How is it that one man can come into a life that has been so hard, so shattered, so disappointed and turn into so much love, happiness, and peace? I posted a picture of my dad on Instagram, and the first comment that came in was Corine: "Oh, I'm surprised by his resemblance to Dad," she said. My cousins commented their shock at the resemblance, and followers, perfect strangers, chimed in and noticed the striking resemblance to my dad.

Until that day, I had not noticed their striking resemblance, although I often remarked that Gil acted so much like my father and reminded me of him in his acts of kindness.

I now know some matches are made in heaven, and others are sent from heaven to make us whole. I believe in our case it is a latter. And I smile up at my dad every day.

My mom and I have a good relationship, although she wasn't the kindest and most nurturing always. My prison sentence weighed down on her so heavily. I will never forget the pain in her eyes when she visited me. She has pulled thru for me at times, but not always when it counted. But, she worked hard her whole life, she has shown resilience, strength and sacrifice for her children. As a parent myself I know for a fact children misunderstand their parents, and misconstrue most of their actions. It may be the case for me. I love her deeply, and I know that she loves me too.

My brother Gilbert was a strong presence in my life, and especially in my struggles. Recently I found out there may still be a warrant on my record, he is the first person I called to resolve it. He has been tough on me, and held me to different standards than anyone else he loves, but one thing he has made clear is that he loves me unconditionally and would do anything for me. I do love him no matter what I felt or thought about him when I was younger. He has shown me love, and devotion when it mattered the most.

My sister Corine is the deepest love of my life. She has filled every motherly void I may have experienced throughout my youth and my adult life, she still does.

My brother Roger didn't get much air time in this book, simply because he is that sweet, supportive, non-judgmental brother, who suffered tremendously from the loss of our father, and dealt with his own shortcomings as a result. Roger supports me whether I am a convict or a superstar. He inspired me to be more myself, and less who I'm expected to be.

I do feel like my dad is watching over me. The people who have hurt me have seen their share of retribution. The judge who sent me to prison stepped down from his chair after his long appointment by President Reagan. The prosecutor who railroaded me was fired from the District Attorney's office the week of my release and is now a Traffic Violations attorney. Gil and Copper had a horrible divorce and custody battle after he caught her cheating on him with her personal trainer. Jaffa (Gil's mother) lost her husband and is now bitter and old. A friend of mine recently saw her at a wedding where she told the groom that marriage is a big mistake and almost fainted at the sound of my name being spoken. She made the proud claim that she was the one who got me to leave NY and never come back. What mother and grandmother feels such pride about uprooting children from their home and the life they know, in trying to send their mother to jail because her son couldn't keep his married dick in his pants? A bitter, sad, old widow, that's who.

Gil's brother, the NYPD attorney who made sure I spent an extra night at central booking in jail (because 14 months wasn't enough), also got a bitter divorce recently.

For my part, my life may have been fucked for a long while, but my adversities have fueled my successes. I have lived in shame of my criminal past for almost a decade and the humiliation and pain of seeing my kids get uninvited from birthday parties. This all ended when my health and wellness venture took off and a notorious diet guru in NY felt threatened enough by my small growing business that she attempted to ruin me by publishing my criminal record on social media.

Dylan was not 18 yet. I had started to write this book but would not finish it, nor release it, before he'd hit come of age. I needed his consent, and I needed him to be okay. I needed his story to be a success story for all the children out there who have special needs and for their moms who are told they don't have a shot at a normal life.

Much of my story was his story. But here I was, faced with what I had always been so afraid of: the truth about my past not catching up to me (that was already done) but catching up to my children.

I had to act, and I had to act fast. Erasing your past, hiding it in a closet will never work, and I have learned as much. In 2016, I had become friends with Lauryn, a successful lifestyle blogger, and well-known podcast host. I loved her for her wits, sass, and her heart of gold. Our friendship became deep and strong so quickly. Her advice was gold. She came to visit me in the South of France with her husband, Michael, (her podcast host), and we were set to record a podcast episode for their show, all about French lifestyle, beauty, weight loss, fitness, and wellness. We went to lunch at La Petite Maison (one of my favorite local restaurants in the region) and over a plate of lobster pasta and La Piscine de Champagne, Michael looked at me and said, "You need to tell your story. You wouldn't be where you are today if it wasn't for what you have been through. When you are ready, Lauryn and I are willing to give you a safe space and platform to own your narrative."

This advice was cathartic, and I will be forever thankful to Lauryn and Michael. After lunch, we headed to my house to record our wellness podcast. Michael set my microphone up, put my headphones on, and gave me a warm look. He said, "At any time, if you feel like going there, I will follow your lead. If you don't want to, we won't." Lauryn is the warmest friend I have, and she makes me feel so safe. She looked at me as though to say, if we go there, it is for you. She often said my story is beautiful and inspiring and nothing to be ashamed of.

"Hello, hello, from beautiful Monaco," Lauryn said as she began the podcast. "We are here today with our friend Ingrid De La Mare-Kenny...We met last year at the Eden Roc in the South of France ... I stalked her because I had been following her for years, and I told Michael I need to see what that girl is eating, move over."

And Michael takes over. "Ingrid, first let me ask you, why did you decide to come to Monaco?"

My heart was pounding. Gil and the girls were sitting on the couch behind us. I took a quick look at them. At that moment, I decided to be honest. No more hiding. No more lies.

And I did it... I was afraid, but I was fearless at that moment, I told my story for the first time to an audience of hundreds of thousands and I never stopped since. I am no longer ashamed. I am not longer afraid.

This is my story, and I own it.

7-7-2017 Our wedding night in St. Barth's

"It has been truly an honor to watch Ingrid own her truth, rise from ashes, write her destiny, create a brand from the ground up and come to dominate the wellness space. As a branding expert, watching Ingrid so expertly build a tribe of women that have coalesced around and have continuously championed has been nothing short of brilliant and beautiful. She is a true trailblazer and cunning marketer in the digital brand building space. To know Ingrid is to know the personification of perseverance and walking in ones truth."

—Dara Kaplan, Partner and Co-Founder of the Manhattan and Miami based, Wunderlich Kaplan Communications. Dara has been featured on Forbes, CNN, Fox News, NYPost, Huffington Post, Daily Mail, Inc.com, Elite Daily and more.

*

"Ingrid De La Mare-Kenny truly changed my life for the better. When I stalked her on Instagram years ago, I was immediately intrigued by her charisma, warmth, unapologetic attitude. Ingrid is a wealth of knowledge when it comes to everything wellness, health, beauty. She has helped me develop a healthy attitude towards food and diet, and continues to be such a mentor to me. Not only is she one of my best friends, she also has a huge community full of women who TRUST her. This industry needs her- she always puts her community first and her book is an absolute gem. Ingrid's adversity has given her depth & relatability which the reader will feel throughout the book. Anyone who reads it will be immediately inspired while feeling her warmth through the pages. Ingrid, there's no one like you."

— Lauryn Evarts Bosstick, Author of The Skinny Confidential: A Babe's Sexy, Sassy Fitness and Lifestyle Guide and Co-Host of entrepreneurial podcast, The Skinny Confidential HIM & HER, which just hit 55 million downloads. Lauryn has been featured in SHAPE, Women's Health Magazine, SELF Magazine, The Gary Vee Show, People Magazine, and Who What Wear.

*

"What drew me to Ingrid was not just her obvious stunning beauty and her exquisite sense of style. I immediately noticed her inexplicable steeliness and alpha intelligence beneath the feminine beauty and sensibility. Ingrid is mystical yet relatable, lovely yet ferocious and elegant yet gangster. She personifies a pendulum of adjectives. She has lived a life of someone you will only read about. Congratulations on your brave journey, my Lethal Beautiful Friend."

—Helena Reich, Founder & Creative Director of Swoon Luxe

*

"I call Ingrid my rags to riches story and I am not just talking wealth. When I met Ingrid, she was on the verge of losing everything. From her home, to her work to her toxic relationship. Ingrid's gift has always been her children. She will protect them at all costs. She truly loves her children and honors them like no other. In my humble opinion, she knows very well they saved her life on many levels!

One day Ingrid asked me what she needed to do to transform her life to the dreams and visions she could see and knew were there but had not shown up in her physical reality. She was at the end of living a life of chaos and ready to enter her dream life which included a man who would love her and cherish her the way she loved others!

What makes a soul successful in life is realizing they need to let go of the past emotionally and embrace the lessons. INGRID DID THIS! A hard day turned into a new beginning. A struggle turned into a gift. A spark of inspiration and creation turned into a passion. She never took no for an answer. She stopped listening to the voices outside of her and started listening to her own inner voice! She connected with her spirit like never before and went deep within and took action. She started to see her dreams manifest before her eyes and every day no matter how hard it was she kept going!

Ingrid's story will inspire you and motivate you to live your dreams on your terms. However, remember she may make her journey look easy but she did her work, she shed her tears, she changed things she knew had to change and it was not easy! Ingrid today lives a life of riches on every level because she faced her fears and let them go. She stepped into her life because she accepted no less because she decided to finally love herself as much as she loved others."

Rev. Tracy L. Clark, Motivational Speaker and Author of GOD WHERE ARE YOU? IT'S ME.

*

Ingrid's story is something you CANNOT miss. She is not only an inspiration to women everywhere but anyone who has gone through hard times and continued to persevere. She is absolutely one of the most brightest lights ever and no doubt that walking through her path to how she has risen on top will take you through a rollercoaster of how to come out on the end of any situation. She is one of the most chic women with extreme intelligence in every area. I don't know where I would be without her and she's my go to for advice. A MUST READ.
  — **Danielle Prahl (Little)- Best selling author and Online Business Expert**

*

Ingrid is transcendent! Beloved by millions, she is a leader who generously shares her talent and her enormous heart, transforming lives in the process. Her energy, wisdom, perseverance and intuition spill out on every page of this book. Readers are sure to be forever changed, as I have been, by her one-of-a-kind insight on living life the gangster chic way. I've never before felt this sexy!
  — **Trish Jacob, Former TV Reporter, Producer & Journalist. Marketing Communications and PR Executive, Publicity Specialist, Philanthropist (& Mom)**

Made in the USA
Middletown, DE
17 December 2020